Developing Safety Systems

DEVELOPING SAFETY SYSTEMS

A GUIDE USING ADA

Ian C. Pyle

Prentice Hall

New York   London   Toronto   Sydney   Tokyo   Singapore

First published 1991 by
Prentice Hall International (UK) Ltd
66 Wood Lane End, Hemel Hempstead
Hertfordshire HP2 4RG
A division of
Simon & Schuster International Group

Typeset in 10/12 pt Plantin
by Columns, Reading

Printed and bound in Great Britain at
the University Press, Cambridge

Library of Congress Cataloging-in-Publication-Data

Pyle, I. C. (Ian C.), 1934–

 Developing safety systems : a guide using Ada/I.C. Pyle.

  p. cm.

 Includes bibliographical references and index.

 ISBN 0–13–204298–3 : $45.00

 1. Ada (Computer program language) 2. Computer
software—Reliability. 3. System safety. 4. Computer
software—Development.

 I. Title

 QA76.73.A35P95 1990

 005.13'3—dc20   90–7753

                       CIP

British Library Cataloguing in Publication Data

Pyle, I. C. (Ian C.) *1934–*

 Developing safety systems: a guide using ADA

 1. Automatic control system. Applications of
computer systems. Safety aspects

 I. Title

 629.8950289

 ISBN 0–13–204298–3

---

1 2 3 4 5 95 94 93 92 91

Ada is a registered trademark of the US Government Ada Joint
Program Office.

For
Elisabeth, John, David and Katy

Contents

Preface

THE LAST FEW YEARS have seen considerable growth in reliance on computer systems, linked with an increasing apprehension about the confidence that we can have in them. There are undoubted benefits to be obtained from the use of automatic systems, but it is important for developers and operators to be aware of the implications of delegating decisions to an automaton, when the consequences of such decisions could be damage to life, limb, property or the environment. The relationship is fundamentally different from responsibility delegated to another person.

Most critical systems are developed by people without recognised qualifications in information system engineering or software engineering. (Indeed, it is not yet established what suitable qualifications for the subject should be.) We are in a collective learning mode, trying to understand how best to develop such systems and to ensure that they deserve the trust we will place in them.

The profusion of guides can be overwhelming. Responsible organisations have sought to give the best advice on system development, recognising that all levels of responsibility need guidance. Each has something useful to offer, but it is often difficult to relate them to one another, because of differences in concepts and terminology.

This book began to take shape in 1986, from which year attention to safety in computer-based systems has grown dramatically. Sometimes it seemed that new material was appearing so fast that it was hindering rather than helping the people involved! Sometimes it seemed that I was never going to find a stable situation in which to stop. But as with program development, there is a time when further tinkering is futile, and a baseline has to be set for change control. The pace of change in the world of safety is still rapid, but the main lines now seem to have been drawn, even if they sometimes appear to be battle lines. We have been through a period of turbulence in software technology, as the use of Ada has become established and we are moving into the use of mathematics for expressing the semantics of automatic behaviour. There is much misunderstanding about this important aspect of software engineering, which I hope is made more intelligible by the viewpoint presented here. The long-term solution to the development of trustworthy safety systems is for aspiring software engineers to be made aware of the challenges and opportunities in this field, to which this book might contribute.

xiii

The book is an attempt to pull together the current ideas, in a practical way, for software engineers. During the period of writing it, I have presented particular ideas in various other places, but I bring them all together here.

I am happy to acknowledge the valuable and perceptive reviews of the developing text by the Prentice Hall referees, which showed up a number of places where the explanations were in need of improvement.

I wish to thank Aeronautical Radio, Inc, for granting permission for substantial parts of their report number 613 to be included as Appendix A here.

I thank SD-Scicon UK Limited for giving me permission to publish the work. The views are my own, and not necessarily those of the company.

But the ultimate credit for the book really belongs to my wife – who kept me aware of the need to finish it or to abandon it! Thank you, Margaret.

Ian Pyle
Guildford, 1990

1

Introduction

SOFTWARE has been used in embedded computer systems since the 1950s, with programmed digital systems replacing (or being designed instead of) analogue ones. As confidence in such systems has grown, they have been applied to more critical situations, and are now increasingly used in systems where safety is of great importance. While the implications of this kind of use have been intuitively appreciated, the consequences for practical purposes have been harder to define, as in most cases little could be done other than insist on great care and checking.

Much more can be done. We introduce the issues concerned by referring to the published material (Section 1.1), explaining the underlying tension (Section 1.2), terminological ambiguity (Section 1.3) and general background assumed of readers (Section 1.4). The structure of the rest of the book is summarised in Section 1.5.

1.1 Software in safety-related systems

Guidelines have been published during the last few years to assist developers of safety-related systems, explaining the criteria for accepting them in safety-related situations: Chapter 2 gives technical details. The documents have stimulated discussion of the increasingly important role of software in the design of safety-related systems. However, since the majority of engineers responsible for producing or accepting such systems are not software engineers, the nature of software and its failure modes are not generally understood. As a result, there is a widespread feeling of apprehension about computer-based systems, and considerable lack of confidence in them. This is not only a technical problem, but a social one. The technical methods are not sufficient in themselves, but must be deployed in a social context where they can be seen to be effective.

While software is not the only component in a computer-based system which affects safety, and the programming language used is not the only contributor to the adequacy of that software, it does nevertheless have a strong effect, since the style of software design encouraged by appropriate linguistic concepts can support the good practices of safe system design. Ada is the most suitable language currently available for safety-related software, and this book presents guidance for software/system engineers working with Ada. The guidance is also applicable to software written in other languages, but the checking provided by the rules of Ada (enforced automatically by Ada compilers) would then have to be applied by hand or by pre-processors.

1.2 Safety is controversial

There are few certainties in life, and safety cannot be made one of them. It is impossible to ensure absolute safety in any system we build – but there are many steps we can take to reduce the risks of potential danger. By forethought and planning we can eliminate, avoid or defuse dangerous situations, either preventing them from arising or ensuring that if they do the effects are not serious. But since forethought is never perfect, these steps carry the risk of inadequacy, and systematic analysis helps to reduce that risk. The resulting safety achieved is determined by the combination of all factors. This is particularly true in systems where the actions are controlled by automata, for which the planning (i.e. software) requires complete forethought.

Herein lies controversy: there is no consensus about the relative risks and importance of different approaches, which depend as much on intuitive perceptions as on technical expertise. There have been major technical developments during the last decade (with more to be expected), and the balance will shift as a result. But there is no general agreement yet as to the best ways of ensuring that a system is as safe as possible, or of estimating the risks that remain in a potentially dangerous system. This book presents an approach that is based on current published guidance from authoritative bodies; so it inevitably tends to lean to the conservative rather than the radical side. However, the advance in high-level languages is now so marked by the availability of Ada that software for potentially dangerous systems cannot ignore it. There is a conservative view of safety that rejects all high-level languages – and there is a radical view that rejects any informality. Here is a middle course: largely procedural, dependent on the skill and judgement of engineers and mathematicians, but taking advantage of the extensive logical ability of automata for formal analysis and checking (through software tools such as an Ada compiler). It is intended to comply with the current guidance rather than to challenge it, although there are a few instances where the concepts and facilities of Ada justify radical rethinking. The public guidelines are on the whole sufficiently robust to bear reinterpretation in this context.

We sometimes have to take decisions when there is no consensus. The analysis and discussion here is intended to illuminate decision-making by those responsible for safety-related software-based systems, even if the decision is to take a more conservative or a more radical approach than is commended.

1.3 Safety is ambiguous

One reason for the controversy about safety in software is an ambiguity in the use of the term 'safety'. While there is general agreement that safety is 'a property of a system that it will never do anything bad' (Oxford, 1986), the more specific identification of the 'bad' features to be avoided range from 'cause risk to human life' to 'deadlock'. This is partly a difference of viewpoint, between the system as a whole and the software that determines its behaviour. Within the software community, a safety property is an assertion that the program never enters an unacceptable state (Lamport, 1980), referring to such features as mutual exclusion, critical section synchronisation, absence of deadlock and partial correctness. In this sense, 'safety' is the counterpart of 'liveness': a property of a system that it will eventually do something good (Oxford, 1986).

But in the systems community, safety relates to the relationship between the system and its environment, which is of course substantially determined (in the case of a computer-based system) by the software in it, but not by that software in isolation. While software safety is undoubtably important, it does not completely address the concerns of the safety systems engineer. Where it is necessary to distinguish the two uses of the term, we refer to the *software* and *system* aspects as 'logical safety' and 'physical safety' respectively.

1.4 Safety is a focal point

Readers of this book are presumed to be practising engineers or programmers, but not necessarily chartered software engineers. Most of the ideas presented here would be part of a graduate software engineering course, but they are not just of academic importance: these are the key concepts for people involved with the development of safety-related, computer-based systems. This approach to software development involves a considerable change of attitude from that frequently held by those who have programmed only in (Real Time) Fortran, Assembler and similar languages: the focus of attention is shifted from *performance* to *comprehension*, allied to the need to cope with complexity and ensure that a safety-related system does not have unpredicted behaviour.

For many purposes, computers are used to carry out calculations *fast*. This is not the focal point in a safety-related system: what is important is that the behaviour (determined by the software) is *consistent*, *predictable*, and *confirmed* as the acceptable behaviour for the automaton responsible for safety.

1.5 Structure of the book

This book is structured according to the different roles involved in producing and accepting safety-related systems, and the corresponding human activities: discovering, inventing and analysing. Often there will be several organisations, with distinct and clearly defined responsibilities, whose actions jointly achieve safety. Within the roles, we broadly follow the characteristic software life-cycle explained in the *STARTS Guide* (NCC, 1987), and explain how safety has to be taken into account from Requirements to Evolution. We show how Ada (particularly through its package construct) provides a framework in which design rules needed for safety can be applied and confirmed.

Part I comprises Chapters 2–6 of the book. It is concerned with investigating the situation in which a software-intensive, safety-related system is contemplated, dealing with general principles, responsibility, the requirements for safety, the classification of safety issues and the continuation of safety during the evolution of the system. The purpose of this part is to focus on discovering the specific goals that must be assured in a safety-related system.

Part II, comprising Chapters 7–10, is concerned with constructing the software needed, dealing with the general principles of software development, the software architecture or program structure and the logical and physical design of software for controlling various types of device. The creation of software in Ada is not directly affected by safety requirements, but the structure of Ada software and its susceptibility to analysis are important, both for achieving the required safety-related behaviour and for giving confidence in its safety integrity. The purpose of this part is to identify the techniques in Ada that should be used.

Part III comprises Chapters 11–15; these are concerned with confirming that the software produced is properly safe, by checking it in various ways during its development. The confirmation covers the general principles of program correctness and software quality, including both analytical checks and explicit tests for safety with several kinds of device handlers. The checks are carried out by both automatic and human methods, with attention drawn to residual defects that automata do not recognise (which must be investigated with particular care). The purpose of this part is to establish the information about a safety-related system that is needed to justify its certification for operational use.

Chapter 16 is the conclusion, which is followed by a number of appendices referring to specific public recommendations.

The book does not replace the official guides, but is intended as a supplement to them, giving specific assistance when the software is designed and written in Ada.

PART I   DISCOVERY

2

Responsibility for safety

SAFETY-RELATED SYSTEMS are likely to be operated under the supervision of some licensing authority, established by law. Safety legislation varies from country to country, but similar principles apply, depending fundamentally on technology and scientific understanding. In the United Kingdom there are different laws dealing with safety in different circumstances: the safety of employees at work (particuarly in hazardous situations such as mining, involving explosives or dangerous chemicals) and the safety of the public (particularly when travelling or from the transport of hazardous substances). Authorities are set up to enforce these laws, such as the Health and Safety Executive or Civil Aviation Authority in the United Kingdom; similar organisations exist in other countries.

Each licensing authority makes its decisions in the light of available knowledge, and publishes guidance about its regulations and procedures for permitting a safety-related system to be operated. In the majority of cases these have nothing to do with software. But an increasing number of such systems *do* depend on software, and a number of authoritative guides have been published to assist producers to make them sufficiently safe to satisfy legal (and ethical) requirements. Because of the low general awareness of software engineering, the guides cover much common ground about software development (as in the STARTS publications which are now widely available in the United Kingdom), but with special emphasis on correctness and safety. The present book can be considered as an amplification and interpretation (for Ada) of the existing guides.

Management concern for safety is fundamental. The safety of a system produced is directly proportional to the amount of attention given by management to the goal of safety: in setting policy, defining the relative priority of safety and other goals, granting authority, and defining responsibility and accountability. In particular, the safety policy must lead to appropriate technical measures being established, and properly experienced staff being engaged for the work. Unless the management give due attention to safety issues, the technical competence of the staff will be dissipated.

The method used to develop the whole system must incorporate safety considerations from the beginning, and must encompass the hardware and software together with the usage of the system. For example, hazard analysis must be done for the whole system, ensuring that the configuration and software design take account of the hazards which might occur, in order to provide leverage for certification. Different kinds of failures may have different consequences which should be distinguished: system-wide modelling and analysis of hazards can identify critical assumptions, and ensure that run-time checks are included when the danger cannot be eliminated by design.

The official guides illustrate different ways by which safety may be established for a software intensive system: the HSE Guide (Section 2.1) provides technical insight and useful checklists; for avionics systems, the RTCA's document (Section 2.2) defines the information that should be recorded for certification; for military software, Def-Stan 00–55 (Section 2.3) emphasises the separation of organisational responsibilities and checks to be carried out; EWICS (Section 2.4) gives general background and advice for industrial computer systems; and the ACARD report (Section 2.5) advocates a legal and professional framework. The draft standard by the International Electrotechnical Commission (Section 2.6) discusses the relationship between hazards, frequency and safety integrity. The actual legal framework in Britain is summarised in Section 2.7.

2.1 Health and safety

The Health and Safety Executive of the Department of Employment is responsible for implementing the Health and Safety at Work Act (1974), and has published guidance on the use of 'programmable electronic systems' (i.e. computers!) in safety-related applications. There are two volumes: an *Introductory Guide* and the *General Technical Guidelines*. The HSE Guide is for use in both production and assessment; its principal concern is the safety integrity of the hardware and software forming a Programmable Electronic System.

The HSE Guide distinguishes between a control system and a (safety) protection system. Although the latter is a kind of control system, it is deliberately treated as a distinct element in a safety-related system, so that it may be simpler than the principal control system, thus avoiding many problems of complexity. A protection system is defined as one designed to respond to abnormal conditions in the plant (which may be hazardous in themselves, or latent in that inaction could then give rise to a hazard). The response of a protection system must be to generate outputs that either prevent the hazard from occurring (if possible) or else mitigate its consequences if it is unavoidable.

The HSE Guide includes several ways of analysing the hazards in a safety-related system (based on identifying the failures that are dangerous because they lead to unsafe or potentially unsafe conditions in the plant), and an assessment framework. These are discussed further in Chapter 6. The Guide identifies three fundamental system elements that contribute to safety integrity, namely the configuration, the reliability of the hardware, and the quality of the procedures used throughout the development process. (Notice that software *correctness* is not specifically identified: the guidance implicitly presumes that it is beyond the current state of the art.)

In addition to these aspects that are particularly relevant to safety, the HSE Guide covers the general principles of design and production of computer-based systems, in order to explain the framework within which the issues of safety must be dealt with. Detailed notes on the HSE Guide are given in Appendix B.

The HSE is also responsible for the Nuclear Installations Inspectorate (NII), which has distinct rules concerning the safety of nuclear power stations (explained further in Chapter 5).

2.1.1 Diversity

A central feature of the HSE Guide is diversity. The protection system should consist of a number of independent elements, sufficiently redundant to guard against failures within the elements of the protection system itself. While replicated elements will reduce the likelihood of failure arising from random hardware failures, they do not help with systematic failures. The elements must be independent to reduce the likelihood of common-cause failures: specification errors, equipment errors or software errors.

Specifically, this excludes reliance on a single computer, however well-checked or formally correct its software. The redundancy may extend to non-programmed devices, to independently designed software or to different execution mechanisms.

Being aware of the risk of common-cause failures, the system designer has to decide how much of the work should be done several times over (in parallel or in series), and how much isolation to impose between those carrying out the work. There are inevitable commonalities: the specification for the work to be done, the technology available and the professional culture of the staff doing the work.

One important (but not initially expected) result of experiments in design diversity (Leveson, 1986) is that they show up diverse defects in the specification. In one major experiment of up to twenty different designs to the same specification, the different designs showed up different defects in the specification – so we should assume that even two or three independent designs are likely to locate some different defects, but fail to detect many more. This is one kind of systematic failure – and the communication between the designers exchanging fault reports introduces another possible common cause of failure, since it reduces their independence.

2.2 Avionics safety

The aviation community recognises several similar (but not identical) ways of categorising the severity of the hazards that might arise in flight. Principally, they reflect the effect of failure or design error on the safety of the aircraft and its occupants (i.e. the crew in the case of military aircraft).

Flight Airworthiness Regulations (FAR 25.1309) and Joint Airworthiness Regulations (JAR 25.1309: Equipment Systems and Installation) apply to the whole aircraft, and give definitions of the criticality category of the effects of various failure conditions or design errors on an aircraft and its occupants.

Each function (of an equipment or of the avionics system) is categorised according to its impact on safety, considering the possibility that the function might not be properly performed. Certification criteria for civil aviation systems are based on the significance to safety of non-performance of the functions involved, taking into account the possibility of malfunctions and unavailability. A function is categorised as critical, essential or non-essential. (Sometimes the 'essential' category is subdivided into major and minor essentials.) The categories in FAA Advisory Circular 25.1309-1 for the effects defined in FAR 25.1309 and JAR 25.1309 are as follows:

- A function is *critical* if the occurrence of any failure condition or design error would *prevent the continued safe flight and landing of the aircraft.*
- A function is *essential* if the occurrence of any failure or design error would *reduce the capability of the aircraft or the ability of the crew to cope with adverse operating conditions.*
- *Non-essential* functions are those for which any failure or design error would *not significantly degrade aircraft capability or crew ability.*

The safety category of some functions may change during operational use, depending on the usage, such as mode, time, condition, or other operational factor. In general, the safety category for the whole system is determined by the highest level of criticality in any function in it, both for the set of all the functions concerned and the time-variation of individual functions.

A refined categorisation is given in a supplementary notice to JAR 25.1309 (ACJ nr 1), dividing the effects into catastrophic, hazardous, major and minor, according to the following definitions:

- An event or combination of events which makes it impossible for the aircraft to continue in safe flight and landing is deemed *catastrophic*; death and/or aircraft loss will result from the event.
- An event or combination of events which gives large reduction in safety margins, physical distress or workload such that the flight crew cannot be relied upon to perform their tasks accurately or completely, or could cause serious injury to or death of a relatively small proportion of the occupants is deemed *hazardous.*
- An event or combination of events which gives significant reduction in safety margins reduces the ability of the flight crew to cope with adverse operating conditions, impairs their efficiency, or causes injury to occupants is deemed to be a *major* effect.
- Events which give only slight reduction in safety margins, slight increase in workload (e.g. routine changes in flight plan) or physical effects but no injury to occupants are deemed to be *minor* effects.

Separate guidance is given for software in avionics systems, defining assessment procedures that are required by the Regulatory Authority for certifying the software that implements each function.

Table 2.1 Tolerable probabilities for hazard categories

Category	Effect of malfunction or design error	Max. probability per operating hour
Essential:		
minor	Reduction of ability to cope	10^{-5}
major	Significant reduction of ability to cope	10^{-7}
Critical:	Prevent continued safe flight	10^{-9}

For avionics systems, the probability of malfunctions or design errors must be extremely improbable (better than 1 in 10^9 operating hours) for critical functions, extremely remote (better than 1 in 10^7 operating hours) for major essential functions, and remote (better than 1 in 10^5 operating hours) for minor essential functions. We show these in Table 2.1. Probabilities in terms of operating hours are significant for usage, and show what redundancy may be required, but they cannot be directly interpreted for design characteristics such as software, since the impact of a fault depends on the variety of situations that must be handled during these periods. Thus the critical software must operate properly even in the extremely improbable combinations of circumstances that arise only once in 10^9 operating hours (i.e. once in about 100,000 years of continuous operation).

2.2.1 DO-178A

Guidance for the production and verification of safety-related software in avionics equipment and systems has been prepared by the Radio Technical Commission for Aeronautics (RTCA, a US government and industry advisory body), and the European Organisation for Civil Aviation Electonics (EUROCAE, the corresponding European advisory body). The joint document, 'Software considerations in airborne systems and equipment certification' (revised 1985) is principally aimed at commercial aircraft, but is also influencing military standards in the United States, Europe and the United Kingdom. For example, the UK Ministry of Defence Interim Standard 00-31/Issue 1 relied heavily on it.

The RTCA Guidelines, known as DO-178A, describe the underlying principles of software development and an approach to software certification, but leave the details of applying these principles (or supplementing them if necessary) to be defined for each specific project and agreed with the certifying authorities. This book is intended to guide software designers in the application of the RTCA principles to software written in Ada.

The document presents guidance and recommendations for performing the major tasks in software engineering, including the categorisation of functional criticality, selection of assurance levels for software (according to criticality of function), techniques and methods for software development, verification and validation suitable for use by an applicant for certification, the range of system software requirements, development planning and testing relevant for certification, disciplines for configuration management and quality assurance, and recommended documentation to justify certification (both initially and after modification).

The guidance is based on partitioning all the activities of equipment and systems as disjoint 'functions'. The software is presumed to be partitioned accordingly, and the presumption is confirmed by analysis for breaches of the partitioning. Each partition is tested comprehensively, with an analysis of the coverage of the tests. This concept fits well with Ada, apart from the need to consider *layers* of software over the hardware in the system design. We discuss this point further in Section 7.4 below.

DO-178A covers the control of software design and its verification, describing how to structure the work to give the visibility needed for the proper management which is needed to support claims for certification.

It distinguishes the following specifications:

- system requirements;
- software requirements (verified against system requirements);
- software design (verified against software requirements);
- software implementation (verified against software design);

and testing based on

- requirements (verifying the performance of intended functions);
- structure (verifying the coverage of all parts of the software);

applied to

- software modules individually;
- integrated sets of software modules;
- software integrated in the real hardware.

All of these are achieved naturally in Ada using the approach advocated in this book.

The structure of the software is critically important (hence the significance of Ada packages), as partitioning into well-separated parts means that no action in package A can cause an action in package B to fail, and no action of one function can cause another to fail. The verification process must assure this, which is significantly easier with software in Ada, but still depends on the underlying software and hardware supporting the execution of the software. If a task runs amok, it must not imperil the behaviour of any other task in the same processor (McCormick, 1988).

Although DO-178A is written as though there were intrinsic differences in the ways of producing the software with different risk factors; the real difference is in the rigour of the checking applied, not in the software itself. Tests have to be verified as well as performed satisfactorily. DO-178A requires reports to be produced on the tests of software at Risk Factors 1 and 2, to verify their adequacy.

For Risk Factor 1 software, each test must be traced back to one of the requirements; any deviations from standards must be justified; any problems must be tracked from detection to cure; and the whole process must be audited to ensure that it is complete. For Risk Factor 2 software, a general statement of compliance is needed, with a summary description of the verification process and problem correction. The kinds of checks implied are discussed in Sections 12.6 and 13.6; further details of the documents called for by DO-178A are given in Appendix C.

2.2.2 ARINC paper 613

The airline community now recommends the use of Ada in order to reduce the cost and economic risk associated with software systems. Airlines Radio Incorporated (ARINC) has published a guide on the use of Ada in avionics systems (ARINC paper 613, reproduced as Appendix A). The Guide deals with the use of Ada in 'the development, testing and maintenance of digital avionics for the commercial aviation industry'. It recognises that the elements of the Ada language are not all equally important for avionics software, but that certain identified features can be recommended for avionics, including major features of the language that compilers should support efficiently, and other operational features that should be supported by all compilers used for avionics software. The ARINC Guide does not specifically address safety, but provides useful motivation on general grounds for using Ada in avionics software.

2.2.3 Assessment

The intensity of the assessment depends on the criticality of the function, in order to ensure that the probability of failure is better than the tolerable value; DO-178A refers to these as 'levels' of software, but MoD Std 00-31 calls them 'Risk Factors'

Table 2.2 Severity scale for categories of effect and tolerable probability

Severity	Effect category	Risk Factor	Tolerable frequency/probability	
				10^{0}
1	normal		frequent	10^{-1}
2				10^{-2}
3	nuisance	3	probable	10^{-3}
4	minor		reasonably probable	10^{-4}
5				10^{-5}
6	major		remote	10^{-6}
7		2	improbable	10^{-7}
8	hazardous		extremely remote	10^{-8}
9				10^{-9}
10	catastrophic	1	extremely improbable	10^{-10}

Table 2.3 Relationship between probability and severity of effects (avionics)

Probability	Category	Severity of effect
10^0	Normal	
10^{-1}		
10^{-2}	Nuisance	
10^{-3}	Minor	Operating limitations; emergency procedures
10^{-4}		
10^{-5}	**Major**	**Significant reductions in safety margins; difficult for crew to cope with adverse conditions; passenger injuries**
10^{-6}		
10^{-7}	Hazardous	Large reductions in safety margins; crew extended because of work load or environmental conditions. Serious injury or death of small number of occupants.
10^{-8}		
10^{-9}	**Catastrophic**	**Multiple deaths, usually with loss of aircraft**

(to avoid confusion with design levels). We follow the latter nomenclature here.

The relationship between tolerable probability for the several categories of effect and the associated Risk Factor, interpreting the above more specifically, is given in Tables 2.2 and 2.3.

2.3 Procurement of safety critical systems containing software

The UK Ministry of Defence policy for the procurement of safety critical systems containing software (with an associated Interim Standard: 00–55, published in draft when this book was written) lays down the respective responsibilities of the MoD Project Manager and the Design Authority for such a system. The policy document defines the information that must be passed between them at the start and completion of the development project, and the ways in which such a project must be carried out, emphasising that the practices and procedures used must be over and above those of conventional software engineering.

The MoD Project Manager must be involved from the concept stage, before any software development contract is let. Any likelihood of Safety Critical Software must be identified, and the Project Requirement Specification written in plain text. The MoD Project Manager also has to be the MoD Software Safety Authority: this responsibility cannot be delegated or assigned to the Design Authority.

The Design Authority must appoint an independent Software Safety Assessor, who will monitor all relevant activities during the software development. Particular kinds of check may be required, depending on the criticality category of the software. (For examples of the kind of check that might be called for, see Appendix D.) On completion of the project, the Design Authority must certify that the prescribed safety assurance activities have been carried out satisfactorily, and the independent Software Safety Assessor must confirm this by countersigning the certificate.

The Safety Certificate (with the Safety Plan and Safety Records for the project: see Chapter 15) shows the evidence on which the MoD Project Manager will decide whether to accept the developed software.

This style of working puts significant technical responsibilities on the Project Manager, and assists him or her in dealing with these responsibilities by providing general guidance. Particular guidance on the issues affected by the use of Ada are given in this book.

2.4 EWICS TC7 guidelines

The European Workshop on Industrial Computer Systems (EWICS) Technical Committee 7 on *Systems Reliability, Safety and Security* has published guidelines for Safety-Related Computers (EWICS, 1985), concerning software development and systems documentation, and has recently prepared further details on System Integrity, Software Quality Assurance and Metrics, Design for System Safety, and Reliability and Safety Assessment (Redmill, 1988, 1989). These guidelines are deliberately written without presumptions about the programming languages used, and the principles include considerations about the language as well as the program itself. This book shows how the principles of the EWICS guidelines apply to programs written in Ada, so that the advances in security and compile-time checking made possible by the rules of the language allow the program designer to devote more attention to the safety-critical issues. Appendix E gives a summary of the guidelines, with notes on their interpretation for Ada.

The EWICS guidelines for the development of safety-related software comprise specific principles with detailed guidelines (at three levels of priority) for the *development* of safety-related software, and guidelines for the *documentation* of safety-related computer systems. Note that the second part refers to hardware as well as to software, whereas the first part is solely concerned with the software.

The EWICS guidelines explicitly advise projects to select from the general recommendations given, and to record the selection. This book can be regarded as such a documented selection, appropriate for systems programmed in Ada. A general principle is that the more critical a package is to the safety of the system, the more straightforward should be the style of programming adopted, and the more restrictive the guidelines. Thus the less critical parts may be permitted to infringe the rules given, although it is still desirable to explain why.

Safety, as we point out in this book, is not a property of software alone, but of the whole system in which software may be a part. The attention given to software in the EWICS guidelines reflects this viewpoint.

2.5 ACARD

The ACARD (1986) report *Software: A key to UK competitiveness* presents a possible scenario in which any life-critical computer system must have a License To Operate, issued by the licensing authority, after the operator has been granted a Safety Certificate. (The operator must also name a Certified Software Engineer as being personally responsible for its operation and evolution or maintenance, that is, rectification and development.) The Safety Certificate will only be granted after a rigorous inspection process, covering the process of development as well as the product itself, taking into account the degree of risk, the severity of the danger and the cost.

This possible scenario is more pervasive than any that yet exists, but forms a valuable basis for thinking about the problems. It is similar to the Ministry of Defence policy described in Section 2.3 above. The inspection process for safety certification has to ensure the competence of the people involved, the soundness of the methods of construction, the proper application of these methods during original construction and subsequent evolution; the soundness of the tools used; and the verification to an appropriate level of the software concerned.

The general principle applied is that the *quality* of the software must be greater when there are potential dangers arising from its use. (Software quality is discussed below, in Section 4.4.) It is significant, however, that the ACARD report deals only with *correctness* in the context of Safety Certification, giving no recognition to the problem of interaction with the real world where the potential dangers lie (i.e. *physical* safety in contrast with *logical* safety). This book puts more emphasis on safety by properly controlling the use of potentially dangerous devices, and isolation of program parts through the use of Ada packages.

2.6 International Electrotechnical Commission

Working groups of the International Electrotechnical Commission (SC65A/WGs 9 and 10) are preparing standards for safety-related systems and for the associated software. When this book was written, a draft of the software standard had been issued for comment, giving a multi-level categorisation of hazard class (like that for avionics systems), but a looser relationship between hazard class and tolerable probability. The hazards to be taken into account are as follows:

- loss of human life or lives;
- injuries to or illness of persons;
- environmental pollution;
- loss of or damage to property.

Tolerable risks of these hazards occurring may be specified as a quantified probability (singly or in combination) depending on the particular industry.

An earlier draft of the standard had listed criticality levels (safety risk to society) classified in the following way:

(B1) wide scale risk to life;
(B2) wide scale environmental risk with no immediate risk to life or limb;
(B3) risk to life or limb on a contained scale;
(B4) wide scale economic risk, not to life or limb;
(B5) no risk to life, limb or property.

The intention is that the *system* standard will combine the severity of the hazard with the tolerable frequency of occurrence to give an overall system integrity level; the *software* standard will then define a software integrity level on a five-point scale (where level 1 is 'very high' and level 5 is 'normal').

All aspects of software development, from architecture to assessment, are then considered, and techniques applicable for each aspect given a recommendation for each software integrity level: Highly Recommended, Recommended, or Not Recommended. For example, under System Design Techniques, Fault Tolerance is Recommended for all safety integrity levels; Fault Avoidance is Highly Recommended for levels 1–3, and Recommended for levels 4 and 5. Under System Assessment Techniques, Fault Tolerance is Highly Recommended for safety integrity levels 1 and 2, and Recommended for levels 3–5; Fault Avoidance is Highly Recommended for all levels.

In the published document, the tabulated recommendations are not definitive, but are given to illustrate how the software integrity level approach can be (and presumably is intended to be) developed.

2.7 Legal considerations

A wide range of legal frameworks exists in the field of safety, and this book does not seek to interpret the law in any sense. For the United Kingdom, the principal major Acts are as follows:

- The Mines and Quarries Act 1954;
- The Factories Act 1961;

- The Offices, Shops and Railway Premises Act 1963 (OSRP Act);
- The Nuclear Installations Act 1965;
- The Civil Aviation Act 1971;
- The Health and Safety at Work etc. Act 1974 (HSW Act);
- The Consumer Protection Act 1987.

There are numerous regulations laid down in addition to these, which may be relevant to a specific application.

A basic feature of the Consumer Protection Act is the notion that the product may be defective (and in consequence harm a person); the Act says that a defect (in the safety of the product) occurs if the product is not as safe as members of the public are generally entitled to expect. The significance of 'expectation' in relation to safety is developed further in Section 11.2 below.

3

Control systems

SAFETY INVOLVES CONTROL: there must be some means of controlling the sources of potential dangers. We therefore first investigate properties of control systems in general, in order to establish the context for the safety or danger that might arise during their use.

We devote this chapter to discussing computer-based control systems, because a safety system is a special kind of control system. A protection system (as envisaged in the Health and Safety Executive Guide) is a further special kind of control system.

In this chapter, we introduce a common nomenclature for discussing control systems (Section 3.1), and describe their structure (Section 3.2). This leads to the important identification of safety interlocks and guards (Section 3.3), and their relevance in control systems of various kinds, particularly when the control loop delay is significant (Section 3.4) or involves human interaction (Section 3.5). Finally, we consider the significance of malfunctions and unavailability of the control system (Section 3.6).

3.1 Nomenclature

The nomenclature we will use in this book is illustrated in Figure 3.1. We are considering the design of software for a potentially dangerous embedded-computer system; we will call the intended software system S; the computer system on which it runs T; the system in which it is embedded U; the people or property susceptible to danger V; and the whole environment in which everything operates W.

Thus the computer system T has input–output peripherals that allow it to control the enclosing system U, and also input peripherals that allow it to sense information from the environment W (particularly about V) that may be relevant to the correct and safe operation of U, to avoid harming V. The software S is responsible for achieving the right interactions between all of these.

The requirements for the control system T (implying S) must be formulated to state clearly its purpose, boundaries and information flows.

Notice the relationships between these elements: S defines the behaviour of T (in terms of its primitive actions); T senses and controls activities in U; U has the possibility (which is to be prevented) of acting dangerously on V; and U and V

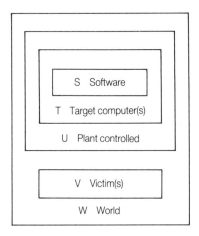

Figure 3.1 Nomenclature

together act within W. T may be able to sense the states of V and W as well as U, but it does not directly control them. There may be part of U (a guard) which can influence the behaviour of V.

3.2 Structure of a control system

In terms of the above nomenclature, we can distinguish three major parts in the world of a control system: the outer environment (W), the system being controlled (U), and the control system itself (T). The system being controlled, together with the control system, constitute the controlled system or plant (U+T). We may describe the system being controlled as the bare plant (that is, the plant without any controlling system). Recognising that the plant comprises the system being controlled *plus the control system* is important for the user, but the combination of the environment with the system being controlled is more important for the control system designer, who has to see the bare plant in the context of its environment, about which information is available as input to the control system, and in which the plant responds to control signals sent from the control system.

The bare plant interacts with its environment in terms of the plant commodities: materials, energy etc.; the bare plant also interacts with its controller in terms of information, through transducers (sensors and effectors). The controller probably needs to include some model of the plant in its environment, with identified states and processes. Information received by the controller from the bare plant is used within the controller to adjust its own model of the plant, subject to some inevitable time delay. Figure 3.2 illustrates this relationship, showing the plant processing the external commodity, and the control loop affecting it through the sensors, controller and effectors.

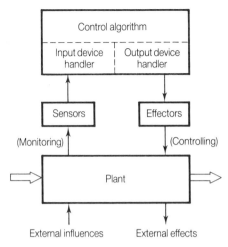

Figure 3.2 Plant and control loop

The fundamental problem of safety in a controlled system concerns the richness of the interaction between the bare plant and its environment. The bare plant is (and has to be) capable of carrying out certain actions which are in some circumstances desired, and in other circumstances definitely to be prevented. Thus it is capable of interacting more richly than is desired with its environment. The responsibility of the safety controller is to ensure that the plant carries out these special (dangerous) actions only when the circumstances are suitable: by using what we call interlocks and guards.

Depending on the nature of the plant and its control system, various effects must be taken into account for their potential impact on safety. The simplest are all-electrical systems (in which an effect is immediate). In any physical system there is a risk of deterioration (random hardware failures), which can cause the physical unit to fail. In an inertial system, there is a delay before control signals are effective (latency). In a communication system, there is latency and fallibility; and in a system involving human interaction as well as automatic information handling, problems of latency, fallibility and perversity may arise.

Another important distinction is between *static* and *dynamic* safety. The plant may have a safe stable state into which it can be set if the control system fails. But if it does not have such a state, the requirements for *availability* of the control system take precedence over the specific considerations of safety. In this book, we concentrate on the design of a control system to achieve static safety, since that is where software and Ada are particularly significant. To achieve dynamic safety, the control system must be structured primarily for high availability (by replication of unreliable components, coordinated by software), and secondarily for safety using the software techniques we describe.

We discuss these possibilities in the following sections. They must be taken into account according to the specific characteristics of the control system and plant, but do not have any special influence on the use of Ada.

3.3 Safety interlocks

We will presume, since otherwise safety is not at issue, that U is capable of some actions that are dangerous, in that they can harm potential victims V. Note that the actions of S are never dangerous in themselves, and that we disregard potential dangers of T. (If we wish to protect users from the risk of the computer falling over on top of them, we must make sure that appropriate sensors and effectors exist, and consider the housing of the physical computer T as part of the plant U.)

> The essence of designing for safety (in a computer-based system) is to ensure that the potentially dangerous actions of U can only take place when it is safe to do so. This means that possible dangerous actions of U must be constrained by suitable interlocks, or the possible victims V must be constrained by suitable guards. The interlocks and guards depend on the existence of suitable sensors and effectors in T, and above all on the correctness of the software S.

So a first level analysis, carried out on the information established as the statement of requirements, is the check that appropriate interlocks and guards can be set up. We must identify the potential dangers in U, establish the criteria for safe use of dangerous equipment, ascertain that sensors can provide the information needed to discriminate between safe and hazardous modes of operation, and ensure that every danger can be protected against by a combination of interlock and guard. The safety requirements for a control system have to be established, which is the topic of Chapter 5. The nomenclature we use for the safety interlocks (including the state of the guard) is the predicate SAFE(U, V, W). This shows that safety in general involves the state of the plant, the state of the possible victim(s) and the state of the surrounding environment.

In accordance with the principles of the HSE Guide, the safety protection system may be separate from the control system. This does not remove the obligation to have safety interlocks in the control system, but provides diversity in the overall safety of the plant, by having it explicitly in the safety protection system as well as incidentally in the control system.

3.4 Control loop delay

In most control systems there are significant delays in the control loop, which ultimately limit the kind of control that can be applied to the plant. Conventional control theory is based on continuous (analogue) devices being used, but the same principles apply to discrete digital systems. The differences are that additional problems (latency and quantisation) arise in discrete systems, which in effect increase the loop delay and limit its accuracy. Safety analysis must therefore take account of the total delay and accuracy of the control system.

Delays occur at all stages in the control loop. Each sensor detects the state the plant is in (with some instrumental delay); it may initiate the sending of state reports to the target computer(s), but more commonly the computers poll the sensors to establish the state of the plant, thus introducing a latency delay comprising the time between successive samples of the state being polled. The calculations based on plant states may take further time, depending less on the individual complexity of the control algorithm than on the total load on the computer (because of the scheduling delay), although the designer can take this into account by combining the calculation with the polling cycle. If the controlling computers are distributed, there is additional delay in the transmission of data from one computer to another.

We can analyse the time responses of the controller by noting that the value of any control signal sent from the controller to the bare plant has to take account of three timing effects: the sampling time from the sensors (inputs from U to T), the computing time within the controller based on values received (execution of S in T), followed by the latency time of the effectors (outputs from T to U). The last is particularly important in mechanical devices because of inertia effects.

The time taken to transmit control signals to effector devices may have to be considered if cable routes are long, if there is a shared communication medium into which the signals must be slotted (in contention with others), or if the target computer system is distributed.

Finally, devices that control actuators on the plant have inherent delays arising from the inertia of the actuators and the response of the plant to them. Thus a feedback control system, even using the simplest control algorithm, has delays between the state of the plant at a particular time and the action taken to change the state to a desired value. Under certain circumstances, this can lead to plant instability (if the control delay exceeds the plant response time) which may be avoided by using more complicated algorithms such as the three term PID (Proportional + Integral + Differential) controller.

The complement of delay is anticipation. Designers can anticipate, even though computers cannot. Thus in planning the software for a safety system, the inherent delays must be recognised as for a control system. The safety software may have to take account of timing delays, both in the state information used in the interlocks and in the protection given by guards.

Interlocks would normally be formulated in terms of instantaneous plant states and detectors of potential victims. The viewpoint now introduced draws attention to the fact that each interlock must be formulated with sufficient prediction to compensate for sensory input delays (treating the interlock plus victim plus guard as a higher-level control system). This may include the use of historical information from the sensors (or other internal data), but always being aware of the need to err on the side of safety in each extrapolation, and remembering that historical dependencies increase the number of regions in the data space that must be tested.

It is even more important to take account of delays in the use of guards, since plant inertia will frequently mean that actuators do not take effect immediately. For example, applying a brake to rotating machinery does not bring the speed down immediately; the safety system must take account of the delay before the brake is effective in slowing the machinery, preferably with a speed sensor to indicate when the rotation is slow enough for safety. An absolute delay provides a default anticipation of the time at which the situation will become safe, assuming that the brake works; but actual sensors are preferable. This point is developed further in Chapter 9.

Control system timing   We can express these delays mathematically as follows. If the state of the plant and its environment are sensed at time t to be $v(t)$ and $w(t)$, and the actions in the plant are effected by $u(t)$, we desire

$$u(t) = f(v, w)$$

where v and w denote the information sensed up to time t. An instantaneous response is not feasible because of two effects: (i) sampling from the plant and environment is not instantaneous; and (ii) the evaluation of the function takes time.

The best possible (nearly instantaneous) response is given by

$$u(t) = f(v(t - \delta t - \varepsilon), w(t - \delta t - \varepsilon))$$

where

δt is the time to compute f and deliver the result to the effector

and

ε is less than or equal to the sample interval for the sensors

In most cases there is contextual and historical information to be taken into account as well, which we denote by $x(t)$. The relationship is now given by

$$x(t) = g(v(t - \delta t - \varepsilon), w(t - \delta t - \varepsilon), x(t - \delta t - \varepsilon))$$
$$u(t) = f(v(t - \delta t - \varepsilon), w(t - \delta t - \varepsilon), x(t - \delta t - \varepsilon))$$

The designer must ensure that the formulae and data values used for the interlocks take account of these delays, either by direct reference to sensors or by calculation of the various transmission time delays involved (feed-forward control).

3.5 Designing for human interaction

When a control loop in a system involves human interaction, there are further issues to be considered. As well as the delays in responding to stimuli and the possibility of failure in communication, there is the need to overcome human weaknesses and perversity, including misunderstanding instructions given, from tiredness or poor training, and deliberate attempts to sabotage the system. The last of these is particularly important in systems where compromising the safety might be used for malicious purposes. The designer must be prepared for human misuse, and ensure that the safety interlocks take account of this failure mode. The problem is to distinguish between legitimate and improper human inputs, which means identifying the range of options which are valid in each situation, in other words putting an extra safety barrier round the human inputs.

It has been estimated that 30 per cent of system faults are due to human (operational) errors (Maxion, 1986). Fault-tolerant user interfaces in experiments showed substantial improvements in human performance, but a significant (80 per cent) increase in the cost of the system to provide tolerance to users' faults.

Vulnerability analysis (Dobson and Martin, 1986) can be used with systems in which people are important, because of their propensity for making mistakes, incompetence or malice.

As well as absolute guards against deliberate misuse, it is desirable to have assistance on-line to guide the operator. The assistance should include prompts (to identify what input is required), may often include option lists, and may include on-line help to explain the circumstances for each option. The particular wording of each of these messages should be carefully prepared, so that the users will understand what they are required to do with all the implications of the decisions.

Specific guidance on the 'Man–Machine Interaction' aspects of computer system design have been prepared by another Technical Committee of EWICS: TC4. The guidance covers planning, designing, operating and maintaining industrial plant involving computers. This is an important aspect of system design, but not one to which specific programming techniques or the use of Ada are relevant, so it is not treated further here.

3.6 Control and availability

The behaviour of a computer-based control system, while determined by its software (in terms of the elementary actions of the actuators in the plant), is dependent on the continued availability of the computer(s) that execute the software. Depending on the nature of the control required (continuous or supervisory) and the intrinsic behaviour of the plant, it may be necessary to give special attention to availability in designing the control system. This could involve the use of several computers in parallel, to provide mutual back-up and stand-by facilities.

The safety of a controlled system depends on the control systems (at least the protection system) being available and working properly. Thus malfunction and unavailability of the control system are potential sources of danger. The HSE guidance on configuration and diversity is intended to take account of this kind of risk. However, a control system that relies on redundancy to mitigate the effects of malfunction or unavailibility is likely to depend on software to coordinate the redundant parts; Built-in Test Equipment (BITE) is likely to be driven by software, causing the equipment found faulty to be de-activated and possibly replaced by spares. Here software provides a positive enhancement of safety.

There is an important role for software in the design of a high availabilty system, but it is not specifically a matter of *safety*. We therefore draw attention to the topic of *system* design of the controller, but do not treat it further in this book, as it is outside the principal scope and does not involve any considerations specific to Ada.

High availability can only be achieved by careful design of the system (taking the software and hardware together), to ensure that appropriate steps are taken when failures occur. This means that the software must be designed to deal with the possibility of system failures, by including detection mechanisms for the possible faults, and providing graceful degradation of the system when they are detected. There are random and systematic faults. Faults may arise randomly because of failures in the hardware or subsystems. Although we cannot predict the occurrence of any individual random fault, we can make statistical estimates, based on past experience of the same or similar equipment. Systematic faults arise as a consequence of deficiencies in the software or hardware design, and are exposed whenever particular (unpredicted) situations arise. Failures of this kind will occur consistently (reliably!) when the same combination of circumstances occur, whether during testing or operational use. Prediction of their likelihood is therefore much more difficult, since it is based on the extent to which the operational situation was not anticipated during the development, depending on the people and environment of the development, not on the particular system.

We have mentioned in Section 3.2 the distinction between *static* and *dynamic* safety, the categorisation depending on whether or not the plant has a fail-safe condition. The difference is important for the designer of the control system, bearing in mind that the control system itself may fail. (Failure of the control system may be due to a random hardware failure or to a previously undetected systematic error being exposed by an unusual combination of circumstances.) If a fail-safe condition exists, the protection system must bring the plant to this condition whenever any failure develops in the controller. But if the plant has no fail-safe condition (e.g. an aircraft in flight), then the *availability* of the control system is of fundamental importance for safety, *even if the software is perfectly correct*.

Thus in such systems, there is a significant additional consideration for safety, beyond the scope of software. We refer to these two kinds of system as requiring static and dynamic safety, respectively, because software provides a static description of the behaviour of the control system, and the availability of the target computers which run it is a dynamic property.

The designer of a control system thus has to consider the impact on safety of both software-determined behaviour and the underlying hardware. If the availability of the raw hardware is adequate for the necessary reliability of the control system, then the designer can concentrate on those software issues immediately related to safety. But in the more difficult case when the raw hardware availability is inadequate, it is necessary to design a high availability system – which introduces significant extra problems for the software designer, not immediately related to safety. Designing software (in Ada or otherwise) for a high availability system is a substantive topic, which is better treated separately from the considerations of safety that form the basis of the present book.

In particular, because failure of the computer running the software is a common cause which would result in the loss of *all* of the software-determined behaviour, there is *nothing* that software (in the same computer) can do to avoid or overcome it. To achieve greater availability, the control system must be designed as a distributed system, with several computers configured for redundancy, thus providing detection and back-up by being suitably programmed, giving mutual protection against coincidental random failures. Software must coordinate and synchronise their actions, ensuring data integrity and substitution when a failure is detected. We do not discuss these topics further here, as they go beyond considerations of safety.

To summarise: the analysis of a system to determine its safety requirements must take account of the risks of malfunction and unavailability; the system design must ensure that the residual probabilities are sufficiently small for the risk to be tolerated, given the nature of the harm that might be caused. Logical design may presume infinite and infallible resources, but physical design must provide mechanisms with suitable (non-catastrophic) reductions when actual resource limits are approached. This principle is significant at many points in system design.

We discuss the implications of this from the point of view of the software designer in Chapter 5 below, and from the viewpoint of confirmation in Chapter 11.

4

Programming for safety

SOFTWARE is not inherently either safe or dangerous. However, software can be used to control devices that are inherently dangerous, rendering them safe. (Fortunately it cannot work the other way, making safe devices become dangerous!) Thus we see that the property of safeness or danger resides in the plant controlled by the computer concerned, not in the software.

The power of a computer is limited by the nature of the peripheral devices that are connected to it; here we are considering systems in which there are potentially dangerous devices directly or indirectly under software control. Such devices have the intrinsic power to harm life or property, but this power is protected from misuse by interlocks and guards that are dependent on software. For example, computer controlled machine tools could cause direct harm, and computer controlled collision avoidance systems (e.g. traffic lights) could cause indirect harm (by giving green in both directions). Similarly, a computer controlled train could cause harm to its passengers and to anyone or anything on its track by virtue of its physical movement and momentum. In the intended mode of operation, interlocks ensure that the potentially dangerous functions occur only when nothing is present that could be harmed.

Thus safety is not an absolute property, but is dependent on the context of use. The role of software in connection with assuring safety is two-fold: it must be correct with respect to the control of the critical devices, and it must implement interlocks for those devices to ensure that their use is safe. Such interlocks depend on the ability of the system to detect and distinguish properly between the safe and dangerous circumstances, in order to restrict the potentially dangerous functions to safe situations. In addition, software can enhance safety by coordinating the use of built-in tests and redundant hardware.

Safety-critical systems require software that imposes context-dependent limits on the operation of certain output devices: a central kind of requirement for safety is that (depending on the circumstances) the system must detect situations when it must *not* carry out particular actions of which it is capable.

Software is thus responsible for the behaviour of the plant. Safe behaviour depends on the software making the appropriate discrimination between safe and dangerous conditions, and controlling the plant properly. Because of this fundamental responsibility, any residual defect in the software could lead to the safety integrity of the plant being lost. This is the nature of automatic control: if the automaton is in control, then we rely on the automaton taking proper decisions and actions.

In discussing the impact of programming on safety, we first consider the problem of specifying software requirements (Section 4.1) as the definition of the required behaviour. The ways in which software affects safety are explained in Section 4.2, and its relationship with correctness in Section 4.3 (which introduces the problem of correctness of components and tools used). The quality of software is a central issue, which is analysed in Section 4.4, leading to a treatment of confidence and reliability in Section 4.5. General guidelines for software development in safety related computers, prepared by EWICS, are summarised in Section 4.6 to conclude the chapter.

4.1 Specifying software requirements

We can recognise three kinds of information in a software requirements specification: the functional characteristics, the constraints, and the quality aspects. Most theoretical work on specifications focusses entirely on the functional properties, which define the behaviour of the automaton. It is important for control systems not to stop there; particularly for real-time systems, it is important also to state constraints, although one cannot sensibly say anything about the constraints until the functional properties have been identified. The quality properties, including safety, provide a kind of back-up and internal redundancy, permitting important consistency checks to be applied within the specification.

The functional part of the requirements specification should indicate what kinds of action the system should take in all situations, normal and abnormal. In other words it should have both positive and negative parts. The positive part is the principal constituent, which describes the intended functionality of the controller in relation to the bare plant. The negative side, however, is important, as it indicates specific safety and security requirements for the controller to prevent any damaging actions that are not intended to occur. In general, there are particular actions possible by the bare plant which the controller must ensure never take place.

It is important to identify and distinguish the positive and negative functionalities in critical areas, as different techniques are necessary to give the assurances of positive and negative properties. Positive functions can be demonstrated, but the software must be analysed comprehensively to give negative assurances. In general, positive functions relate to individual software components (subprograms and packages in Ada), whereas negative properties depend on the system structure (package separation and context clauses in Ada).

The constraints need the framework established by the functional part as the basis for their description. They fall into two parts: constraints on the target system being produced, and constraints on the project whose goal is to produce that system. Constraints of the first kind relate to resources needed in the target system (such as storage space, processing time, input–output bandwidth, back-up facilities, etc.);

those of the second kind relate to the resources needed in the course of producing the system (such as manpower, elapsed time, and facilities in a host development environment).

The qualities in the specification summarise intentions and more general properties required. These are often subjective and difficult to confirm beforehand; they include user-friendliness of the man–machine interfaces, ease of maintenance, robustness, and dependability. Safety also comes into this category, as it depends on the relationship between the software-controlled plant and its environment (not on the software alone). A fruitful analysis of these properties comes from considering the effect of *negating them*, and examining the consequential effect on the resulting design; in the case of safety, this leads us to look for the potential dangers, which in the proper system we have to prevent. Dependability in particular depends on the prospects of physical failures, and the availability of back-up facilities to take over in such situations. The transition from primary facilities to back-up (and even more, the reverse transition after the primary has been repaired and has to resume its proper role) is particularly tricky and a significant source of risk. We develop this idea further in Chapter 6.

The first two parts of the requirements specification are involved differently in the subsequent development activities: the functional part is the major input to the logical design activity; the constraints part, together with the result of the logical design, is needed for the physical design. Both the logical and physical designs determine the program.

DO-178A document 2 (see Appendix C) illustrates the information that must be provided as software requirements:

- functional and operational characteristics of the software;
- each operating function or operating mode;
- performance, test, design and criticality for each function;
- sizing and timing;
- hardware/software interfaces;
- built-in test and/or monitoring;
- performance (degradation and function) under fault conditions.

These fall into the categories we have identified above, but are broken into a number of sections to ensure that attention is given to all modes of operation, both intended and unintended.

The HSE Guide gives a useful checklist (10A) for reviewing the software requirements. We discuss the designer's use of software requirements further in Chapter 7, and the verifier's use of them in Chapter 11.

4.2 How does programming affect safety?

Software is fundamentally important for safety because it prescribes the behaviour of the control system in an explicit and formal way that is susceptible to analysis and reasoning. As control systems have become more complex, such analyses have become increasingly necessary, both of the intentions and of the actuality. The concepts and notations of software permit behaviour to be described, whatever technology is used to implement it – whether it is by relays, hard-wiring, pneumatics, firmware or stored program computers. Software in a computer-based system controls the actions of all the potentially dangerous devices. The principal contribution of programming to safety is the visibility it gives to this control activity, allowing it to be analysed and assessed.

4.2.1 Choice of programming language

Programming languages differ in their focus of attention – what features they make highly visible, what they hide or cannot express. Ada has brought the issue to a head by its explicit focus on embedded-computer systems, where safety is often significant.

Few high-level languages recognise the need for input–output programming, particularly of the unconventional peripherals that are concerned as sensors and effectors in a safety-related system. Encapsulation of input–output operations into Ada packages provides for the controlled access to critical operations, limiting the parts of the program that must be given special attention to verify their correctness (and consequently to justify the trust that is placed in them). By treating input–output devices in this way, the logical and physical (representational) aspects of device handling can be clearly distinguished; as a consequence, analyses can be carried out to show that the sequences of statements correctly provide the required control and data to the sensors and effectors, taking acount of the circumstances.

Ada has been criticised (e.g. by Hoare, 1981) for certain 'unsafe' characteristics, but this serves to show how close Ada has come to the needs of system programmers. No previous programming language was even close to meeting the safety requirements: assembly languages provide no visibility of intention; BASIC, C, Forth, Fortran, Pascal (and even Algol-68) are all significantly deficient, particularly in their input–output and modularity features. The features of Ada that can lead to unreliability have now been studied by several authors (particularly Wichmann, 1988), and the position is reviewed in Section 8.3 below.

4.2.2 Formality in software

Formal techniques are fundamental to all computer-based systems. The information handling in a computer is always formal, being based entirely on the form of the data (ultimately the bit-patterns) regardless of any meaning or interpretation. Programming languages such as Ada are formal, so that inferences can be made about them and programs in them by manipulating the texts. (This is essentially what tools such as SPADE and MALPAS do: see Chapter 12.)

Package declarations in Ada are formal, and Ada compilers check that the body corresponding to each specification is consistent with it; however, the information contained in an Ada package declaration is limited to the declarations of its constituents (and certain representations) with no formal specification of its intended or claimed semantics.

4.2.3 Limitations of software

No software can (without its operating environment) determine the time-performance of the plant. Ada was criticised in its early implementations for not making adequate use of the speed of the processor on which the software ran; however, this criticism is no longer applicable with second generation Ada compilers and run-time systems.

This is not to say that Ada is perfect for the purpose: only that it is the best language we currently have available. Its major defects reflect the state of the art in programming and software engineering in 1980, when it was designed: the absence of any way of expressing the intended semantics of program units, and the weak linkage between the software and its associated hardware.

We can conclude that the important programming features for safety are visibility of program structure and separation of concerns, leading to identification of critical parts. This partitioning allows the critical parts of the software system to be checked adequately, thus justifying confidence that the control system will take all proper actions.

4.3 Correctness and safety

A strong distinction must be made between correctness and safety. It is easy to leave errors in programs, even after extensive analysis and testing. Errors in a safety-critical program could result in serious danger, but this is not the only source of danger. Experience has also shown that a large proportion of the problems originate in the specification, so that even if the program is correct (with respect to its specification) it could still be unsafe. Thus correctness is not sufficient for safety. Because of the practical impossibility of eliminating all errors from large software systems, we know that it is futile to strive for correctness of the whole of a large program. However, we can focus on a safety-critical kernel, provided that we can be sure that this is adequately isolated. The great strength of Ada is that it allows the program to be so partitioned that a safety-critical part can be isolated, and the rest of the program written to use it without the risk of inadvertent misuse of the safety-critical part. This is the approach of the present book.

4.3.1 Which parts must be correct?

The overall situation is therefore:

- safety requires certain parts of the program to be correct;
- safety requires the whole program to be disciplined in using them;
- correctness is not completely achievable;
- correctness of small parts is achievable;

from which it follows that

- safety-critical parts must be kept small;
- those program parts must be adequately isolated;

which can be done using Ada; but in any case

- correctness is not sufficient;

and checks are needed beyond those that test for correctness.

Software faults can be traced back to errors in three basic sources: specifications, assumptions and the logic of derivation. Extensive checking is needed to search for such faults. Explicit formulation is the effective way of making the information from these sources visible, so that any errors can be detected and corrected before the fault has serious consequences. This analysis of correctness and safety shows that the most important contribution of Ada to safety integrity is its support for programs written in distinct parts (packages) which can be made sufficiently small for the critical ones to be verified with complete confidence, and sufficiently isolated from one another that they do not interfere, with explicit dependencies throughout the whole program. The most important consideration for the Ada programmer in the achievement of safety is the identification of the critical and sensitive packages, so that appropriate rigour can be applied to their checking, in accordance with their criticality.

DO-178A requires the software to be partitioned, so that the failure of one element cannot cause the failure of another element. The partitioning of a system is the fundamental aspect of system design, which is discussed further in Section 7.4.

4.3.2 Using unreliable components

If we had to insist on the perfection of every element that contributed to a control system, we would never be able to start. The secret is to be able to build a system with *greater* reliability than any individual component. We do this by knowing the failure modes of the components, and designing the system so that any actual failure is detected and counteracted before it impairs system integrity.

This principle is most conspicuously applied to the hardware design, but it also has a place in the software design, through the technique of defensive programming. Where the behaviour of some part of the system has to be highly reliable (by which is meant that the raw reliability of the hardware and software is not good enough), one way of improving the reliability is to operate run-time checks on the states that the system is expected to be in on entry to, and exit from, critical parts, with an alternative formulation of acceptable behaviour to be carried out if the checks indicate a failure. The conditions which the state is intended to satisfy at these positions are known as the pre- and post-conditions for the pieces of program concerned; Sections 8.4, 9.2 and 12.4 discuss this idea in more detail.

This general idea can be applied in a number of ways, including recovery blocks (Randell, 1975) and exception handlers. With recovery blocks, the state of the system is captured at the pre-condition, and reset if the post-condition is not achieved; with exceptions there is no automatic capture and resetting. Ada provides for exceptions, as explained in Section 9.3 below.

Other contributors to a computer-based system are the software tools used to develop and check it. These must not be assumed to be perfect, but, rather, are likely to contain faults, particularly in the parts that are rarely used. Here, however, we see the benefits of a software tool, since any deficiency in it will be systematically visible. Thus wide use of a tool gives visibility to its problem areas; conversely, the extent of successful use gives confidence for further use within its well-used range. Sections 7.7. and 11.7 develop this theme further.

4.4 Quality levels in software

Since the software is responsible for the safe operation of the plant, it is of course necessary that the program itself should not introduce further errors. The confidence that can be placed in a software system depends on the likelihood that it does not contain serious residual defects. This depends in turn on two principal characteristics: the sheer size of the software concerned, and the techniques used for checking it. We equate this with the *quality* of the software.

Errors may be in the specification or the design of the software. The definition must cover errors of all kinds (trivial to catastrophic), because the significance of a software error is not intrinsic, but depends on the context of its use. If there is a certain possibility that an error might be present, the software cannot determine what the consequences might be.

A fundamental source of error is our understanding of the nature of the real world with which the software deals. The specification of the program is bound to rely on assumptions about the real-world behaviour, which inevitably affect the software. (Lehmann, 1988, has estimated that one in ten lines of a program depends on such assumptions.)

Confidence in software can best be expressed by indicating the probability of errors remaining after all checking. The development and checking techniques will provide assurance that certain kinds of defect are absent. These are different orders of magnitude, depending on the effort and rigour applied to the processes.

In addition to checking individual programs, in the case where alternatives are acceptable, design diversity is a valuable technique for achieving reliability (see Section 7.5). This has an unexpected added bonus, given the problem of being sure that the specification is right in the first place: if several teams are independently trying to design a system from the same specification, then each will detect a different selection of mistakes in the same specification, and the resulting specification will be better even if only one of the resulting designs is used (see Section 7.5).

The ACARD report described in Section 2.5 recommends various levels of rigour in the inspection process, adjusted to the degree of risk, the severity of the danger and the cost. Several levels of certification are envisaged, ranging from normal quality to a disaster level of importance depending on the nature of the danger that has to be averted: inconvenience (normal quality), financial loss (high-quality level), one death (safety level), and more than ten deaths (disaster level). Here we develop this ACARD idea.

4.4.1 Size and error rate

As programs get larger, the probability of an error being present (for a given development technology) obviously grows in proportion to the size, or faster. To indicate the size of a program, it is common to count the number of 'lines', which in Ada really means the number of structural semicolons. With this definition, 'lines' include statements (simple and compound), declarations and specifications, but not semicolons in strings or comments. (One of the reasons why more lines have to be written in Ada than in earlier languages is that it gives more attention to the non-executable information that is otherwise given in documentation, if at all.) All lines that might interact must be counted, although the visibility rules of Ada reduce the risk of unintended interaction between distinct packages.

Note that error rates expressed in terms of 'lines of code' are independent of programming language, provided that the real source program texts are used rather than any texts generated automatically from an earlier source. Various other definitions of size, with greater attention to complexity, have been advocated (particularly by Halstead, 1977 and McCabe, 1976), but they have been shown (by Bache and Tinker, 1988, and Shepperd, 1988) to give no significant advantage over the 'lines of code' counts.

Target error rates in software for these ACARD levels of certification are shown in Table 4.1. They are given as residual errors per line, i.e. per structural semicolon in an Ada program unit. These error rates (10^{-3}, 10^{-4}, 10^{-5} and 10^{-6}) should be compared with 10^{-2} (i.e. 1 per cent), typically achieved currently.

The major contribution of Ada in this respect is the encapsulation of program units into well-isolated parts, so that (provided design rules are followed to control the possible communication paths) critical parts can be kept small and hence have a high probability of correctness.

4.4.2 Quality scale

This description suggests a scale for indicating quality levels, based on the residual error rate, using a negative logarithmic scale (like the pH scale used to measure

Table 4.1 Quality-dependent checks

Risk	Quality level	Technique (style)	Residual error rate
	2	**Conventional testing**	10^{-2}
	3	Strong type matching	10^{-3}
High	4	**Mathematical specification**	10^{-4}
Safety	5	Rigorous analysis	10^{-5}
Disaster	6	**Formal correctness proof**	10^{-6}

acidity). On this scale, software with a residual error rate of 10^{-3} errors per line has a quality level of 3. A quality level of 0 means that there is likely to be an error in every line! Different techniques capable of detecting a wider variety of errors must be used to achieve the lower error rates, and to justify the confidence that will be placed in the resulting software (see Table 4.1).

Current manual technology for programs written in languages less rigorous than Ada leads to errors (bugs) at a rate of order one per hundred lines of program; to get better levels of correctness we must use greater rigour, at least in the checking, but preferably (to avoid waste) during the creative phase. The automatic compile-time checks of Ada, with careful inspection and preparation of test cases, can raise this to one per thousand lines of program. Further improvement, to give error rates of one per 10,000 lines, requires that the intended effect of the program must be adequately specified, in a form suitable for checking against the way the designer has chosen to achieve this effect. Independent, thoughtful verification of the program text must check it for consistency between design and specification. The next kind of improvement, for error rates of order one per 10^5 lines, is by proof sketching: justifying the assertion of consistency between design and specification. The highest level of correctness currently achievable, giving error rates of order 10^{-6} per line, is by complete proof of consistency between design and specification. Each of these regimes is discussed in more detail below.

The above error rates are at best approximations, and should really be interpreted as indicators of the largest program that should be written using a particular technology for a particular total error rate: a program containing 100 lines with an error rate of 10^{-4} has a 99 per cent probability of being correct.

As checking techniques become more laborious, it becomes more and more essential to use automatic processes to carry them out, because of the natural frailty of human checkers. Indeed, as automatic program analysers become more practical, it becomes feasible to apply powerful checks to a wider class of programs and thus achieve a lower residual error rate in them than could be achieved by the use of unaided intelligence.

Thus we can distinguish several styles of software development and checking, with indicated residual error probability per line and corresponding *quality levels* as shown in Table 4.1. A 32k line program tested conventionally is likely to have over thirty errors remaining on handover, whereas with a mathematical specification it is likely to have only three or four. By rigorous analysis or formal correctness proof, a program of this size is likely to have had all errors detected before handover (but persistent change control is essential to prevent new errors being introduced during evolution). These probabilities are not guaranteed, but simply indicate the expected likelihood of different kinds of error, and the consequent reliability of programs checked for errors by progressively more intensive methods.

4.4.3 Techniques to achieve the quality levels

The quality level of most current software is 2, which implies an error rate of order one error per hundred lines of program text. This is achieved in current practice (described in the STARTS Guide and Handbook), by the controlled exercise of programs using sample input data. The parts of the program which are exercised, and the data used, are chosen according to the project on the basis of a test plan, taking account of the software requirements specification, the particular program design, and the target environment.

The error rate can be improved to 3 (of order one error per thousand lines of program text) by comprehensively using strong typing with *basis path* testing, stochastic data and perturbation analysis of the test data. This implies that all compile-time consistency checking has been provided by an Ada compiler, followed by independent inspection of the resulting program, and careful testing of the compiled code for fulfilment of the original specification. (In general, there are an infinite number of paths through a sequence of statements. A *basis set* of paths is a set such that 'linear' combinations of them can form any path through that part of the program. This is the idea underlying basis path testing (McCabe, 1982; Walsh, 1979).)

A quality level of 4, with an error rate of at most one error per 10,000 lines of program text, is appropriate for software sold commercially (where an error could bring financial loss to the buyer), and for software used to construct other certified software. To achieve this level, the ACARD report recommends that rigorous development methods should be used, and all programmers involved should be competent in mathematical methods of software design and construction. The production process should be inspected to check (by sampling) that the methods used are properly applied. The resulting software should be held under strict change control, with monitoring of the error rate actually achieved. If the actual software is found to have more errors than the stated target rate, then any certificate of high quality is withdrawn. Mathematical specification means having explicit pre-conditions and post-conditions for every operation involved, and invariants for every data type. These are used as the basis for the inspection and test preparation. This degree of formality and precision gives an order of magnitude improvement in confidence, but is not yet applicable to input–output peripherals.

Quality level 5, with an error rate of at most one error per 10^5 lines, is appropriate for software whose failure could cause someone to be killed, but where further danger could be averted by switching off the equipment. The ACARD report recommends that this be the level required for safety systems. The whole of such software (assumed to be smaller than 10^5 lines) should be constructed by rigorous proof-oriented methods, under the responsibility of a named software engineer, and checked by a named competent mathematician. The inspection is of the tools used in the production process, the people using them, and the adequacy of the proof-sketches that link specifications with designs. Rigorous development means taking the mathematical specification as above to be the starting point for the development of the software, making a series of transformations from the specification to the eventual program, each component being mathematically specified and the logic of each transformation being justified informally. The selection of components and transformations depends on the skill of the designer, using mathematical rigour throughout the development process. This requires considerable effort but results in significant benefit. Rigorous analysis requires the developed program to contain assertions about the state of the system at critical points, and involves carrying out symbolic analysis through each stage of the program between critical points to confirm that the state reached is consistent with what it should be.

Quality level 6 software, with an error rate of at most one error per million lines, where the software itself is substantially smaller than a million lines, is for software whose failure could involve more than ten deaths, or where it is not feasible to switch off the equipment to avert danger. ACARD calls this 'disaster level', and calls for the whole of the software to be checked under the responsibility of a named competent mathematician by formal mathematical proof, using tools that are themselves certified to high-quality level, and with independent checks on the correct working of support software used (for example, by checking the binary code against the higher-level source program). The inspection here is of the checking process, and the people and tools involved in it, assuming that potential errors are in the logic, not in the specification or assumptions. Formal correctness proof takes the mathematical specification and the developed program (containing invariants and assertions), and shows by explicit rules of inference that they are logically consistent. (It completes the feedback loop of rigorous development.) The given program is treated as a mathematical object, which is proved to imply the given specification. Note that this proof does not cover the underlying infrastructure or computer used to execute the program; a full proof requires the same thoroughness to be applied to all levels of the system design, including micro-code and electronic circuits.

Software (including software components and software tools) for use in safety-critical situations must be inspected to ensure an adequate level of correctness, and named individuals should be responsible for the software engineering and mathematical checking. Inspection of safety-critical software implies concern for the production process as well as the software produced, and proof obligations in addition to thorough testing. ACARD recommends certification for both people and software, to ensure that proper standards are applied (although suitable standards do not yet exist). From the present analysis, the ACARD approach seems to ignore the most likely sources of errors: the specifications and assumptions on which the software is based.

4.4.4 Relevance to Ada

Ada, having been designed before formal specification was well-established, is primarily intended for conventional testing, gaining its order-of-magnitude improvement over conventional development by the use of strong typing rules and package specifications. Several authors have invented ways of linking mathematical specifications with Ada (see Chapter 12), and the improvements are significant for programming in Ada just as for earlier languages. Rigorous analysis has hardly yet been applied to Ada, and formal correctness proofs are only feasible for small programs. These techniques, suitable when the level of confidence required is higher than can be obtained by conventional testing, are explained in Chapter 12. In addition to checking the software, it is vital to check that its interaction with the plant is correct for safety by investigating the feedback loops with safety implications. This is not formal, and is discussed in Chapter 14.

4.5 Confidence and reliability

There is currently much concern about the best way to take into account the possibility of systematic faults in a computer-based system. Techniques are available to determine the reliability in the face of random faults (principally hardware), but it has been found to be impossible to bring the concept of 'software reliability' into the framework of those techniques. This section suggests an approach based on the random occurrence of operational situations combined with possible systematic faults arising from residual (undetected) defects in software or hardware design.

Reliability requirements are conventionally expressed as an expected period of time before failure, with the connotation of progressive (stochastic) deterioration. Software does not fail in this way, so how can we interpret the concept of expected time to failure?

The various checks described produce a body of evidence concerning properties of the target computer's behaviour, which gives confidence that the operational behaviour will be safe. But currently we have no way of assessing this confidence in order to put a figure of merit or probability factor on it. Thus there is a significant intellectual gap between the best available practice and the desired prediction, with scant basis on either side for making the link between them. In this section we discuss the problem and its implications.

Conventionally, the reliability of a system is determined from its hardware design, taking account of replication of components to provide redundancy. There is no room in such a structure for design defects. In a computer-based system, there is the possibility that mistakes have been made during the development, and the certainty

that omissions have been made during the pre-release checking. The present
approach takes these into account as an additional random mode of failure. It can
thus be combined with the hardware reliability elements.

4.5.1 Three-term formula for software reliability

Although the software is constant (at each version during evolution) and therefore
already contains any faults that might lead to danger, these faults are latent rather
than manifest in the running system, since the actual behaviour depends on the
particular data, plant states and operational conditions: on the *variety* rather than the
intensity of use. It is the combination of operational situations and executed software
on the target computer that changes stochastically with time, and from this
observation we can interpret 'expected time to failure' for software.

The basic contribution of systematic (principally software) faults is given by a
three-term formula:

$$S = p_D \times p_V \times p_E$$

where

> p_D is the probability rate for data input being outside the tested domain;
> p_V is the proportion of possible situations that are not verified before operation;
> p_E is the proportion of software that is faulty (in any path),

and

> S is the rate of operational data causing execution of a path that contains a
> fault.

Note that these three terms reflect activities at significantly different periods relevant
to the system: its operational use; its pre-operational checking; and its invention.

The error density p_E depends on the software development technology and quality
control before verification; it can be estimated by determining the proportion of
software faults discovered *during* the pre-operational testing, on the assumption that
the faults are equally likely to be made in the checked as in the unchecked parts.

Verification can be considered as the software analogue of accelerated life testing
in hardware. Whereas it is necessary to find ways of increasing the probabilistic rate
of random errors in hardware (by, for example, running the unit at a higher
temperature) to establish the raw failure rate, in the case of systematic errors this is
no problem: if the error happens once, it will happen every time, and whatever
happens with a particular situation will always happen in that situation. Thus the
situations that arise frequently need be tested only once, giving time for testing the
situations that arise only rarely during operational use. The domain of test data
inputs must take account of all values that are significant for the activity of the
system. It is a charactistic of software-based systems that the *variety* of behaviour is
too great for exhaustive testing. Verification (including factory tests) covers some

proportion of this domain. The proportion of operational situations that are exercised during pre-operational checking is (usually) intended to be completely representative. Bougé (1982 and 1983) has analysed the implications of representative testing. Various techniques are available for estimating the proportion of paths in the program that are exercised by a particular test set. If a particular situation exposes a fault in the software, it can be corrected before operational deployment. Sources of such faults are (a) deficient or ambiguous specification; (b) unjustified assumptions; and (c) bad logic in the development. The faults are likely to occur in any part of the design. Verification gives both an estimate of their density, and the feedback for exposure of a proportion of them. The result of the combination is that the software contains a (static) proportion of undetected faults. In Section 4.4 we have taken this as the measure of the software quality.

Operational conditions generate data and situations at a certain rate, covering a range that is dependent on the elapsed time of exposure. When an operational situation arises that is outside the verified domain (in other words, was not anticipated when the verified situations were prepared), it will execute software which has the original susceptibility to error, without the benefit of the verification exposure. Thus we get a time-dependent probability, which can be combined with the hardware failure rates.

The above analysis applies for a single item of software, without considering its design in any greater detail. As with hardware, a more significant analysis can be carried out after the system has been designed. The impact of software fault-tolerant design, with exception detectors and handlers, is to qualify the above analysis for individual software units, and to indicate how the static measures for each unit should be combined according to the pattern of data and situations which it has to handle.

4.5.2 Other approaches

The *STARTS Purchasers' Handbook* (NCC, 1989) explains the relationship between reliability and availability in safety-related systems by contrasting the causes of failure. The major reason for a failure in software is said to be due to the designer missing, or incorrectly implementing, a requirement (in contrast with the wear and tear or fatigue under stress). Since the presence of any such fault is unknown, the result of the fault cannot be predicted or even (STARTS says) estimated. The analysis given above shows how the techniques used for the construction and checking of the software can be combined with the incidence rate of operational situations to estimate the failure rate. STARTS actually confirms this idea by illustrating the three following possible methods for predicting the reliability of software:

1. Empirical evidence has shown that software developed by process 'x' will contain y errors per 1000 lines of code. Software developers must choose a process (x_i) which should lead to an acceptable rate of errors (y_i) for their

application. The process can be supplemented by design approaches which will lead to the software tolerating certain faults.

2. Software can be executed in a test environment close to the expected operational environment. However, for most safety-related applications, the number of faults, and the rate of detecting faults, should be so low that the results would not be sufficient to calculate a statistically significant MTBF over any practicable test period.

3. If the software is only used occasionally, on a 'demand' basis (for example, the control software of a reactor when overheat has been detected), the number of demands during the expected life of the software can be predicted. The software can then be tested to a higher number of demands, using random data, and a MTBF calculated.

(Note that the last method disregards the fact that any fault exposed by the testing should be corrected, and the software thus changed.) With regard to availability, STARTS points out the significance of being able to stop the system safely after it has started operation: the distinction we have made between static and dynamic safety. (The concept of 'mission time' may be important here – but it is not mentioned in STARTS.) Periods of unavailability provide opportunities for corrective maintenance, enhancements, and for recovery in the event of failure.

The IEC standard points out the importance of being able to carry out tests of the system without taking it out of service. If it is necessary to include facilities to by-pass the safety interlocks (for example during maintenance of the plant), then alternative safety controls must be provided, not necessarily under programmed control. A watchdog timer should be applied during any such period when the safety checks are inhibited, to raise an alarm after a predetermined time if the inhibition period persists for too long.

4.6 EWICS guidelines

The general guidelines and checklists prepared by EWICS TC7 under the general title *Dependability of Critical Computer Systems* (Redmill, 1988, 1989) cover the issues relevant to high-quality computer systems. There is a guideline for the development of critical software, including the selection of the programming language, software development and documentation techniques. Other guidelines are given on the production of system requirements specifications, the design and production of hardware (for safety-related computer systems), the verification and validation of critical computer systems, and the verification and validation of critical software.

A system integrity guide addresses the operational phase of a computer system; it advises on how to keep the system safe and reliable throughout this period, while it is subject to changes (maintenance and enhancement) for operational or environmental reasons. Software quality assurance and metrics are presented in another guide, which identifies software metrics for measuring software qualities required in order to achieve safe and reliable systems, or are suitable for use in the QA function.

A guide on design for system safety (Bishop, 1989) reviews and evaluates design techniques which can be applied to both hardware and software throughout the system's life. The reliability and safety assessment guide gives information about specifying the safety and reliability criteria for a system, and techniques for assessing the reliability and safety of the system development process.

Much of the advice is about software engineering in general, with the safety-specific parts focussing on the susceptibilities of software to analysis and checking. The EWICS Guides go beyond this book in breadth, and are valuable checks with which to back up the details given here.

The EWICS TC7 view on critical software is that a program used to achieve safety must be predictable in all significant behaviour. This means that each version of the program must be analysed before it is in operational use, and all the situations that may arise during its life must be anticipated. Its behaviour for all possible operational situations must be deterministic. In particular, the storage requirements and use of other resources must be known before execution time, and the overhead in time during execution must always be predictable.

The general principles for the design of safety-related software are given by TC7 in terms of human understanding. The basic rule is:

> The program structure should be easy to understand, both in its overall design as well as in its details. The program should be readable from start to end.

Only if this rule is followed can the developers expect to be able to detect possible faults or dangers. From this rule a number of derived recommendations (which closely match the concepts and practices of Ada) have been formulated. These recommendations, with the interpretations for Ada are:

- *The program should be divided into modules*: in Ada these are packages.
- *Good documentation must be provided*: in Ada much of the information is automatically checked for consistency. We explain where additional information is needed.
- *Retrospective attempts to optimise memory space or execution time should be avoided*: Ada allows an overall programming style to be chosen that localises such decisions, with disciplined evolution for improvement of performance characteristics when found necessary.
- *The program should be written in such a way to allow easy testing*: Ada package bodies have this property.
- *Programming tricks should be avoided*: programmers resort to these when they cannot express their design in the language used. Ada provides facilities to render this unnecessary, but checks are still necessary.
- *A central idea of system structure should be adopted*: again, Ada packages, with their context clauses and subunits, provide precisely this. Ada establishes a uniform approach to the kinds of program unit and data types used. It also

provides for clear identification of the parts of programs in which different tasks or processes can compete for resources, and where they refer to the potentially dangerous devices.

The EWICS Guide also mentions the need for verification that all the recommended criteria have been met, but is not as comprehensive as DO-178A. Where particular criteria are set for safety-related software, EWICS recognises that it is important to verify that they are met in the software produced, and all infringements of the criteria identified and justified. Thus the acceptability criteria (e.g. target error rates) should be agreed as a constraint in the initial requirements. The development procedure should include production of documents to show that the criteria are met, with complete audit trails. The verification should be carried out by qualified people independent of the developers. Specifics are left to individual developers: which in practice means to the recommendations of DO-178A.

5

Safety requirements

SAFETY BEGINS with the analysis of the requirements of the control system: how the plant is to be controlled, and particularly how any dangerous actions are to be prevented. How the requirements are established is not directly relevant for the present discussion – various methods, such as Core and SREM, assist the analyst in the acquisition of the necessary information about the requirements. The requirements for the system T (implying S) must be formulated to state its purpose, boundaries and information flows clearly. Here we concentrate on the examination of this information, particularly with regard to safety, looking ahead to the ways in which the requirements may be achieved and be shown to have been achieved.

Our analysis begins by identifying the various dangers that might arise (Section 5.1) and classifying them (Section 5.2). We discuss the criteria for safe operation of the plant (Section 5.3) and how to relate these to the reliability requirements (Section 5.4) and the safety integrity requirements (Section 5.5). We summarise the safety requirements (Section 5.6) by reference to DO-178A and the HSE Checklists.

5.1 Identifying the potential dangers

Dangerous actions are presumed to be possible during the operation of the controlled plant in its world. In preparation for subsequent design, we must identify which dangers can occur, by considering the various kinds of equipment in the plant (U) that can harm life or property, and the nature of the effectors in the target computers (T) that can influence them.

If a danger cannot be avoided by any action of T, then the system as currently specified is intrinsically dangerous. This discovery may precipitate a change to the specification to make the system controllably safe.

For each output from T to U, we must consider whether any dangerous action of U is initiated, and note those output operations that are potentially dangerous.

Independently, we must review the potential dangers in U as a whole: are they all included in the list so formed? If not, we must revise the specification to include the outputs that cause them.

The Health and Safety Executive Guide describes some techniques of hazard analysis for use in various circumstances, including Fault Tree Analysis and Failure Mode Effect and Criticality Analysis.

MoD draft interim standard 00–56 defines the process of Hazard Analysis for investigating the potential dangers in a military system, including all the documentation to be maintained.

Ways of analysing the system for its potential dangers are discussed in Chapter 6 below.

5.2 Classification of danger

In the light of the analysis of Chapter 3, we can classify the potential dangers in terms of controllability, independently of any other classification (by severity or tolerable risk, etc.). There are three classes of danger, which we call immediate, indirect and persistent.

The simplest kind of danger (as far as control is concerned) is the immediate danger that arises from an adverse effect on a victim of a directly and explicitly controlled item of the plant, for example a high voltage source (without capacitance). The target computer controls the switching on and off of the voltage, so ensuring safety by controlling U in SAFE(U, V, W). To avoid this kind of danger,

do not start the hazardous action *until it is safe* to do so.

At the other extreme, we have indirect danger where the victim is at risk from some action by an item of the world which is not directly controlled by the target computer, but which is indirectly influenced by the plant. An example of this is a level crossing, where the train causes the danger but the plant extends only to the signals. In this case the system is made safe by the use of guards on potential victims (the barrier gates of the level crossing), so that safety is ensured by the target controlling the guards that control V in SAFE(U, V, W). To avoid this kind of danger,

keep potential victims away from the hazardous place *while it is dangerous.*

The intermediate case arises when there is persistent danger, arising from a directly controlled item of the plant with inertia. Such an item may continue to be in a dangerous state after the target computer has commanded it to become safe. An example is rotating machinery, where there may be control of the power input and the brakes but where the machine is still dangerous after power has been cut off and the brakes applied. In this case the system is made safe by both of the above techniques, controlling U so that it only starts being dangerous when V permits, and controlling V by guards so that the system cannot become dangerous given the state of U in SAFE(U,V,W). To avoid this kind of danger,

do not start any hazardous action *when victims are present,*

and

keep victims away from the hazardous place *until it becomes safe.*

Summarising:

> Harm = dangerous action in presence of susceptible subject
> Danger = potential harm
> Guard = means of preventing subject from being susceptible
> Interlock = means of inhibiting action when it would be harmful

So our first level analysis, based on the information established as the statement of requirement, is the check that appropriate interlocks and guards can be set up.

We must identify the potential dangers in U, establish the criteria for safe use of dangerous equipment, and ascertain that sensors can provide the information needed to discriminate. The following considers in detail only the simplest case, that of immediate danger. Similar analyses may be carried out for the other cases, when guards are needed. These are explained in later chapters.

5.3 Criteria for safe operation

We assume that each potentially dangerous action is sometimes safe to perform: otherwise there can be no safe operation. Conversely, we assume that it may sometimes be dangerous if *no* action is performed. Thus there are risks both of performing the action in the wrong circumstances, and of not performing it when it should be carried out.

The situation in which the action is safe may depend on the state of other parts of U and W, or cooperative actions by distinct (and distinctly controlled) parts of U, or timing relationships.

For each output from T to U that initiates a potentially dangerous action, we must establish and record the condition(s) under which the action is safe. This will in general be a formula, SAFE(U, V, W), that depends on other characteristics of U, V and W, not necessarily instantaneous. (In other words, in general it may also depend on time, but we do not explore that possibility here.) In any case, it will depend on time-dependencies in the above characteristics.

In general it is preferable for each hazardous output from T to be associated with a distinct interlock: an internal predicate that determines whether or not it can be operated safely. If a single output from T can, depending on the circumstances, cause distinct dangerous actions, then the formula is correspondingly more complicated, and the risk of mis-design or mal-operation of the safety system is increased. This analysis may precipitate reconsideration of the specification, in order to separate the information flows for the distinct actions.

We should note particularly which inputs to T from U or W are involved in each of the safety-interlock conditions, and consider the effect (fail-safe or fail-dangerous) of malfunction of each. This analysis may precipitate introduction of some additional sensors in order to detect situations that are important for safety, or to the redesign of sensors to reduce the risk from malfunction.

We must record all the safety-critical inputs to T, grouping them according to the danger they protect against, and associating them with the corresponding interlock formula. (As explained above, it is preferable that each input be involved in at most one interlock; if it is involved in more, this should be particularly noted.)

In addition to the above considerations, there is the basic issue of availability of the control or safety protection system (introduced in Section 3.6), and the risk of malfunction in the physical control loop. The safety of a controlled system depends on the control system (at least the protection system) being available and working properly when it is needed. Thus malfunction and unavailability of the control system are potential sources of danger. The HSE guidance on configuration and diversity is intended to take account of this kind of risk. To ensure proper functioning of all safety critical functions, the safety system should be automatically monitored or made self-checking. The proportion of failures detected by self-monitoring are given by the HSE Guide as 90 per cent for failures detected by an external watchdog, and 98 per cent when in addition there are extensive self-checking programs. (The self-checking programs must be executed regularly as part of the normal running sequence, not only at power up, and must exercise the fundamental operations of the computer: memory, internal registers and processor functions. A program structured in Ada, as we recommend, should apply the same principle at each layer in the software structure.)

A control system that relies on redundancy to mitigate the effects of detected malfunction or unavailability is likely to depend on software to coordinate the redundant parts. Built-in Test Equipment (BITE) is likely to be driven by software, causing the equipment found faulty to be de-activated and possibly replaced by spares. Here software provides a positive enhancement of availability (and consequently of safety).

It is vital that no circumstances should lead to unidentified, undefined or unsafe conditions (e.g. from data stored in volatile memory), including the programmed response to mode changes such as the following:

- power switch-on;
- power restoration following a failure;
- power supply interruption and resumption;
- switching between manual and automatic modes of control (if provided).

In all cases, the software and hardware in combination must ensure that the program can only be entered at a point where it is safe to do so, and only after completion of any necessary resetting of the system. The Ada structure described in Chapter 8 below can provide precisely this kind of protection, using a technique called 'double insulation' to ensure that checks cannot be by-passed.

The analysis of safety requirements has to identify the sources of information and the checks that must be made for safe operation; for example, in order to protect against faults at switch-on or power resumption, the power-supply detector must be treated as a significant input device, and the start-up check as its interlock function.

Emergency shut-down systems need to be tested; this involves simulating fault conditions to check that the system responds correctly, but without activating a real shut-down. Thus the safety functions must be 'muted' during the on-line tests of the emergency system. The maximum time allowable in the muted condition for a specific safety function must be determined as part of the design. The design must include steps to detect periods longer than this during operation, and to take appropriate action.

The analysis of a system to determine its safety requirements must take account of the risks of malfunction and unavailability; the design must ensure that the residual probabilities are sufficiently small for the risk to be tolerated, given the nature of the harm that might be caused if the control or protection system does not work properly.

5.4 Reliability and availability requirements

The safety of a controlled system depends on the control systems (at least the protection system) being available and working properly when it is needed, as explained in Section 3.6. Thus malfunction and unavailability of the control system are potential sources of danger. Different industries and regulatory bodies lay down different requirements for the reliability of safety or protection systems. Target reliability rates may be sought of order 10^9–10^{11} hours to failure.

The analysis of a system to determine its safety requirements must take account of the risks of malfunction and unavailability; the design must ensure that the residual probabilities are sufficiently small for the risk to be tolerated, given the nature of the harm that might be caused if the control or protection system does not work properly.

For civil avionic systems, the probability of malfunctions or design errors must be better than 1 in 10^9 operating hours for critical functions (extremely improbable), better than 1 in 10^7 operating hours for major essential functions (extremely remote)

Table 5.1 Avionics reliability requirements

Risk factor	Category	Effect of malfunction or design error	Probability per operating hour
1	**Critical:**	**prevent continued safe flight**	10^{-9}
2	essential:		
2a	major	significant reduction of ability to cope	10^{-7}
2b	**minor**	**reduction of ability to cope**	10^{-5}

Table 5.2 Nuclear reliability requirements

Automatic control function	Class of danger	Risk of failure
Plant tripping		10^{-7}
Plant interlocking	**A+**	10^{-9}
	A	10^{-6}
	B	10^{-4}
	C	10^{-2}
Plant sequencing		10^{-1} to 10^{-2}
Plant regulation		10^{-1} to 10^{-2}

Table 5.3 Proposed classification of computer systems in nuclear power stations in the Federal Republic of Germany

Class	Description
I	Highest requirements of nuclear safety: Systems that release automatic actions for protection of human life and environment.
II	**High requirements of nuclear safety: Systems that act for the protection of human life and environment by:** **– guiding safety variables under abnormal conditions;** **– causing operator actions deterministically.**
III	Normal requirements of nuclear safety: Systems that – limit plant variables to specific values; – avoid scrams; – report disturbances in systems of class I and II.
IV	**High requirements of plant safety: Systems that** **– release actions automatically for protection of persons in the plant;** **– protect important parts of the plant;**
V	High requirements of plant availability: Systems that – increase plant availability; – protect normal parts of the plant.
VI	**High functional requirements: Systems that serve for optimal plant operation, e.g. with respect to efficiency or manoeuvrability.**
VII	Component related control: Systems for simple requirements.

Table 5.4 Proposed reliability demands for computers in nuclear power plants in the Federal Republic of Germany

Class of system (see Table 5.3)	I	II	III	IV	V	VI	VII
Max unavailability (total)	10^{-5}	10^{-4}	10^{-2}	10^{-4}	10^{-2}	10^{-1}	10^{-1}
Max unavailability (safety related)	10^{-7}	10^{-5}	10^{-4}	10^{-5}			
Max probability of failure (per year)	10^{-4}	10^{-2}		10^{-2}			
Max probability of dangerous failure (per year)	10^{-7}	10^{-5}	10^{-4}	10^{-5}			
Max probability of failure during an accident	10^{-6}	10^{-4}	10^{-3}	10^{-4}	10^{-2}		

and better than 1 in 10^5 operating hours for minor essential functions (remote). We tabulate these in Table 5.1 below.

The Nuclear Installations Inspectorate has laid down mandatory requirements for the integrity of automatic control functions which contribute to safety in nuclear power stations, depending on the kind of control function at risk (see Table 5.2).

Similar tables have been proposed for the safety of nuclear power stations in the Federal Republic of Germany. Table 5.3 gives a proposed classification scheme for computer systems involved for safety-related purposes, with the corresponding reliability demands shown in Table 5.4.

The HSE Guide contains figures for hardware failures and common-cause failures that contribute to these, but not for software. No software techniques have yet been found that can be proved to achieve these or any specific failure rates; indeed, all software techniques are based on detecting certain categories of fault, with the assumption that *all* detected faults can be corrected (if the effort is justified) before delivery. (Of course, after the defects have been identified, it is possible to decide consciously to correct only a limited proportion of them.)

Probabilities in terms of operating hours are significant for usage, and show what redundancy may be required in the configuration of the whole system, but they can not be directly interpreted for design characteristics such as software, since the impact of a fault depends on the variety of situations that must be handled during these periods, not in any direct way on the elapsed time. For example, critical software must define proper behaviour, even in the extremely improbable combinations of circumstances that arise only once in 10^9 operating hours (i.e. once in about 100,000 years of continuous operation).

The analysis of Section 4.5 shows that failure rate probabilities can only be sensibly interpreted as referring to the distribution of operational situations with which the control or protection system must cope, not directly with the software that determines its behaviour.

We discuss the implications of this in Chapter 7 below (for the designer) and in Chapter 11 (for confirmation).

5.5 Safety integrity requirements

The HSE Guide uses the phrase 'safety integrity' in two senses: applied to the plant, and applied to the safety-related system that controls or protects the plant. A safety-related system is defined as 'a system upon which the safety integrity of the plant is to be assured', while safety integrity is defined as 'that characteristic of a safety-related system relating to its ability to perform its required functions in the desired manner under all the relevant conditions and on the occasions when it is required so to perform'. Thus the concept is essentially about performing functions properly on demand.

Safety integrity criteria are also introduced, defined as 'the criteria used as the basis for the safety integrity design and analysis of the safety-related system'. The required level of safety integrity for a safety-related system must be known and specified; for a Programmable Electronic System this would normally be in terms of the configuration, reliability and overall quality of the system. In some cases, the safety integrity criteria for a plant may be determined from other sources (e.g. guidance relating to a particular industry), but when there are no existing safety integrity criteria they must be developed for the particular plant by application of the safety principles in the Guide and by considering those properties of non-programmable systems that have been or might be used in similar circumstances. The exact criteria to apply will depend on the potential harm to people and the environment, in magnitude, intensity and risk. For the design, this may mean taking the configuration, reliability and quality of acceptable non-programmable systems; the assessment is mainly qualitative (particularly for the software), combined with quantitative analysis of hardware reliability.

The IEC draft standard explains how the magnitude of the software safety integrity requirement is to be derived from the system safety integrity requirement, depending on the severity of the hazard and the probability of occurrence. Key influences for achieving software safety integrity are given as follows:

- software development methods and techniques;
- software architecture techniques;
- quality assurance;
- project management.

Broadly speaking, the requirements for safety integrity in the HSE Guide and the draft IEC standard correspond to the validation requirements of DO-178A: they all deal with confirmation that the equipment (and/or system) will carry out the proper actions when it is supposed to do so.

5.6 Review of safety analysis of requirements

The preliminary safety analysis should be carried out as soon as the principal operational requirement has been established, because the resulting information (derived from the given requirements before the design starts) may show up fundamental shortcomings that need to be put right at this early stage. In particular, the safety analysis draws attention to the outputs and inputs of the control system relevant to safety of the plant, and the necessity for interlocks between them.

The analysis shows where additional sensors may be needed to achieve safety, and ensures that all the inputs and outputs are identified before software design begins.

DO-178A provides a list of typical requirements to be established, which fall into several categories as follows:

- Desired positive behavioural characteristics:
    functions to be accomplished in software;
    built-in test and/or monitoring requirements;
    test requirements.
- Tolerable negative behavioural characteristics:
    performance degradation and/or function loss under fault conditions.
- Characteristics of the desired behaviour:
    partitioning requirements;
    criticality of the functions;
    timing requirements.
- Underlying mechanisms assumed to be available:
    hardware/software interfaces;
    characteristics of the processor utilised.

The HSE Guide includes checklists (1A and 1B) which should be used for reviewing the safety requirements specification.

6

Analyses of safety and danger

WE CAN ANALYSE a safety-related system using the assessment framework of the HSE (see Table 6.1).

In this chapter, we are concerned with steps 1 and 2 of Table 6.1. Step 3 has been addressed in Sections 5.4 and 5.5. Part II of the book is concerned with step 4, the constructive step. Part III is concerned with step 5, the analysis and checking step, and recording the information in preparation for certification. Chapter 15, corresponding to step 6, brings the threads together by the process of certifying that the desired criteria are actually met.

6.1 Methods of hazard analysis

There are several methods of analysing a safety-related system for danger, such as: Event Tree Analysis, Fault Tree Analysis, Failure Mode and Effect Analysis, Failure Mode Effect and Criticality Analysis, and Hazard and Operability Studies. As mentioned in Chapter 2, the Health and Safety Executive (HSE) has published guidance for the use of these analyses in connection with Programmable Electronic

Table 6.1 HSE safety assessment framework

1 Analyse the hazards
   a identify the potential hazards
   b evaluate the events leading to these hazards
2 **Identify which systems assure the safety integrity of the plant**
   a check that all their failures are included among events 1a.
   b select appropriate safety integrity criteria
3 Decide on an acceptable level of safety integrity for the Safety-Related System
4 **Design the Safety-Related System using the selected safety integrity criteria**
5 Determine (by analysis) the level of safety integrity achieved in the Safety-Related System
6 **Ensure that the safety integrity level achieved (in 5) satisfies the level that is acceptable (in 3)**

Systems (PES, i.e. computers); notes on the guidance are given in Appendix B.

Event Tree Analysis (ETA) works from each event which the system can sense, and traces forward logically to the possible situations that might follow the occurrence of the event. In systems of any complexity, this leads to large trees, as all the circumstances following each event are included, both safe and hazardous.

Conversely, Fault Tree Analysis (FTA) works backwards from each identified hazard to the circumstances that could cause it, using logical combinations of the basic events that might occur. The basic events are those with known or assumed frequencies, failure rates or probabilities of failure. The HSE Guide includes indicative values for basic events involving mechanical devices in factories.

Failure Mode and Effect Analysis (FMEA) works from possible failures anywhere in the system to the resulting effect on the safety of the plant, using either a hardware approach or a functional approach. The hardware approach treats the system as a combination of physical devices (any of which might fail), including the plant sensor and effectors, the operator communication devices, inter-computer data-links, backing storage devices, etc. The principle is to consider the effect of failure of each; however it is difficult to follow this analysis through the programmable electronics, which can only be treated as a black box. The functional approach treats the system as a combination of control functions (any of which might fail), such as feedback loops, interlocks, and safety trips. The requirement specifies what the Programmable Electronics in the System should do in particular circumstances; the FMEA considers in what ways the function might deviate in practice from the required specification.

Since the process of analysing the system by FMEA starts from the intended function of the system, it is particularly advantageous for revealing unforeseen hazards. It exposes potentially hazardous single failures (but at the expense of covering all non-hazardous failures). It does not consider combinations of failures.

Failure Mode, Effect and Criticality Analysis (FMECA) attaches a criticality measure to each possible failure, in order to focus attention on those with greatest frequency, highest probability, or most serious effects. This can be linked with the functional criticality categories of DO-178A (critical, essential and non-essential, as explained in Chapter 2). The configuration defines how the system is partitioned into distinct elements, each providing functions of a particular criticality category, determined by the effects of malfunctions or design errors in the total safety. The most critical function of each of these determines which part of the failures tree should be given close attention.

Hazard and Operability Studies (HAZOP) studies (developed for the chemical industry) work from the instrumented flow diagram of the plant (the pipes and vessels carrying the active materials, with their normal ranges of flow rates, temperatures and pressures), and considers the effect on the plant of deviations outside the normal ranges in each phase of operation (including maintenance, commissioning, testing, start-up, close-down and failure of services). Such studies are particularly important for computer-based control systems, as they show the importance of the range checks on parameters, which may be sensed or controlled by the computer system. The subtypes of Ada (with range constraints defining the legitimate values in proper operation) provide a convenient and useful notation for describing the situation. Programmable Electronic Systems can detect any excursions outside the normal ranges, and initiate suitable protection actions. Failure of a PES combined with such a deviation outside normal parameter range could result in a directly consequent hazard.

6.2 Multi-viewpoint analysis for safety

The following guidelines are based on analysing the system from several different viewpoints, and using each to check the others.

The viewpoints we take (in order) are: victims, plant (dangerous devices and guards) and the target computers (concentrating on their inputs, detecting safety states; and then their outputs, controlling guards and dangerous devices). These lead the designer progressively from effects to causes, and use a single list of interlock conditions that are eventually incorporated into the software (Table 6.2). Each viewpoint deals first with the system as it is intended to operate, then considers the possibility that it might not operate properly.

(a) *Viewpoint of victim*   The victims are those elements of the system that are susceptible to harm if the system is not safe; so we begin the analysis by identifying them and locating the harm which they might suffer if the plant is not safely controlled.

Begin the safety analysis by listing all the possible categories of people or property that might be harmed by the plant (see Table 6.3). These are the victims. Make an entry for each on Form 1, and fill in the rest of the information, recording what undesired action would cause the harm, either by an item of the plant itself, or by an item of the world outside the plant with which it works but does not control. In the

Table 6.2 Viewpoints for safety analysis

Viewpoint	
1 Victim	Safety
2 Plant	
a effector	Danger
b guard	Protection
3 Target computer	
a sensor	Detection
b output to guard	
c output to effector	

Table 6.3 Headings for multi-viewpoint safety analysis

Form 0 – Interlocks

Ref	SAFE (U,V,W)	Source	Cause	Guard	Danger Detector
	criterion	constituent of U or W that can directly cause harm	action by U that must be constrained to eliminate the danger	action by U that will prevent the harm	state sensed by U about effectors, guards and V

Form 1 – Safety

Ref	Possible victim	Danger	Source	Protection	Safety criterion
	V	potential harm to V by action of U or W	dangerous effector in U or W	Guard in U	(reference to Form 0)

Form 2 – Danger (direct)

Ref	Source	Danger	Cause	Control	Safety criterion	Timing constraint:
	effector in U	potential harm to V by action of U	controlled action by U	output to effector from T	interlock for start of action (ref)	how long danger persists

Form 3 – Protection (indirect)

Ref	Protection	Cause	Danger	Control	Safety criterion	Timing constraint
	guard in U	action by U or W that cannot be controlled	harm to V by unprotected action of U or W	output to guard from T	interlock for application of guard (ref)	how long guard protects

Form 4 – Detector

Ref	Sensor	Dependent Interlocks (refs)	Confirmation of controlled actions	Latency of detector t_{det}	Effect of malfunction of T
	input to T about U, V or W				

Table 6.3 continued

Form 5 – Effector

Ref	Control	Action	Safety	Latency of effector t_{eff}	Effect of malfunction of T
	output to effector in U from T	of effector in U	of effector action (ref)		

Form 6 – Guard

Ref	Control	Action	Safety	Latency of guard t_{gd}	Effect of malfunction of T
	output to guard in U from T	of guard in U	by guard action (ref)		

latter case, record which item of the plant should act as a guard to prevent the victim from being harmed.

Define the safety conditions for the action of the relevant items of the plant, and record these explicitly on the interlock form (Form 0). Put the reference to the interlock on the safety analysis form.

(b) Viewpoint of plant   The plant contains both effectors that might cause harm to the victims and guards that are designed to prevent victims from being harmed. In both cases there are proper conditions for use, and we analyse the system for each of these kinds of device.

(i) Begin the danger analysis by listing all the possible constituents of the plant that might inadvertently cause harm to people or property, if they are not controlled properly. These are the dangerous devices. Make an entry for each on Form 2, and fill in the other information required, recording the specific danger and the undesired action that would cause it. State the output from the target computer that controls the dangerous device.

Now define the safety condition for each action of the relevant items of the plant, and record it explicitly on the Interlock Form, with the reference on the Danger Analysis Form. (The interlock criterion should be the same as for the corresponding safety analysis; if there is any discrepancy, we must investigate it and reconcile the two viewpoints.)

The system should be safe with respect to a particular dangerous device if the device is *never* operated, but this would mean that the system did not achieve other desirable effects. Therefore the safety criterion for a dangerous device must identify explicitly when it is safe for the device to be operated.

(ii) Begin the protection analysis by listing all the constituents of the plant that exist to prevent victims from being harmed, either by the plant itself or by other actions in the world by entities outside the plant but of which it is aware. These are the guards. Make an entry for each on Form 3, and fill in the other information required, recording the action that could be harmful and the harm that the victim will suffer if the guard does not work properly. State the output from the target computer that controls the guard.

Now define the safety condition for each guard, and record it explicitly on the Interlock Form, with the reference on the Protection Analysis Form.

The system should be safe with respect to a particular guarded hazard if the guard is *always* applied, but this would mean not achieving other desirable effects of the system. Therefore the safety criterion for a guard must include explicitly identifying when it is safe for the guard to be removed.

(*c*) *Viewpoint of target computer*   The target computers have both inputs and outputs relevant to safety. The inputs are critical for applying the safety criteria, while the outputs control the dangerous devices and the guards.

(i) Begin the detector analysis by listing all the inputs to the target computers about the status of the raw plant, the victims and the world, that might be involved in safety interlocks. (This list must be checked against Form 0 for completeness.) These are the critical inputs. Make an entry for each on Form 4, and fill in the other information required, recording the reference to each interlock that depends on the specific input.

Consider the possibility of malfunction of the target computer (e.g. failure to detect a critical input), and discover the effect that such a malfunction would have on the plant and the victims. If the effect is not acceptable, the design must be revised.

(ii) Begin the effector analysis by listing all the outputs from the target computers to potentially dangerous devices. (This list must be checked against Form 2 for completeness.) These are the danger-critical outputs. Make an entry for each on Form 5, and fill in the other information required, recording the dangerous device that is controlled by this output, and the reference to the interlock table defining the conditions under which it is safe to operate the device.

Consider the possibility of malfunction of the target computer (e.g. failure to send a control signal to a dangerous device) and record the effect that such a malfunction could have on the plant and the victims. If the effect is not acceptable, the design must be changed.

(iii) Begin the guard analysis by listing all the outputs from the target computers to the guard devices. (This list must be checked against Form 3 for completeness.) These are the safety-critical outputs. Make an entry for each on Form 6, and fill in the other information required, recording the potentially dangerous action that is prevented from being actually harmful by this guard. Refer to the interlock table to define the minimum conditions under which the guard must be applied.

Consider the possibility of malfunction of the target computers (e.g. failure to send a control signal to a guard) and record the effect that such a malfunction would have on the plant and the victims. If the effect is not acceptable, the design must be changed.

(*d*) *Cross-checks*   As well as several checks already mentioned, there are further cross-checks to be carried out between the forms now filled in:

- that the same dangerous devices are listed on Forms 0, 1 and 2;
- that the same guards are listed on Forms 0, 1 and 3;
- that the same detectors are listed on Forms 0 and 4;
- that the same danger-critical outputs and devices are listed on Forms 2 and 5;
- that the same safety-critical outputs and guards are listed on Forms 3 and 6;
- that each interlock on Form 0 is referenced from each of its components: detector device (if relevant), and guard (if relevant).

If any of these checks show up a discrepancy, the relevant analyses must be repeated to resolve the situation. The viewpoints must be consistent.

Tables 6.1 and 6.2 give the headings for collecting the information for each of these viewpoints. The timing constraints and latency refer to the times between the situation occurring and the computer receiving the sense signal, or conversely of the computer sending a control signal and the device responding to it.

6.3 Malfunction, unavailability and backup

In Section 5.4, we discussed the requirements for availability which affect safety. This is a significant motivation in the HSE Guide for system configuration, ensuring that there are sufficient safety-related systems in the overall configuration to be capable of maintaining the plant in a safe state or of bringing it to a safe state when required.

We should note which inputs to T from U or W are involved in each of the safety-related interlock conditions, and consider the effect (fail-safe or fail-dangerous) of malfunction of each. This analysis may precipitate the introduction of some additional sensors in order to detect situations that are important for safety, or to the redesign of sensors to reduce the risk from malfunction.

We must record all the safety-related inputs to T, grouping them according to the danger they protect against, and associating them with the corresponding interlock formulae. (As explained above, it is preferable that each input be involved in at most one interlock; if it is involved in more than one, this should be explicitly noted, for the dependency implications in change control.)

The particular relevance of Ada to this topic is the attention given to run-time error detection by the exception mechanisms in Ada, including application-specific exceptions. This means that malfunctions are likely to be detected throughout the running program, and appropriate recovery actions initiated.

Recovery from a malfunction is only feasible if there is an alternative way of achieving an acceptable effect, which might involve hardware changes (e.g. reconfiguration), or reloading software.

The danger of this approach, of having automatic substitutes for faulty components, is that the substitute itself may be faulty, and in the normal course of events it is less extensively tested. This same argument is used against having exception handlers at all in an Ada program; since the handler is only operative in rare circumstances (on detecting something unusual that should never happen in normal operation), it is quite likely to be faulty itself. This argument is defective, because it applies with equal force if the substitute component is activated in response to a condition detected by an **if** or **case** clause. The **exception** condition may, however, be difficult to stimulate in a test environment. The special notation draws attention to the situation, and indicates the need for specific testing, as mentioned in Section 14.2.3 below.

Calculations of system availability based on the hardware structure and component availability, taking account of common-cause failures, can be carried out using techniques explained in the HSE Guide. Software reliability can only be incorporated by different techniques, explained in Section 11.2 below. Corresponding to the repair time for hardware, we can use the time to reload the software (which is the time to reinstate a perfect copy of the current version) followed by any initialising process needed to bring its data to correspond with the current state of the plant.

More general techniques are available for achieving high availability, by the use of hot and cold stand-by computers, but we do not discuss this subject further because the techniques are not specific either to safety or to the use of Ada.

PART II DESIGN

7

Software construction principles

PART II of the book comprises this chapter and the following three, giving details of software construction. Since software is intrinsically neither safe nor dangerous, there are no specific differences relating to safety in the *creative* aspect of software development. In contrast there are significant differences in the checking to ensure that the software is satisfactory and acceptable for certification. All the guides for software development, including STARTS, JSP188 and DO-178A, emphasise the need for discipline, systematic working and orderliness, so that the software is traceable, testable, maintainable and understandable. The significant aspects of software development that affect safety are its structure and predictability. This chapter is about the general principles of software construction (with Ada in mind, but not specific to Ada). Chapter 8 deals with the structural properties of a program, using the concepts and facilities of Ada. Chapter 9 covers the logical design of critical modules (packages) in an Ada program (with safety in mind, but not specific to safety), and Chapter 10 focusses on particular points in the physical design of safety-critical software in Ada.

The most important differences between ways of producing software concern the definition of what it is intended to do and how the particular algorithms and data structures are obtained, given the defined intentions. To achieve low error rates in the software, it is essential that the intended behaviour (of the target computer and the plant it controls) be well-defined. The different methods are more about defining the intention than about deriving the algorithms and data structures. Indeed, it can be argued that it is better to regard 'software' as including the formulated intentions as well as the executable programs. The HSE Guide analyses the sources of failure that could lead to danger, along with strategies that are effective against them.

Rigorous and mathematical methods of software development rely on starting with formal definitions of the intended behaviour, the states to be achieved or maintained, and the state conditions under which actions are to be carried out.

Ada contributes significantly to these goals, as the language enforces discipline and enhances maintainability and understandability. Text books such as Booch (1983), Watt, Wichmann and Findlay (1987) and Somerville and Morrison (1987) explain the general principles of programming in Ada.

The present book supplements these general principles by focussing on the areas needing special attention in potentially dangerous systems. The same principles apply (but with some differences in terminology) to software written in other modern languages such as Modula-2 or C++. (The principles still apply but are less easy to interpret in languages that do not have modular structure, such as Pascal, C, Fortran and Coral-66.)

Although our emphasis in this book is on software, the central point about safety is that it concerns the whole system; so we must begin by considering the *system* design (Section 7.1) before we discuss the development principles for software (Section 7.2), subject to change control (Section 7.3) as it evolves. The issues of partitioning (Section 7.4) and diversity (Section 7.5) are critical for safety and reliability. We show that formal notations including the programming language (Section 7.6) also contribute significantly, but raise the issue of unreliability of the software tools that are used in the development process (Section 7.7). The system performance (Section 7.8) may also have a bearing on its safety. Documenting the software requirements (Section 7.9) provides a checklist for this chapter.

7.1 System design

The best approach to system design (in a safety-related system) follows from the analyses of safety and danger described in Chapter 6. Step 4 of the HSE assessment framework is 'Design the Safety Related System using the selected safety integrity criteria', having analysed the hazards and identified which systems ensure the safety of the plant. We have shown how to identify the dangerous devices in the plant, and established safety criteria for constraining their activities (which require certain information to be sensed about the plant and its environment).

The HSE Guide gives an analysis of sources of failures that can cause danger, and recommends strategies to avoid them. The sources of failure, which may occur singly or in combinations, are as follows:

(a) errors or omissions in the safety requirements specification;
(b) systematic failures (including software);
(c) random hardware failures.

It is important to take account of common-cause failures, since any fault in a unit of software will be present in all copies of it, whenever it is used. The HSE Guide discusses common causes in redundancy systems, and includes checklists for qualitative assessment of common-cause failure (CCF) aspects. The model recommended by the HSE relates the common-cause failure rate in a system comprising several channels to the independent failure rate of an individual channel by a numerical ratio known as β. Values for β are given in the Guide as 10 (typical), ranging from 3 (min) to 30 (max) in replicated identical systems, and a factor of 10 smaller in diverse systems. However, the HSE Guide also says that if the specific requirements aimed at the avoidance of CCF in the programmable electronics are met, the CCF rate need not be included in the calculations of reliability.

The HSE strategies against the sources of failure are as follows:

- configuration (against sources (b) and (c));
- quality (against sources (a) and (b));
- reliability (against source (c)).

The strategies relevant to software are configuration and quality. Quality is pervasive. (We have discussed software quality in Chapter 4.) The specific concern in the design of the control and protection system is its configuration, to ensure that all the interactions required can be handled adequately, and that there is sufficient robustness (redundancy, internal checking and correction) to cope with the random hardware failures.

The configuration should take account of the principles of partitioning and diversity explained in the following sections, including non-programmable devices as well as computer-based systems. The HSE Guide indicates that an acceptable configuration would have a number of systems which are capable, independently, of maintaining the plant in a safe state, or of bringing the plant to a safe state when required. For example, there may be primary protection by physical containment, then mechanical forces, followed by electro-magnetic forces, controlled by natural and artificial logic. The number of such independent systems must depend on the hazards created by the plant, regardless of any programmability, and may include replicated devices. If some of the safety systems are programmable, this is no justification for reducing their total number.

A Programmable Electronic System used for control of safety is envisaged as consisting of a number of channels, any of which might fail. The configuration should be such that no failure of a single channel causes a dangerous mode of failure in the total configuration of safety-related systems. The control loops identified in the safety and danger analysis (Chapter 6), with their interlocks to ensure safety, can be considered to be channels in this sense.

Failures may occur in the hardware or the software associated with a channel. Random hardware failures can be detected by Built-In Test Equipment (BITE) and taken into account by software, thus diminishing the severity of their impact. As well as random hardware failures, there might be systematic hardware failures that affect all identical designs of the hardware, which are treated as common-cause failures. Similarly, a software fault affects all identical units in the software. If the configuration relies on software for several channels, the principles of software diversity should be applied, so that different channels have independent faults (although, as explained in Section 7.5 below, there is a growing body of evidence that small-scale software diversity is not effective).

7.2 Development principles

All software qualities, not only safety, are affected by the approach used in its development. The STARTS Guide explains steps to be taken at each stage in the software life-cycle for real-time systems, but with no specific attention to safety.

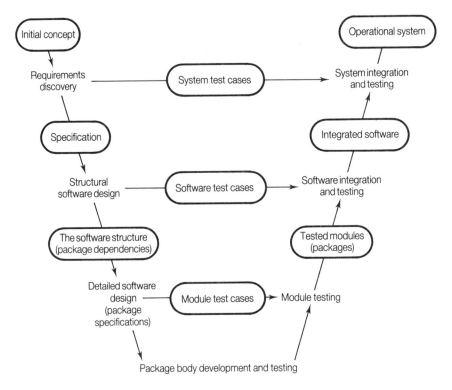

Figure 7.1 STARTS Life-Cycle model (adapted)

However, the regulatory agencies are not primarily interested in the specific approach or development method used, only in the resultant level of safety, as evidenced by the verification carried out. Thus the emphasis for certification is to ensure that the information obtained at each stage is adequate for verification.

Software development consists of a series of stages during which the requirements are interpreted and transformed into an executable program, by progressively deciding how the desired effects are to be achieved by some combination of more elementary effects, and later confirming that the combination of these elementary effects does have the effect required.

This progressive decision-making is very difficult to do by thinking and writing alone, without experimentation. It is distinctly easier to see the implications of tentative decisions (in order to confirm them for subsequent work) if they are embodied in executable programs. Such intermediate, experimental programs are usually described as prototypes; they typically deal with some functional aspects of the desired software, but not the totality, and not the infrastructure on which it rests. For example, there may be separate prototypes for the interaction with users and for wide-area communication, neither being comprehensively robust or fault-tolerant.

Prototypes are frequently written in languages with weaker binding and less imperative control than the final production version of the software. Functional and declarative languages are useful for this purpose: languages such as ML, Miranda, OBJ; or rule-based systems such as ART or AnimAID. Sometimes the prototype can be automatically transformed into an imperative form (thus binding the rules, and making subsequent changes less easy), giving an initial vesion of parts of the eventual program.

At each stage, the software should be verified (reviewed, analysed and/or tested) to confirm that the interpretation is effective, and the transformation does result in all the desired effects, and no undesired effects, being achieved.

The STARTS Guide shows this process in a V-diagram (Figure 7.1), in which the left-hand side indicates progressive expansion of decisions about how to achieve the effects, and the right-hand side indicates progressive integration of the results of those decisions. There is a fan-out of detail on the left, and a corresponding fan-in on the right. Apart from the lowest level (the vertex of the V), the period of time between the design decision and the corresponding integration is significant, and two verifications are necessary: one immediately after the design (in which it must be assumed that all the subsidiary effects *are* achieved), and the second after the integration has been carried out, based on the *actual* effects of the constituents.

The EWICS Guide presents recommendations for the design of safety related software systems, comprising two apparently conflicting principles, as follows:

1. A top down or mixed approach is preferred to a bottom up one.
2. They should incorporate verified and previously used components.

The conflict can be resolved in Ada because of the distinction between package specifications and package bodies. The first recommendation refers to package specifications used in the system architecture; the second to their bodies. This issue is discussed further in Chapter 8.

The development stages identified in DO-178A are as follows:

- generation of software requirements (which define the functions to be implemented in the software);
- detailed software design and test plan generation;
- implementing the software design in executable code, with progressive integration and testing.

During the integration steps, it is expected that modules will be revised in the light of testing so that earlier mistakes are corrected.

Note that DO-178A expects the coding (i.e. formalisation) to be delayed until the third stage – a hangover from earlier programming styles, in which the programming languages could not express detailed software design (or software structure). Using Ada, the structural and detailed software designs should be formulated (coded) during the earlier stages, in order to obtain the benefits of automatic checking before any algorithms or data structures are written.

In the following chapters we discuss the information called for by DO-178A, and recommend how it should be expressed in Ada.

The discipline described in all the guides amounts to being clear about what one is trying to do before starting to do it, with agreed acceptability criteria. We call this the *intention* principle, which is about formulating the requirements an element is intended to satisfy, and how it is intended to show that it eventually does satisfy them. This principle gives us the basis for completeness and adequacy checking: we can compare what each element actually achieves with the formulated intention.

Another important principle is *improvement*. At each stage in software development, there is an 'initial' solution that is followed by a number of improvements as the development continues. It is essential to have an initial solution (even though it is difficult to produce, because the author knows it is likely to be wrong) as a baseline for the subsequent improvement, under configuration control. After a baseline has been established, there is a structure within which subsequent changes can be controlled. Configuration control expresses this principle, by requiring the constitution of each baseline to be established (with the components identified in specific configurations) and changes made to it only when properly authorised.

This principle gives the basis for consistency checking. When development is based on descriptions or definitions in natural language with implicit semantics, there are likely to be different interpretations by different designers (or even by the same designer at different times). These different interpretations appear as inconsistencies in the developed design, and have to be resolved as part of the whole process. In database technology, the resolution of similar inconsistencies is known as 'normalisation' to avoid any suggestion of incompetence on the part of the designers. Walkthroughs and reviews of software have the same goal as normalisation, namely to achieve consistent interpretations in the designs from several people or viewpoints. Normalisation of software designs should be carried out, expecting to improve them before they are submitted for external verification.

DO-178A requires a document to be written (document 12: see Appendix C) recording the standards or discipline used for the processes of software design, implementation and testing. If there are any aspects of software design or implementation that may jeopardise meeting the functional objectives of the system (such as the use of natural rather than formal languages, or the use for other reasons of bought-in components), they should be identified, and corresponding steps taken in the verification (analysis and testing) stages to ensure that the objectives are still met in spite of them. If changes to the standards or disciplines are made during the course of the project, the document should be amended to record them.

The Ministry of Defence Standard 00–55 has focussed attention on formal techniques for software development, and stimulated considerable discussion which has not yet been resolved. Formal techniques are fundamental to all computer-based systems: the information handling in a computer is always formal, being based entirely on the form of the data (ultimately the bit-patterns) regardless of any meaning or interpretation. Programming languages such as Ada are formal, so that inferences can be made about them and programs in them by manipulating the texts. (This is essentially what tools such as SPADE and MALPAS do.)

Package declarations in Ada are formal, and Ada compilers check that the body corresponding to each specification is consistent with it; however, the information contained in an Ada package declaration is limited to the declarations of its constituents (and certain representations) with no formal specification of its intended or claimed semantics.

There are a number of techniques for formalising the semantics of an Ada package specification, mostly based on annotating the program text with additional information about the intended effects of the constituents. The situation is reviewed in (Goldsack, 1985). Ada itself can be used to describe intentions within certain limits (Pyle, 1984), but in general more powerful notations are needed, such as Anna, Asphodel, SPARK and MALPAS; these are discussed in Chapter 8.

An Asphodel specification supplements the Ada text with information about the intended semantics following the ideas of the Vienna Definition Method (VDM: Björner and Jones, 1980; Jones, 1986).

In Chapters 8 and 12, formal specification and formal proof are described for use with safety-critical software elements, and for high integrity elements when the application merits them. For Ada programs, this implies formally analysing all category 1 packages and selected category 2 packages.

7.3 Evolution and change control

All significant software will be modified during its operational life, for correction, improvement and enhancement. Change control procedures must ensure that changes are properly justified; the rules of Ada will ensure that the internal integrity

Table 7.1 Persistence of faults (from Bishop et al., 1986)

Phase	Local faults found	Previous faults detected	Faults found later
Customer specification	Unknown		68 $= 52 + 0 + 0 + 14 + 2$
Manufacturer specification	**38**	**52**	**15** $= 6 + 6 + 3 + 0$
Design	14	0 + 6	5 $= 3 + 2 + 0$
Code	**24**	**0 + 6 + 3 = 9**	**2** $= 2 + 0$
Acceptance testing	6	14 + 3 + 2 + 2 = 21	
Back-to-back testing	**1**	**2 + 0 + 0 + 0 + 0 = 2**	

of the program is maintained. Here we discuss the special considerations related to safety assurance in an evolving system.

It must be expected that errors will be discovered at all stages during the development process (and afterwards), particularly during the integration and verification stages. Table 7.1 shows the distribution of errors detected, related back to the stage at which the mistake was made, from Bishop *et al.* (1986). The way in which any error becomes apparent does not necessarily show its real origin, nor does it show any other errors arising from the same source. For safety systems, it is therefore essential to trace back each detected error to its prime cause:

> a specification or design decision that is now known to have been wrong,
> and the subsequent checks that are now known to have been inadequate.

Correcting an error will require changes to one or more modules and to one or more tests. The earlier in the design process that the error occurred, the more pervasive its impact is likely to be (although with Ada, the consequences will be limited by the dependency relationships shown in the context clauses). The decision now to be changed will underlie the design of some module, which might have consequences in other modules mentioning it in their context clauses. All the work from that decision point must be done again, with as much care as each previous time, and the changes or amendments logged.

For example (anticipating the software to be presented in the following chapters), where the modifications to the program involve change to a critical package like SAFE_DEVICE, the normal rules of Ada are not adequate. If the change is to an actual device (sensor or effector) and its associated UNSAFE package, or to the interlock SAFE_TO_OPERATE, then the safety analysis must be repeated on the whole SAFE_DEVICE package (within which the change is bounded).

However, if the specification part of a package such as SAFE_DEVICE is changed (for example introducing more modes of operation, more operations, new parameters or more exceptions), there will have to be corresponding changes to the body to provide their implementation, as well as new parts of the higher-level parts of the program that make use of these additional facilities. The complete V&V check must be repeated, including a repeat of the safety analysis concerning all relevant dangers and interlocks, with all the checks of representation specifications explained in Part III. The results of pre-design safety studies (such as Failure Modes and Effects Analysis) can usefully be carried forward to the maintenance phase (Baudoin, 1986).

In order to resist the natural temptation to short-cut such work, the first priority should be to locate the test set that ought to have detected the error at some stage of integration, and amend it now that the specific problem has been identified. Only then should the program itself be modified, and the new tests applied.

7.4 Partitioning for safety

The design of safety-related systems is fundamentally about the way in which they are structured. The HSE Guide gives general principles for configuring safety and protection systems; DO-178A rules for software require partitioning into distinct modules; a similar concept is expressed by EWICS in terms of human understanding. The basic rule is:

> The program structure should be easy to understand, both in its overall design as well as in its details. The program should be readable from start to end.

While this rule is not specific to safety, its importance and relevance can be seen in Section 1.2 above: we strive for safety by forethought (largely expressed in software); forethought is never perfect, but is improved by understanding and systematic analysis. Monolithic programs are deprecated for many reasons, but they cannot be tolerated in safety-related systems as they impair the human understanding that is a prerequisite for responsibility.

7.4.1 Partitioning rules

Good structure is essential. Only if this rule is followed can we expect to be able to detect possible faults or dangers. From this rule we can derive a number of recommendations, which closely match the concepts and practices of Ada, as follows:

- The program should be divided into modules: in Ada these are packages.
- Good documentation must be provided: in Ada much of the information is automatically checked for consistency. We explain where additional information is needed.
- Retrospective attempts to optimise memory space or execution time should be avoided: Ada allows an overall programming style to be chosen that localises such decisions, with disciplined evolution for improvement of performance characteristics when found necessary.
- The program should be written in such a way to allow easy testing: Ada package bodies have this property.
- Programming tricks should be avoided: programmers resort to these when they cannot express their design in the language used. Ada provides facilities to render this unnecessary, but checks must still be appplied.
- A central idea of system structure should be adopted: object-oriented design is encouraged by Ada packages, with their context clauses and subunits. Ada establishes a uniform approach to the kinds of program unit and data types used. It also provides for clear identification of the parts of programs in which different tasks or processes can compete for resources, and where they refer to the potentially dangerous devices.

The architecture of a safety-related program in Ada is discussed in Chapter 8, including the way of handling critical peripherals. A package encapsulates all the operations on a device, making it available to any other package that mentions it in its context clause, but always in a disciplined way through the access facilities provided in the package. This is just the same principle of encapsulation as is needed for safety and security, which is the recurring theme of the guidance.

7.4.2 Layered facilities

Within an Ada program, each package collects a set of service facilities that are used in a variety of situations. The package body provides facilities that may be used elsewhere in the program, as defined in the package specification. Thus the natural structure is to have the packages in *layers*, forming a partially ordered structure where the packages in each layer may be implemented using the facilities specified in the packages in the lower layers. Underneath all the software layers there is common underlying hardware: the processor(s), memory, input–output peripherals (and under those, the power supply), which provides the facilities on which all of the others are built. Table 7.2 illustrates a typical layered structure.

This layered structure is common in large programs such as operating systems, but does not seem to have been taken into account in most guides for safety-related software. The concept of partitioning in DO-178A does not explicitly recognise the layered structure of software. In such a structure, the reliability of each layer depends on its usage of the layers below it (including the hardware). Our interpretation of DO-178A for layered partitions must therefore be that each layer is as critical as the criticality of the layers above that depend on it. Thus high criticality descends through the layers, and the lowest layers are likely to have Risk Factor 1. The consequence of this analysis for integrated software is discussed by Pyle (1989).

Thus, specifically, the hardware (processors, memory, busses, communication links and peripheral drivers) are highly critical, leading to the same concerns as in the HSE Guide, but from a different starting point. This principle has now been recognised in the case of processors: the development of the VIPER chip (Cullyer

Table 7.2 Layered structure of a software-based system

Command facilities		Automatic facilities	
Data Base Management	Network Comunication		User Interaction
Operating System		Device Drivers	
Backing Stores	Computers		Data Links

and Kershaw, 1984) was intended to provide a firm base on which the software layers could be built. Viper is a Verifiable Integrated Processor for Enhanced Reliability; its design has been expressed formally, with an associated proof that it has the intended behaviour. Because the design is published openly, any deficiencies in it can be discovered by analysis (as has been reported by Manuel in *The Engineer*, April 1990). If an actual system is built on a less well established base, the principles of using unreliable components (Section 4.5.3) must be applied.

Precisely the same principles apply to the lowest level of software (the Ada run-time system, which provides facilities to implement tasks, exceptions, and dynamic memory allocation), but little practical advice has been published about this topic other than recommending abstinence. Since such software would *not* be written in Ada, the construction and checking should receive the same degree of independent verification as has the VIPER chip, as its impact is similarly pervasive. In the short term, the Ada run-time system must be treated as an unreliable component (Section 4.5.3).

7.5 Diversity for reliability

The idea of diversity is that several independent varieties of a unit should be made, so that if there is a fault in one of them, there will be another unit that does not have this fault. Applying this idea to software, we have to think of independent design, not just re-executing the same program (with the same faults in it). Total diversity of software is difficult to achieve because there is a common element in the design of diverse software, namely the requirements specification. To eliminate foreseeable commonalities, there must be careful isolation of the design teams, and deliberate variety of specifications, algorithms, languages and technologies. A safety-related design should at least develop diverse versions of applications software and use them to check one another and to detect any deficiencies in their common specification; in high reliability the diversity should extend to the system embedded (executive) software. The N-version design approach emphasises the customer–designer interaction rather than the designer–verifier interaction, but does not address the problems that arise from resulting incompatibilities.

The HSE Guide (see Section 2.1.1 and Appendix B) provides checklists for diversity in redundancy systems. Diversity of software is required in a PES (according to the HSE Guide) in the following situations:

- the sole means of achieving the required level of safety integrity is by a programmable safety-related system; *and*
- there is the possibility that a fault within the software associated with a single channel might cause a dangerous mode of failure of the total configuration of the safety-related system.

The rôle of diversity in system design shows the importance of considering software and hardware design together. Major experiments have been carried out in Europe

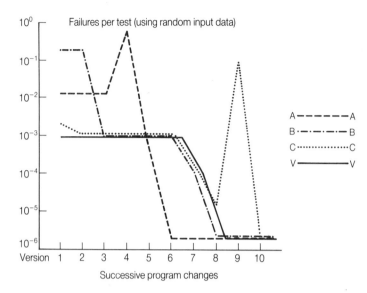

Figure 7.2 Failures in diverse software (source: Bishop *et al.*, 1986). Pseudo-random test data were applied to successive versions of three programs, A, B, C, together with the majority vote, V, on the program outputs. The broken lines show the failure rates in the individual programs, and the solid line the failure rate for the majority votes. Each disagreement with the final 'perfect' program version was considered to be a failure. The failure rate of the majority vote is generally lower than the individual program failure rates (but not in every version), as majority voting enables an independent fault in a single program to be ignored. The 'spikes' at A4 and C9 are due to correction-induced faults.

and the United States to investigate the effect of diversity in design *and also in specification.*

In one experiment on multi-version software development, Kelly *et al.* (1986) investigated specification and design diversity. A system was specified in three ways (informally in English, semi-formally in PDL and formally in OBJ); it was then designed by eighteen different people. The range of errors was found to be very wide, mainly arising from deficiencies in the specification. This showed the importance of multi-versions as a means of uncovering specification faults. (The formal specification in OBJ was not as good as had been hoped, because of the difficulty people had in using it.)

Another experiment (Leveson, 1986) had twenty teams at four universities designing programs to the same specification, to discover how effective the diversity would be. In spite of the specification having had extensive thought beforehand, it was still found to be defective (about six major faults in sixty pages, with thirty significant points of uncertainty). However, when programmers were given a revised (corrected) specification, they were able to incorporate the corrections into their programs very rapidly and effectively.

A project on diverse software (PODS: Bishop *et al.*, 1986) investigated software failures for the control of electrical power stations. Programs were developed independently at three sites, in England, Finland and Norway. Successive versions of each program were tested with the same pseudo-random test data. The experiment found that current 'software engineering' implementation methods were quite effective, in that 93 per cent of the development faults were detected before the acceptance phase. Figure 7.2 shows the proportion of tests that failed for the programs, and Table 7.3 shows the distribution and persistence of faults at one of the sites.

In an ingenious combination of design diversity and expert systems, Theuretz-bacher (1986) wrote a control system in a procedural language, but linked it with a separate safety system containing safety assertions in a declarative language.

The implication of this work for safety software in Ada is that it is not worth while expressing a minor variant of a design as another Ada program. If software diversity is justified, the first improvement will be in the specification, and the result in the software should be a completely different style of program, complementing the Ada software.

7.6 Programming language

Although the public guides (apart from ARINC Paper 613) do not recommend a specific programming language, the basic rules they give all point to Ada, with suitable design rules, a properly validated compiler and a supporting environment. For example, the EWICS Guide gives the following criteria for consideration, all of which are satisfied by Ada (and by no other generally available language):

- Only languages with a thoroughly tested translator should be used.
- Problem oriented languages are strongly preferred.
- The language should be completely and unambiguously defined.
- A programming language and its translator should preferably provide:
    error limiting constructions (subtypes in Ada);
    compilered-time type checking (types in Ada);
    run-time checking of parameters, type matching and array bounds (all in Ada).
- Automated testing aids should be available (e.g. test case generators and monitors).

Conventionally, the work of expressing a program in a machine-readable (and machine-checkable) form is known as 'coding'. This terminology is inappropriate to Ada, since the connotations of concealment and subsequent decoding do not apply (Tooby, 1986). The terminology is also misleading if it is taken to imply that formalisation of software design in Ada should be delayed until a 'Code and unit test' stage. It is better to regard Ada as a language for formally documenting a software design, which can be automatically converted into code by an Ada compiler.

7.6.1 Program design language

Extensive studies (Goldsack, 1985) have shown the importance of Ada for expressing all aspects of program design (not just algorithms): the static structure in terms of packages used, and the dynamic structure in terms of major operations (before the details of those operations are decided). The rules of Ada require modules to identify the package specifications containing the (syntactic) specifications of the operations they use. Thus, if the designer has been able to compile a design module, the rules automatically ensure that subprogram specifications exist for all the operations involved.

During software development, there is a progressive acquisition of information from the initial functional requirements to the program design. Ada has been shown to be appropriate for expressing the morphology of the design, i.e. its structure in terms of modules, specifically packages, representing the entities involved. Ada package specifications give the data types used to carry the necessary attributes of entities, and the operations that can be applied to them, with the appropriate parameters.

Ada package specifications, subprogram specifications and task specifications define the syntax of the respective constituents, but not their semantics (and certainly not their performance).

Various notations have been advocated for expressing the semantics of an Ada program unit. Ada itself can be used to describe intentions within certain limits (Pyle, 1984), but investigations of the use of Ada to express the semantics of operations have identified significant limitations: in practice, the semantics must be specified in other ways. Informal methods are currently the most common, but more powerful notations are becoming available: Anna, Asphodel and the annotations of SPARK and MALPAS (see Chapter 11).

Techniques for formalising the semantics of an Ada package specification are mostly based on annotating the program text with additional information about the intended effects of the constituents. Such formal notations are becoming practical and are important for critical components in safety systems. The situation is reviewed by Goldsack (1985). Formal semantic specification of the program units can be related by the V&V (Verification and Validation) contractor to the respective bodies that are eventually produced, as well as to to the test sets produced to check the implementations. Chapter 11 discusses this issue further.

The main requirement here is that the designer's choice of formalism should be made early, and the decision conveyed to the V&V contractor in order that preparations can begin.

7.7 Reliability of software tools

Compilers and other software tools may be defective. How then can we have confidence in software based systems that have been produced using them? We discuss this issue further in Chapter 11, with the emphasis on confirming that the software that is used to control the target computer is doing what it is required to do; here we consider how the use of potentially unreliable software tools affects the software construction process.

Tools are useful for construction, analysis and management; they can be classified as (a) *translators*; (b) *aggregators*; and (c) *analysers*: the first convert information from one form into another (supposedly equivalent); the second collect information from several sources and produce a (supposed) combination; and the third derive information from the sources to expose some (supposed) logical deductions. Compilers and assemblers and loaders are examples of the first kind; library managers and linkers are examples of the second; conformance checkers and static code analysers are examples of the third.

Often a single tool fulfills more than one role – for example a traditional compiler or assembler applies a limited analysis to the source text (e.g. syntax check) as well as converting the information into linkable or loadable binary. Ada compilers carry out extensive analyses of the source text, ensuring consistency of use of each entity in the program (according to its declaration) and the managerial control throughout the recompilation rules (flagging potential inconsistencies between compilation units). Similarly, library managers and linkers also carry out analyses such as transitive closure of calls and aggregation of memory requirements.

Software tools are as prone to error as any other software, are but subject to the same maturation process (as initial defects are discovered and corrected). Indeed, the maturation is faster in software tools than in other software, because the users tend to be more sophisticated and demanding. Failures can be construction errors (e.g wrong code generated, overlapping memory allocations) or analysis errors (e.g. confusion of categories). A fault of the first kind would affect the executable code, and should be detected by testing. A fault of the second kind would affect the evidence about the executable code, but not the code itself. Thus the solution, as always, is to use diversity and variety of tools, with feedback loops to confirm that results are adequate for the intended use.

Ada compilers are still in the maturation period (some more advanced than others: an Ada Evaluation Service is now available to give information about specific compilers), and other tools are relatively immature. It is therefore prudent to be aware of the risks of possible errors in them, and to cross-check extensively. In practice this means (a) relating confidence to the usage of the facility; and (b) using different tools to check one another. As an example of the first point, most optimisations in compilers are less well exercised than the straightforward translations, so it is wise to avoid program constructs that rely on the compiler for optimisation: keep the source program constructs simple, using source language transformations for optimisation (which can be checked). As an example of the second point, source text analysers need to parse the Ada program (which is non-trivial); this is checked by the analysis done by an ordinary Ada compiler. The same rationale during the checking period (Verification and Validation) justifies the use of a different Ada compiler to check the analyses done by the one used by the developer.

Thus the software developer should use software tools with care and scepticism, relying on their systematic ability to apply rules exhaustively, but being aware that the rules they apply may be wrong. The more widely used a tool is, the more confidence it deserves. Thus project-specific tools should be particularly suspect, although they are nevertheless welcomed for their ability to carry out processes which otherwise would be done less exhaustively by manual methods.

7.8 Performance

No current method of software development addresses the problems of storage and timing constraints, or of traffic capacity in communication. This is beyond the realm of software and high-level languages (as can be recognised by considering different compilations of the same program on different computers). The designer has always to bear the performance in mind, but there is no formal way of expressing what is desired or intended, and certainly no way of ensuring that a given performance target can be achieved automatically by a given compiler and target computer. The features of Ada relevant to this are identified in Section 9.4 and discussed further in Section 13.5.

Each package body will require space for its code and local variables (possibly a variable amount if dynamic storage allocation is used). Each procedure body and task body will require time for its execution, dependent on the values of its parameters and non-local variables. The designer will have to estimate and record (systematically) the intended values and dependencies of these resources; the V&V contractor can provide an independent check that the estimates are both internally consistent and reasonable for the state of the art in programming, compiler technology and hardware to be used.

These issues may be investigated using models of the target system, but must eventually be addressed by testing the software in an appropriate operating environment, initially perhaps using a representative target computer in a representative plant (perhaps simulated), but eventually on the real target in the real plant. The software/hardware integration is of central importance in performance testing: see Section 14.5.

7.9 Software requirements documentation

To conclude this chapter, we list the software requirements that must be properly documented. The topics to be covered in the software requirements document are defined by DO-178A (see Appendix C, especially Section C6). This summary of the topics to be covered is intended to act as a checklist on software construction principles, with particular relevance to software in Ada.

The topics that should be covered fall into four main categories, as follows:

(a)   General characteristics of the desired system:
       criticality of each function;
       sizing and timing constraints;
       partitioning requirements.
(b)   Desired behaviour of the system:
       functions to be accomplished in software, in normal and abnormal
         circumstances;
       built-in test and/or monitoring requirements: error detection and
       recovery;
       test requirements, off-line and on-line, including real time diagnostics.
(c)   The effects of anticipated faults:
       failure modes and their expected probabilities;
       performance degradation and/or function loss under fault conditions.
(d)   Underlying mechanisms assumed to be available to provide the desired
       behaviour:
       hardware/software interfaces;
       characteristics of the processor and other underlying facilities used.

The software requirements document must of course define the effects that the
software is required to achieve. DO-178A goes beyond this and also requires the
document to define the underlying facilities that will be used to achieve these effects:
category (d) above. Modern practice would treat these (particularly the choice of
processor) as part of the solution rather than part of the problem, since the software
should be designed in a machine-independent way, and the processor chosen on the
basis of its performance, availability and reliability. With software written in Ada,
this would be the natural way, and the most important characteristic of the
processor would be the existence and quality of the Ada compiler for it.

8

Software structural design

THE STRUCTURE of software has a central role in the safety of the system whose behaviour it determines. The rules of Ada (with its strong type checking and encapsulation of program units) provide access restrictions which can ensure that there are no contraventions of the safety features within the high-level program, by the use of safety interlocks and suitable design rules. (Safety verification checks must then concentrate on those parts of the program that use the insecure features of Ada.) We explain in this chapter how a program should be structured to localise the safety-related areas, and how design rules for Ada can be used to give the protection needed for adequate isolation of the safety-critical parts.

The program structure is based on the use of Ada packages, which are categorised according to their degree of criticality, so that suitable rules can be followed to constrain their design and facilitate appropriate checks. The safety rule applied within this structure applies to critical packages, and consists essentially of enveloping the handler for each potentially dangerous output device in a package containing the safety interlock, with the package specification making available for external use only those operations that include the necessary safety checks. (We call this technique 'double insulation'.)

The documents that define the structure must be carefully and precisely written, to underlie the checking that will have to take place to confirm that the software is adequately safe. They must cover the software requirements (a common cause of failure in software), the software design definition, and the subsequent integration. All changes after the initially checked baseline must be rigorously controlled.

In this chapter, Section 8.1 explains the structure of a program in Ada as it relates to safety, showing the connection between the functional specification and the program design; Section 8.2 presents the principles of package categorisation that underlie the checking for reliability of the software. The next two sections deal with specific Ada topics that are important in this context: deliberate restrictions on the use of certain Ada features (i.e. language subsets: Section 8.3), and the need for additional concepts to permit verification of Ada texts (i.e. claims about intentions: Section 8.4). Section 8.5 describes the double insulation technique for encapsulating the critical packages, which is the fundamental technique for writing safe programs in Ada. Section 8.6 summarises the documentation required, as a checklist.

8.1 Program structural design in Ada

The role of software in connection with safety is two-fold: it must be correct with respect to the control of the critical devices, and it must implement interlocks for those devices to ensure that their use is safe. The structural design of the software must be such that it strongly separates the critical software from the rest, so that the interlocks cannot be by-passed. Ada packages provide precisely the isolation required, which we now explain.

The fundamental structure of a program in Ada is as a collection of packages which should form a partially ordered set of abstractions, each being implemented in terms of lower-level packages. A group of packages at a uniform abstraction level can be treated as a subsystem in a layered structure, each with its own distinct requirements. The top layer of packages determines the external functionality of the system, implemented by means of the lower layers (as has been mentioned in Section 7.4).

8.1.1 Subsystem identification

During structural software design, the application and infrastructure concepts are named and formulated as package specifications for appropriate data types, which form the subsystems in the target software system. The work of elaborating the subsystem requirements begins when the subsystem has been identified, as an element of the overall design. Typically, in a control system, infrastructure subsystems will be identified first, one corresponding to each kind of peripheral hardware subsystem that the software has to handle. Application subsystems will be identified subsequently, depending on the different areas of concern in the target system. Application subsystems will expect to rely on infrastructure subsystems to provide their interactions with the peripherals.

In formulating the data types involved in the target subsystem, the designer must choose the level of abstraction and the way of dealing with similar entities of the same type. This choice could well affect the ease of evolution of the software after the system has been designed (during pre-delivery checking as well as during operational use).

Each main package may either export a data type (so that packages in higher layers can declare many instances of the type), or it may declare the objects internally and export only the functions for communicating with them. The former uses the idea of Abstract Data Types (or ADTs); the latter is based on the ideas of Object-Oriented Design (OOD). There are many similarities between them; both styles have their proponents, and either can be used for programming safety-related systems. The significant difference between them in Ada concerns the way the package representing a subsystem is used in a multi-tasking context. This is explained in Sections 8.4.4. and 8.4.5(d) below.

Similar work has to be done for each subsystem. The designer should explicitly state the attributes of the concepts with their intended relationships, together with the operations or manipulations that involve them.

8.1.2 Subsystem design

Most of subsystem design work can be done in parallel, as the inter-dependencies do not arise until package bodies have to be developed. However, familiarity with the overall system is essential, and anticipation of future stages is well worth while. As in most kinds of software development, there is a creative phase, when information is discovered and invented, followed by a review phase, when the information is checked. The review must be carried out by someone other than the original designer: often the designer of an adjacent subsystem (see Chapter 13).

The list of questions in Table 8.1 gives the points that should be considered by

Table 8.1 Guide for designing a software subsystem

1   *What is it intended to do?*
1a *Identify* all the operations that the subsystem can carry out, including:
        normal operations, major and minor functions;
        start-up, close-down, recovery, reconstitution;
        built-in testing and diagnosis.

1b *Define* the desired effect of each operation (but not yet how to achieve it).

2   *What information does it handle?*
2a *Identify* all the kinds of data relevant to the use of the subsystem, including:
        inputs to operations (explicit and parametric), used but not changed;
        outputs from operations, produced or modified from input;
        common data shared by several operations of the subsystem, but not for external
        use.

2b *Define* the information content of each and what is done with it (but not yet how to
        represent it).

3   *What can go wrong?*
3a *Identify* all kinds of failure that might happen with the subsystem, including:
        faults in dependent peripheral devices;
        faults in usage or improper attempts to carry out operations.

3b *Define* the situation in which each kind of failure occurs (but not yet how to avoid it or to
        recover from it).

4   *How good must it be?*
4a *Identify* all the performance and quality attributes desired for it, including:
        typical time and expected relative frequency of operations;
        criticality for safety or security;
        resource allocation, in space, time and channel capacities.
4b *Define* the criteria for acceptability of performance and quality targets, e.g. testing/verifi-
        cation obligations (but not yet how to achieve them).

the subsystem designer, and recorded both in Ada text and prose documentation. The properties of the concepts are defined in package specifications, as declarations of appropriate entities. For each entity there should be assertions of the intended (time-independent) relationships, using Ada to express types and relationships. In addition to the assertions about individual entities, there should be some property that holds for the package as a whole, integrating the properties of the individual constituents. (If there is no such overall property, why are the entities together in the same package?) We call this the *claim* for the package (see Section 8.4 below). Each package may be verified by demonstrating that the given program design satisfies the claim, and will cause the intended relationships to be maintained, assuming correct lower-level design.

Note the two-stage approach on each issue: first identify the items concerned (giving them appropriate names), then define the relevant information for each. There is always a temptation to continue giving more and more information, so we note in each case when to stop at this stage, before going on to the logical design (discussed in Chapter 9).

8.2 Package categorisation

Packages may be categorised in a number of ways which we explain here. The primary difference in a safety-related system is its risk factor, which indicates the importance of each safety or protection control loop of the plant (described in Chapters 2 and 3). The risk factor might be directly related to the functionality of the software that controls the loop, or it might arise from the position of a package in the layers of software on which safety-critical functions rely. Thus any package that is *used by* a critical control loop must be categorised as critical, since a deficiency in any underlying package would be as serious as though it were in a package that used it. Similarly, any package *used by* an essential (non-critical) control loop must also be categorised as essential.

In Section 2.2, we distinguished three risk factors: critical, essential and non-essential. The risk factor of the control loop handled by each package should be stated explicitly (as a comment in the header of the package specification). However, as was pointed out in Chapter 7, the distinction between critical and essential functionality does not directly influence the construction of software (in contrast with checking it); the over-riding principle is that of Section 4.3 on correctness and safety:

- safety-critical parts must be kept small.
- those program parts must be adequately isolated.

The significant difference in the software structure is therefore between:

- packages that handle safety-related devices (whether critical or essential);
- packages that ensure proper isolation; and
- other packages.

Since the packages must be written in ways that take account of the differences, the above categories are the relevant ones for software development. We call this the criticality categorisation of the packages. Category 1 refers to packages handling input–output for potentially hazardous devices; category 2 to the packages that protect these from interference; and category 3 for the rest.

In addition, since the safety category of a package determines the kind of checking to be applied, there is a further categorisation based on the ease of verification of the package (see Section 8.4). The general principle we apply is to keep most critical packages as simple as possible, so that they can be rigorously checked by formal analysis and intelligent inspection. We must also ensure that other packages cannot subvert these checks. Thus the criticality category determines the allowable contents of the package, and the associated checking/verification regime.

The approach presented in Chapter 9 below uses the linguistic structure of Ada to ensure that the critical packages (category 1) are kept simple, protected by other packages of trusted software (category 2) that handle anything which might have an adverse effect on the critical software, with the general software in category 3 packages which do not contain any input–output or facilities that could by-pass the category 2 protection.

The design rules are formulated in terms of Ada constructs and thus may be interpreted as recommended subsets of Ada for the different categories of package. Note that these are subsets for programmers, not subsets for compilers.

8.3 Use of Ada features

Ada contains a wide variety of features, with differing degrees of power and sensitivity. One approach to the use of Ada in safety-critical systems is to limit programs to particular subsets of the language in order to prevent hazards being written in. However, this approach runs up against fundamental difficulties when attention is given to the *system* as well as the *software*. Here we present an alternative approach based on package categorisation, and design rules for the use of Ada constructs appropriate to the criticality category of the package.

Ada includes features allowing a program to deal explicitly with its implementation, known as 'unsafe programming'. It also includes features that are deliberately defined to permit variety of implementation. In addition, certain features are notorious for exposing weaknesses in compilers (i.e. where they might be defective, even though validated). Full details of these issues, known as insecurities in Ada, are given by Wichmann (1989), and summarised in Table 8.2.

The Ada features used in any part of a program can have significant implications for the rest of the program. Specifically, the confidence in a program (after static semantic analysis and dynamic testing) largely rests on the features that have been used in it. Most guides for using Ada in safety-related systems recommend avoiding certain features throughout the program, applying global rules to the software development.

Table 8.2 High-risk insecurities in Ada (source: Wichmann, 1989)

UNCHECKED_DEALLOCATION
UNCHECKED_CONVERSION
shared variables, with tasking
changing discriminant values
dependence on the parameter-passing mechanism
pragma SUPPRESS
use of undefined value
order of elaboration of library units
use of priorities for synchronisation
abort statement
use of locally updated global variables after an exception
address clause
MACHINE_CODE
pragma INTERFACE
LOW_LEVEL_IO
optimisation (in compiler)
pragma STORAGE_UNIT
fixed point types with extra precision and/or range (allocated by compiler)
representation specification
record type with unconstrained dynamic bounds

For example, the Southampton group (responsible for SPADE and SPARK: Carré and Jennings, 1988) recommend avoiding features that cannot be handled by their automatic semantic analyser: see Table 8.3. By analysing the requirements for predictability of execution, Systeam KG have developed a set of thirty-five rules which jointly ensure that the space and time needed for a program are bounded. The Systeam rules (for the development of software for the European Fighter Aircraft: Holzapfel and Winterstein, 1988) avoid features that carry risk to system integrity; they are shown in Table 8.4. GEC Sensors (Gordon, 1988) recommend avoiding certain features for safety or portability.

Unfortunately the Southampton subset eliminates all input–output, thus guaranteeing (logical) safety by avoiding any actions controlling a hazardous (or even non-hazardous) device. To achieve physical safety, the software has to deal with input–output, and consequently lose logical safety. This is the fundamental conflict to be faced by the system designer: if the software is logically safe, it cannot affect the safety or danger in the world outside. In order to reduce physical danger, it must rely on features that are logically insecure. (This is not a special feature of Ada, but an inevitable characteristic of software or any formal language.)

In all the subsets, some of the restrictions are not directly relevant to safety, but, rather, express preferences of programming style.

This book persues a somewhat different approach, relating linguistic features to package criticality. Tables 8.5–8.8 below summarise all the Ada features that have been noted by other authors as needing care, classified under general program

Table 8.3 SPARK: features omitted from Ada (source: Carré and Jennings, 1988)

no fraction part in based literal
no number declaration
no tasks (hence no entry, abort, accept, select)
no generic declaration or instantiation
no exceptions (hence no raise, no exception part)
no renaming declaration
no constraint on type mark in object declaration
no constrained array definition in object declaration
no initial value for variable in object declaration or for component in record
no access types (hence no incomplete type declaration, no null, no allocator)
no derived types
must have constraint in subtype indication
no fixed point values (constant, constraint, accuracy definition)
no discriminant constraint (hence no variant record, no variant part in types)
no dynamic range (must be static)
enumeration type must have at least two literals
no character literals in enumeration type
no anonymous subtypes (hence no constraint on type marks in arrays or record components;
    loop parameter must have type mark)
choice must be static, and not others
no use clause in declarative part
no character literal, operator symbol, attribute, slice or all in name
aggregate constituents must be all named or all positional
no go to (hence no statement label)
no block statement
exit from innermost loop only
return in function only (not in procedure)
function must have parameters
no redefinition of operators
no default values of subprogram parameters
parameters must be all named or all positional
no automatic type conversion in subprogram parameters
no context clause on secondary unit
no subprogram body as library unit
no multiple use clause in context clause
no multiple names in with clause

Table 8.4 Systeam rules for Safe Ada (source: Holtzapfel and Winterstein, 1988)

R1: Access types shall not be used.

R2: All constraints shall be static.

R3: Subprograms shall not be called recursively.

R4: The result of a function shall not be of an unconstrained array type.

R5: Tasks and tasking statements shall not be used.

R6: Machine code insertions shall not be used.

R7: Functions shall have a **return** statement immediately before their **end**.

R8: Actions shall not raise a predefined exception.

R9: Objects shall have program defined values before they are used.

R10: Subprograms shall assign a value to all parameters of mode **out** before returning.

R11: Functions shall not change (directly or indirectly) non-local objects, i.e. functions shall have no side effects.

R12: Record components that depend on a discriminant shall not be used as actual parameters of mode **out** or **in out**.

R13: A subprogram shall not be called with an object as an actual parameter that is also used within the subprogram (directly or indirectly) other than via the corresponding formal parameter.

R14: If the same object is associated with two different formal parameters in a procedure call then both shall have mode **in**.

R15: The components in a record type declaration shall not have default expressions.

R16: Address clauses shall not be imposed on program units.

R17: Address clauses for several objects shall not make these objects overlap.

R18: Unchecked type conversion shall not be used.

R19: Initialisation expressions (within object declarations) shall not involve the invocation of a user-defined function.

R20: The sequence of statements in a package body shall not contain the call of a user-defined subprogram.

R21: If an entity is declared by a renaming declaration then within the scope of this declaration only the new name shall be used and not the old one.

R22: Formal parameters shall not have default values.

R23: Default generic formal subprograms shall not be used.

R24: Generic formal objects shall not have default expressions.

R25: Derived types shall not be used.

R26: An exception shall not be propagated out of its scope.

R27: An exception handler shall not have the choice **others**.

R28: A case statement shall not have the choice **others**.

R29: Variant parts in record type declarations shall not have the choice **others**.

R30: Array and record aggregates shall not have the choice **others**.

R31: Character literals shall not be overloaded.

R32: Positional and named parameters shall not be mixed within the same subprogram call or within the same generic instantiation.

R33: A **use** clause shall immediately follow a **with** clause or a package declaration.

R34: Anonymous (array) types shall not be used.

R35: Array and record aggregates shall be qualified.

Table 8.5 Program structure features relevant to safety

Generic units (not in SPARK): use but thoroughly test each instantiation.
Library subprogram body (not in SPARK): permit.
Low level IO package (not in GEC; insecure): cat 1 unit; justify use.
Machine code programming (not in GEC; insecure): cat 1 unit; justify use.
Order of elaboration of library units (insecure): avoid dependence by claims.
Secondary unit context (not in SPARK): encourage; document with layer number.
Unchecked conversion (not in GEC or Systeam; insecure): cat 1 unit; justify use.
Unchecked deallocation (not in GEC, SPARK or Systeam; insecure): cat 1 unit; justify use.

Table 8.6 Declarations relevant to safety

Access type (not in GEC, SPARK or Systeam): cat 2 unit; document the invariant.
Address clause (insecure): treat as representation specification.
Anonymous subtype (not in SPARK): permit as arrays.
Anonymous type (not in SPARK or Systeam): permit with range constraint.
Declared initialisation (not in SPARK): encourage, with invariant.
Default value (not in SPARK or Systeam): encourage, with invariant.
Derived type (not in SPARK or Systeam): encourage, with documentation.
Dynamic choice range (not in SPARK): permit.
Dynamic range constraint (not in SPARK or Systeam): permit with documentation.
Exception (not in SPARK): use; document scope and top handler
Handler for predefined exceptions (not in Systeam): permit.
Implementation-dependent pragma (not in GEC): permit, documenting non-portability.
Operator re-definition (not in SPARK): permit, with documentation confirming axioms.
others in aggregate (not in SPARK or Systeam): permit.
Parameterless function (not in SPARK): permit, with documentation.
Pragma INTERFACE (not in GEC; insecure): permit, documenting non-portability.
Pragma STORAGE_UNIT (insecure): treat as representation specification.
Pragma SUPPRESS (insecure): do not use.
Record type with unconstrained dynamic bound (insecure): treat as variant record.
Renaming (not in GEC or SPARK): permit, with documentation.
Representation specification (not in GEC; insecure): cat 1 unit; justify use.
Shared variable (not in GEC; insecure): cat 2 unit; permit with claim.
Task entry (not in SPARK or Systeam): cat 2 unit; use, with claim for passive task.
Use clause (limited in GEC and SPARK): permit only immediately after **with** or package
    declaration.
Variant record (not in SPARK): cat 2 unit; permit with documentation.

Table 8.7 Statements relevant to safety

Abort (not in GEC; insecure): permit, with documentation for task.
Block (not in SPARK): permit.
Change to discriminant value (insecure): treat as variant record.
Dependence on parameter mechanism (insecure): note potential non-portability.
Exit to outer loop (not in SPARK): permit.
Go to (not in SPARK): cat 2 unit; prohibit unless specifically authorised.
Label (not in SPARK): permit, with state condition assertion.
Mixed styles of component association (not in SPARK): permit.
Recursive call of subprogram (not in Systeam): permit with documentation.
Return in procedure (not in SPARK): permit.
Slice (not in SPARK): permit, with documentation and special check.
Type converted subprogram parameter (not in SPARK): cat 2 unit; permit.
Use of priority for synchronisation (insecure): do not use.

Table 8.8 Expressions relevant to safety

Fixed point arithmetic (not in SPARK; insecure): permit, with deep testing, noting potential non-portability.
Implementation-dependent attributes (not in GEC): permit, noting non-portability.
Locally updated global variable used after exception (insecure): do not use.
Optimisation (insecure): avoid.
Undefined value (insecure): declare initial value.

structure (compilation and program units), declarations (entities the unit might contain), statements (imperative executable statements concerning the visible entities), and expressions (formulae to be evaluated in the declarations or statements). The notes indicate which groups forbid the feature, and what the present recommendation is – in particular identifying the criticality in terms of the categories identified in Section 8.2. The default category is 3 when no other is indicated.

Note on SPARK annotations   Packages in SPARK have two kinds of annotation, as follows:

- **import,** identifying which named entities from other packages are used;
- **proof declaration** (in a package specification only), being a proof function, a proof rule, a proof constant or a proof type.

The import annotation shows which entities from other packages are accessed inside the package. Ada applies an 'all or nothing' rule to the visible entities of other packages: whenever a package is in context, all its visible entities can be accessed; whenever a package is not in context, none of its entities can be accessed. The SPARK import annotation allows the programmer to note that only a restricted set of visible entities are actually used in the package. Proof declarations link a claim to the program text, providing the justification that the claim is valid.

Subprogram annotations in SPARK are of four kinds, as follows (of which two are applicable only to procedures):

(a) **global:** a list of non-local (entire) variables involved in the subprogram;
(b) **derives:** a conjunction of dependency clauses, stating which imported variables determine each exported variable of the subprogram;
(c) **pre-condition:** the predicate presumed on entry to the procedure;
(d) **post-condition:** the predicate intended on leaving the procedure.

These use variables to make any connection between constituents of the package, rather than having a package-wide claim. Relationships expressed through variables are intrinsically weaker and less abstract than those expressed as a direct claim.

8.4 Verifiable Ada

Ada does not include features for stating *intentions* about programs. Supporting information (in the associated documentation if not in the program text) should therefore state what each significant unit is supposed to be or do. We call this a *claim*. Any software that is to be verified must have such a claim, since the verification must be a check that the program (whole or part) does or is what it intends. The claim must be formulated as part of the software creation, to be used subsequently (and usually independently) to check the software created and the tests that exercise it. Each constituent of a package might have a claim. Specifically, there should be a claim for each critical package, for each subprogram contained therein, for each exception and each label.

The questions to be addressed with regard to a package are as follows:

1. What kinds of claim might be made for a package, in comparison with the claims that might be made for the constituent declarations in its visible part?

2. How would different ways of writing a package, in relation to the claim, affect the ease of verifying the claim?

From the first question, we are led to another classification of packages, according to the kind of claim that can be made, based on the package visible part. From the second question, we reach recommendations for verifiable Ada in the several categories of package, by considering which features of Ada in the package private part and body make verification of the claim trivial, easy, difficult or impossible.

The kinds of claim possible have a bearing on the kinds of annotation needed for Ada units, as in Asphodel and SPARK. The formulation of the claim for appropriate constructs is a significant step in developing a program.

8.4.1. Constituent declarations

Individual declarations that might occur in the visible part, according to the basic declarative item, can have claims as follows:

- Basic declarations:
    - object declaration: constant has fixed value; variable is within constraints determined by its type mark;
    - number declaration: identifier denotes fixed value;
    - type declaration: implies claim for objects of the type;
    - subtype declaration: implies claim for objects of the subtype;
    - subprogram declaration: claim relationship between pre-condition and post-condition in terms of parameters and visible objects;
    - package declaration: everything here and for a complete package;
    - task declaration: anything for a task;
    - generic declaration: implies claim for instantiations;
    - exception declaration: claim situation in which exception is raised;
    - generic instantiation: claim as package or subprogram;
    - renaming declaration: no specific claim, only local visibility;
    - deferred constant declaration: constant has fixed (implicit) value.
- Representation clauses:
    - no verifiable claim possible.
- Use clauses:
    - not relevant to claim (only local visibility).

8.4.2. The package as a whole

The claims for a complete package may concern inter-relationships between the claims for the constituents, but need not do so. A package may be simply an administrative convenience for collecting declarative items, with no additional claim.

With the above point in mind, we first classify packages into two kinds: those in which no claims are made for the package as a whole (beyond those made for the constituents individually), and those in which there is a claim beyond those that can be made for the visible declarations. We call packages in which there are only the claims of the constituents 'loose', and a package that has an additional claim 'tight'.

A loose package may include 'common' data declarations, application-specific type definitions and various subprograms for an application (with no particular connections).

The kinds of claim specific to a tight package may be about:

●   relationships between the claims for constituent subprograms;
●   objects of a constituent private data type;
●   state-dependent calls (i.e. functions, procedures and task entries whose results do not depend solely on their parameters).

These depend significantly on whether they are used within a single task or usable from several tasks. We discuss each of them, with examples, below. (In Chapter 12 we consider the problem of verifying such claims.)

8.4.3. Loose packages

A package consisting only of type declarations and constants is useful for collecting application details, implying claims that may be relevant for a number of other packages. (Note that such a package needs no body.) A package containing visible variables needs a strong claim about their intended properties, which may depend on the order of elaboration and will depend on its usage (single task or multi-task). The claim will be very difficult to verify; hence such packages should be avoided.

For a different kind of loose package, consider the claim for a package of trigonometry functions. Regardless of the claim made for the sin and cos functions individually, there should be a claim that sin and arcsin are inverse functions, and that sin and cos differ by a constant phase difference in the argument. Similarly, a package containing exp and ln should claim that they are inverse functions. As well as inverse functions, there may be compositions such as $f(g(x)) = h(x)$.

An important special case of this kind of claim is for the set of operations on an output device that may be dangerous: the operations in the package may ensure the safety of its use by being individually safe and comprehensive, so that no other actions are available for the device.

8.4.4. Tight packages

The claim made for a private type would be that all objects declared (outside the package) to be of that type should comply with an invariant defined for the type, at every point outside the package. This would include internal consistency within the components of objects whose type is private; and distinctness as well as internal consistency in objects whose type is limited private.

> An example of this is a type STACK allowing multiple stacks to be declared outside the package.

(This is the basis of 'object-oriented' programming, and the Ada interpretation of abstract data types.)

A different kind of claim is needed when the result or effect of a subprogram depends on the state of the system when it is called, not only on its parameters. These are very important in conventional 'procedural' programming (and excluded from 'functional' programming). We call them 'state-dependent' subprograms to emphasise that the normal expectation for a subprogram (same result for same parameters) does not apply. The claim must take account of previous actions, which may be expressed in terms of an internal state (not directly visible to the outside). This strongly depends on whether the calls come from a single task (with implied ordering and atomicity) or from several tasks: a secondary classifying principle. Single-task claims can be satisfied in packages with their own variables in the package body, hidden to the rest of the program but accessible to all the internal subprogram bodies.

> Examples include reading the value of a variable, obtaining a pseudo-random number, input operations, taking a value from a stack or queue declared inside the package, and any use of a variable of an **access** type.

The package normally contains other subprograms which have no particular claim individually (and perhaps no immediately observable effect), such as assigning a new value to a variable, setting the seed for pseudo-random number generation, output operations, putting values in a stack or queue, and changing the value to which another points by an **access** value.

The claim for such a package as a whole refers to the history of use of the particular constituents, and perhaps even to occurrences completely outside the package (e.g. protocol handling).

Multi-task claims for state-dependent packages can also have *own* variables in the body, but the accesses to them must be through entry calls rather than subprogram calls, to ensure mutual exclusion.

> Examples are buffers for communication between tasks, multiplexing and demultiplexing operations.

8.4.5. Design rules to facilitate verification

The ease of verification of a loose package is not significant. Each constituent must be verified individually, so the influence of the packaging is marginal in this case.

(a) The ease of verifying a tight package will obviously depend on the specific claim, but will always be made more difficult if unnecessary constituents are present. Thus any constituents not relevant to the package-specific claim should be taken out.

> **Recommendation:** Every package should be *either* loose *or* have one kind of claim, with only components relevant to the claim in the package.

(b) The ease of verifying a tight package concerning related subprograms should depend on the manipulation of the claims themselves, but may be adequately covered by the Ada text, particularly when the individual claims are difficult to verify (as with mathematical functions). The bodies of the functions for sin, cos, arcsin, etc. may well have sufficient commonality to support a claimed relationship, even without a full claim for the individual subprograms (that they are good approximations to the mathematical functions indicated by their names).

> **Recommendation:** The bodies of related functions should be written so that the relationship is evident, e.g. by using internal subprograms and renaming.

(c) For a tight package involving private types, the verification of an invariant must show that it is true initially and implied by the post-condition of every operation.

It is important in this case that nothing outside the package should affect the components of the private type. Objects declared as **private** may be inspected using attributes, so details of the representation are not strictly hidden; but unless UNCHECKED_CONVERSION is used, the components cannot be *changed* outside the package. Since the type is **private**, and there is no way of altering its values other than by these operations, the same (claimed invariant) condition can be assumed to be a pre-condition for every operation. However, no assumption can be made for individuality of instances of the type, unless it is also declared to be **limited**.

> **Recommendation:** In a package with a **private** type, limit the other visible constituents to proper subprograms that construct and manipulate the values of that type. If there are operations that involve data of more than one **private** type, make a package for each **private** type and a further package for the combination.

If two **private** types are related so that the implementation of each needs to use the other, they do not fit into a layered structure. The relationship can be resolved by considering the relative timings required for the operations on the two types – one must be faster than the other. The faster one must be implemented in such a way that it does not depend on the slower one.

(d) For a package involving state-dependent subprograms, the enclosing task structure is critically important. The constituent subprograms are in principle re-entrable, but the data objects declared in the body are the same for all tasks. This means that the package must be written in different ways for single-task and multi-task use.

> **Recommendation:** In a package with state-dependent subprograms, *either* restrict its use to a single task *or* write the operations as task entries and rename them as procedures.

(e) For a package involving input operations, the enclosing task structure is also important, as the values provided to each task will depend on the relative timing. The claim made must take account of this.

> **Recommendation:** Ensure that a package handling input on a single channel is used within only one task. (If necessary, split multiplexed data into one package for the raw data and a distinct package for demultiplexing the data into several tasks.)

(f) For a package involving output operations, the enclosing task is also important (even though it cannot affect the claim for the programmed side of the operation).

> **Recommendation:** Ensure that a package handling output to a single channel is used within only one task. (If necessary, merge data from several tasks in a multiplexing task, and pass it for raw output to a distinct single-task package.)

8.4.6. Summary

Safety-related packages should be constructed with claims in mind. Each critical package should claim at most one kind of inter-relationship between its constituents, and should contain the minimum amount of program necessary to satisfy the claim for the package (beyond the claims for its constituents).

8.5 Encapsulation in critical packages

Each critical (potentially dangerous) output device should be encapsulated in *two* enclosing packages. The innermost package handles the operations on the device, for all circumstances: normal operation (including innocuous as well as dangerous actions) and unusual (e.g. maintenance or adjustment) operations; this package will eventually contain all the specific device controls. The outer package handles the interlock(s) on the device operations, and makes use of information from relevant sensors; it provides to the rest of the program only the interlock-protected operations, so that any attempt to carry out a potentially dangerous operation when it is not safe to do so would be rejected. Because the inner package is encapsulated within the outer one, no other parts of the program can by-pass the interlocks. We call this technique 'double insulation'.

We describe (in Section 10.5) two alternative methods that may be used in the nested packages to assure safety, which differ in their presumptions about device timing and the way of dealing with averted danger; we call them *passive* and *active* interlocking. The designer chooses between them by considering what is to be done if the program attempts to carry out an operation when to do so would be dangerous. Can these circumstances be known in advance? What is to be done in such a situation?

The difference centres on whether the requester of an operation can check whether it is safe (at a particular time) before initiating the operation. If the safety criterion is dependent only on the instantaneous values given by available sensors (which should be bound in a package), passive interlocking is indicated. But with more complicated criteria, it may be preferable to incorporate the check at a lower level (active interlocking), and design the requesting process in such a way that a rejection of the request (when it is unsafe) is part of the normal logic of the requester, programmed as an **else** alternative rather than as an exception.

The first way of dealing with the problem is to define some alternative action to be taken immediately such a situation arises; the second way is to do nothing at the time, but make the plant wait until it is safe to carry out the requested operation. The first way is based on the presumption that the program should know when it is safe to carry out a potentially dangerous operation, and should not have tried to do it when the state is wrong (so the check provides run-time detection of an error). The second way presumes that the timing of the operation is not predictable, and the device will eventually be capable of carrying out the requested operation safely.

Both ways use interlocks to ensure safety, but the nature of the interlocks is different. Passive interlocking is the simpler, the interlock being an instantaneous check, without any further implications. In active interlocking, the interlocking process has not only to indicate whether the situation is safe or dangerous at any time, but to issue stimulus signals whenever that situation changes.

8.6 Design descriptions

With the software written in Ada, each package should be responsible for a distinct objective. This principle relies on partitioning the functionality of the system, including service functions as well as application functions, in a layered structure. Where the functions have different criticality categories, the partitioning permits the software to be treated appropriately for the different risk factors, provided that the packages are isolated and the functions traceable and verifiable. Software elements that share resources (such as common service packages or processors) will in general be in lower layers; execution of any such element must not cause failure of another element. For this reason, mutual exclusion and blocking must be particularly investigated (see Chapter 13).

DO-178A (see Appendix C) requires a document to be written about the software design, showing how each unit performs its intended functions (as defined in document 2). There should be one design description document (DO-178A document 3) for the software as a whole, describing the program structure and tracing its derivation from the requirements document. The design description document for a program in Ada should contain or define the following:

- list of library units, giving layers and dependencies;
- top-level data flow (in application packages);
- active tasks, identifying the units in which they are declared;
- references to package specifications for interface definitions;
- verifiable claims for critical units (as in 8.4);
- timing specifications;
- memory occupancy information;
- interrupt entries, and units in which they are declared.

The document should be written to supplement the Ada program text, referring to the program for most detailed information, and giving explicitly only the information that cannot be expressed in Ada.

9

Logical design

DETAILED LOGICAL DESIGN of software in Ada is expressed in the bodies of the library units that were specified in the structural design, together with all their subunits.

The majority of this work is not specially affected by safety considerations, so we do not cover it extensively in this book: others such as Booch (1983), Watt, Wichmann and Findlay (1987), and Somerville and Morrison (1987) deal with the general problems of software engineering in Ada. The issues that do need special consideration in safety-related systems fall into two categories: those that enable the checking to be done rigorously, and those that deal with the safety-critical control loops in the plant. In this chapter we concentrate on the former areas, including the structural aspects of the latter. Chapter 10 following deals with the specific issue of physical design for the safety-critical control loops, including some notes on design to improve availability.

This approach to logical design in Ada for safety-related systems starts from the risk category of each package, using the category to determine the features of Ada that are appropriate (Section 9.1), making a claim for the purpose of each package and significant state (Section 9.2). Dynamic checks on the assumptions underlying normal operation are incorporated as defensive programming (Section 9.3) with due regard to the issue of timing in software (Section 9.4). The general structure of subunits for double insulation of the handlers for safety-related devices is explained in Section 9.5.

9.1 Design rules concerning Ada features

In Chapters 7 and 8 we discussed the risk factors associated with the software units; each package should be marked (by a comment in the header of the specification) according to its risk factor. Appropriate design rules, which determine the allowable contents of the package (and the associated checking/verification regime) can then be determined.

The general principle we apply is to keep the most critical packages as simple as possible, so that they can be rigorously checked by formal analysis and intelligent inspection. We must also ensure that other packages cannot subvert these checks.

The Ada features that are intrinsically significant for this safety package categorisation are as follows:

- tasks (callable entries and interrupts);
- exceptions;
- access types;
- representation specifications;
- machine code;
- unsafe conversion;
- unsafe deallocation.

We also make recommendations concerning aliasing and the use of **go to** statements, to facilitate the checking (basically for stylistic reasons). In addition, for checking purposes, it is important that certain packages and internal subprograms have a *claim*: a definition of the intended properties of the unit (e.g. invariant, pre-condition, post-condition). We summarise the position on these in Table 9.1. The

Table 9.1 Critical package constituents

	Category 1	2	3
Claim	Must	Must	May
Machine code	**May**	**No**	**No**
Rep. Spec.	May	No	No
Interrupt entry	**May***	**No**	**No**
Normal entry	No	May	No
Unsafe	**No**	**May**	**No**
Task w'out accept	No	May	May
Exception	**May***	**May**	**May**
Access type	No	May	May
Alias	**No**	**May**	**May**
Go to	No	No	May

table entries indicate whether packages of the designated category must, may or must not contain the particular Ada features. The asterisks in column 1 mark important contentious entries: some authors reject the use of interrupts and exceptions in safety-related systems. We have developed the present approach based on the use of interrupt-based input–output and exceptions to frustrate and report attempts to perform a potentially dangerous action when it would be actually dangerous.

9.1.1 Principal package constituents

Note that any machine code or representation clause puts a package into category 1;
such packages must have a claim (see Section 8.4), and the package must be
independently, rigorously and (as far as possible) formally verified (see Section
12.3), to ensure that the claim is met. Such packages must not include any of the
other complicating features, both to facilitate the analysis and to avoid any further
risk arising from the code generator in the compiler (in the translation from the
linguistic semantics of the Ada program to the executable binary code).

Unsafe programming and tasks with callable entries (i.e. passive tasks) put a
package into category 2; such packages must also have a claim, and the package
must be independently checked statically to ensure that the claim is met. (Note that
the unsafe programming and task interactions can cause problems in the package
containing them, but not in any packages that they depend on.)

General packages, in category 3, should then contain no entries, representation
specifications, unsafe programming, machine code or unsafe deallocation.

We recommend that all packages in categories 1 and 2 contain a *claim* about their
intended semantics. Ada package specifications, subprogram specifications and task
specifications define the *syntax* of the respective constituents, but not their semantics
(and certainly not their performance). Various schemes have been advocated for
providing formal semantics for Ada programs (see Goldsack, 1985), mainly by
introducing special annotations. These use the Ada comment convention to 'hide'
the semantic information from an Ada compiler, while allowing it to be seen by an
analyst or analyser. Thus they significantly extend the language (possibly as well as
restricting the conventional Ada part) by introducing new rules concerning the
annotations.

ANNA (Luckham *et al.*, 1984) is a notation for annotating Ada programs based
on the predicate calculus. An annotated package contains Boolean expressions that
state the invariants for the data objects in the package and for the subprograms that
are visible in the package. It does not deal with tasks. Asphodel (Hill, 1988)
similarly annotates Ada text, but uses different typefaces in the printed form to
distinguish the semantics. Formal specifications in Asphodel include the assumptions
about properties of generic parameters and subprograms used, as well as pre-
conditions, post-conditions and invariants. SPARK (Carré and Jennings, 1988) has
mandatory annotations, which specify dependencies and input–output relationships;
they may also include proof rules.

The purpose of formalising the semantics is to permit automatic checking of the
consistency between the executable parts of the program and the claimed intentions.

Such formal semantic specification is desirable in any case, and particularly so for
the critical software. It allows the V&V contractor to make automatic checks on the
respective bodies that are eventually produced, as well as to assess the coverage of
the test sets produced to check the implementations.

The main practical requirement here for the designer is that the choice of
formalism should be made sufficiently early (and the decision conveyed to the V&V

contractor) in order that preparations for checking can begin. The corresponding considerations for checking the software are discussed in Chapter 12.

This strategy is related to, but different from, the approaches of other work on safety systems in Ada, in which a single subset of Ada is used throughout the program. The difference in the approaches is that here we concentrate on the safety of the *system*, not only the software, and accordingly recognise that the output operations are essential for effective operation. They cannot therefore be banned in the interest of safety.

9.1.2 Aliasing

It is possible in a number of situations for the same variable to be identified by more than one name. Obviously, if two variables are given the same explicit address by representation clauses, they will be aliases of one another. Several other cases can occur: for example, a variable given as an actual parameter to a subprogram may be referenced inside the subprogram by both the actual and the formal names (if the subprogram is declared within the scope of the actual name); an array element may be referenced by using different expressions for the index, which may have the same value; and several variables of the same access type may have the same value, in which case they would denote the same variable.

This situation is described as *aliasing*, and is important in analytic checking of software because in certain respects there can be unexpected (and undesirable) consequences.

A sequence of statements appears to show visibly which variables are changed when the statements are executed: those whose names occur on the left-hand sides of assignment statements, or in call statements as actual parameters of mode *out* or *in out*. For the purposes of checking, it is often important to know which variables are *not* changed when particular statements are executed: all variables out of scope, for example. Were it not for aliasing, the rule would be very simple: only those variables in the above positions are changed, others are not.

But because of the possibility of aliasing, a variable may be changed even though its name does not occur in any susceptible position. Disjunction of name does not imply disjunction of the referenced variable.

Consequently it is much more difficult to analyse software in which there is aliasing, and automatic analysers may not be able to cope with it. Rules for guidance have therefore been framed to avoid aliasing in order to simplify analysis. It is not that aliasing is intrinsically bad, but that it hinders checking.

Specific rules to avoid or cope with aliasing in Ada are as follows:

● Do not use **rename** declarations (which explicitly introduce alisases).
● If representation clauses are given for the addresses of variables, make the addresses all disjoint (taking account of the lengths of the variables, dependent on their types). This prevents physical addresses causing aliasing.
● Declare subprograms (in packages) *outside* the scopes of the packages in which

they are used, relying on the context clause to gain access to them. This
ensures that actual parameters are out of scope, thus avoiding formal/actual
aliasing.

● Use complete arrays and aggregates in preference to individual elements and
slices. When individual elements and slices cannot be avoided, use a uniform
style for the expressions in them. Check the relationship between the index
values, and write the program so that it does not presume that the values are
different.

● Whenever **access** values are used, aliasing may occur. Write the program so
that it takes account of the possibility that distinct access variables may refer to
the same referenced variable.

Note that aliasing is intrinsically possible with array elements and access types;
hence some authors recommend that such data structures be absolutely forbidden in
safety-related programing. The present recommendation is to forbid aliasing only in
category 1 packages.

9.2 Claims and state conditions

The properties of entities in the program used to represent significant concepts are
defined in package specifications, as appropriate declarations. Entity-relationship-
attribute (ERA) analysis of these properties establishes the essential characteristics of
each entity, and of the relationships between them. (We describe these as
'characteristics' since Ada uses the term 'attribute' to denote special characteristics
of linguistic entities.) The following intended (time-independent) relationships
concerning all the entities in the package should be stated:

● type of each characteristic;
● relationships between characteristics of the same concept;
● relationships between characteristics of distinct concepts;
● changes in relationship required for each operation.

In addition to these assertions about individual entities, there should be some
property that holds for the package as a whole, integrating the properties of the
individual constituents. (If there is no such overall property, why are the entities
together in the same package?) We call this the *claim* for the package. Each package
may be verified by demonstrating that the given program design satisfies the claim,
assuming that the constituents of the program all behave as specified (i.e. correct
lower-level design). This assumption is in turn verified by the checking of the lower-
level packages.

Safety packages of categories 1 and 2 should therefore have *claims* to define what
they are intended to be or do. Subprograms within them should also have claims to
define their pre-conditions and post-conditions (which may involve the state of the
plant as well as the state within the target computer). Smaller program constituents

should have claims in particular cases to identify their intentions. The corresponding design rules are explained below. Thus each exception should have a claim (defining the intended circumstances it refers to, in the opposite of which it is raised – namely the condition that it indicates has been found not to hold); and each statement label should have a claim (defining the condition that the system is presumed to be in at that label, no matter which statement led to it).

9.2.1 Content of claims

The claim for a package might be that it maintains an invariant for all values of a particular data type, or that it establishes correspondence between an internal state and an external state (in the plant).

The claim for a subprogram will define the actions it intends to carry out, which may be entirely internal or relating the internal and external states. Specifically, output subprograms will claim that they make the external state satisfy certain conditions (perhaps within a certain time).

The significant effect of an action in a program is to change the state of the system containing it in some way. For each possible initial state, the program claims to change it into a corresponding final state. The logical design of the program consists of defining a feasible trajectory in the state space to achieve the required effect. The executable statements in an Ada program define individual steps in such a trajectory, from an initial state (with certain properties) to a final state (with other properties). In normal programming, the statements are written to define the transitions without explicitly defining the conditions that the system is intended to pass through. In safety-related programming, as a means of ensuring that the intended transitions are actually achieved, the intended state conditions should be written additionally at certain positions, as claims. The subsequent verification of the program can then confirm that the given statements do cause the system to make the transition from the given initial state to the given final state.

It is not always necessary to define the state condition before and after every statement. In a sequence of statements, the condition at each semi-colon is both the condition after the preceding statement and the condition before the following statement; unless other reasons require it, the state condition can be omitted at all the internal states in a sequence, leaving only the claims at the start and finish of the sequence needing to be defined. These are typically the positions of the **begin** and **end** in a simple sequence, the **loop** of a repetition, or the **then** or **else** to **end if** in a conditional statement. Note that Ada has compound statements (in which one or more sequences of statements may be included), and that most statements are executed one after the other in the order written.

In this section, we list the situations at which a state condition should be written; we call them check-points and break-points in anticipation of the use that will be made of them during verification. In general, a check-point is where a particular sequence starts, and a break-point is where it finishes.

The notation used to express the state of the system at each of these has to be some combination of Ada (for the constituent variables and expressions involving them) and logic (for quantifiers and deductions). All the assertions should be expressed in terms of concepts established in the context of the subprogram: all Ada identifiers used within them should be in scope.

9.2.2 Check-points and break-points

Rigorous analysis requires the developed program to contain assertions at certain well-defined positions, and justifications to be given that the assertions hold at other well-defined positions. The assertions include the pre-conditions, post-conditions and invariants of the specification.

The check points, at which there should be assertions of the intended system state, are as follows:

(a)   at the beginning of each subprogram body or **accept** statement;
(b)   at the end of each subprogram body, package initialisation or **accept** statement;
(c)   at the beginning of each loop, before the **loop** statement starts;
(d)   at the end (after completion) of each **loop**;
(e)   at the end of each **if, case** or **select** statement;
(f)   at each declared **exception**;
(g)   at each «label».

The break-points are those at which the sequence of execution may break from the textual sequence of statements. By asserting the intended system state at each of these, we have the basis for static verification of the semantics of the program. The positions of the break-points, and the checks that must be made there, are explained below in Sections 12.4 and 13.3.

The dynamic sequel of each break-point will be at a check-point which may not be
the written sequel. The state determined by the program at the break-point will have to be shown to satisfy the assertion of the corresponding check-point.

9.2.3 Annotated Ada

We illustrate this style by showing Ada constructs annotated with state conditions, using the Ada comment convention with an 'equals' sign to mark a state condition.

```
begin                    —=    pre-condition
S1;                      —=    [derived condition]

                         —=    common condition before test
if                       —     [implied additional clauses]
end if;                  —=    common condition after test
```

```
                              —=   p1
if CONDITION then             —=   p1 and CONDITION
 .  .                         —
                              —=   p2a
else                          —=   p1 and not CONDITION
 .   .  .                     —
                              —=   p2b
end if;                       —=   p2a or p2b

                              —=   common condition before
case                          —    [implied additional clauses]
end case;                     —=   common condition after discrimination
loop                          —=   invariant for all iterations
end loop;
 ‹‹label››                    —=   state condition
                              —    (derived condition]
   goto LABEL;                —=
end;                          —=   post-condition
```

(Other authors use similar conventions with different characters to denote the annotations.)

9.2.4 State transitions

Within the sequences of statements, the elementary transitions are achieved by assignment statements and procedure calls. Each assignment statement puts the system into a state in which the assigned variable has a specific value and other variables are unchanged. Consider the assignment statement:

$$X := F(A);$$

If the state condition before executing this statement consists of a predicate p1 independent of X and p2 dependent on X, with the value of A being A0, then after execution of the statement, we have a state condition p1 (the same as before) and p3 dependent on X (not necessarily the same), where p3 is the predicate

$$X = F(A0)$$

Note that it is essential to distinguish between those parts of the state condition that do and do not depend on X. Section 9.1.2 above has explained the concept of aliasing, where different identifiers do not necessarily denote independent data items. The state condition must be written with the possibility of aliasing in mind – preferably by writing the program unit concerned in a style that avoids aliasing altogether, as explained in Section 9.1.2.

A procedure call has the effect of making a transition determined by the corresponding procedure declaration. The subprogram specification in Ada defines the 'signature' of the call (i.e. the number and types of the parameters), but it does not say anything about the semantics of the subprogram, which we have therefore to handle in a different way. Since the body of the subprogram achieves the effect by a sequence of statements, we can define the semantics of the subprogram body as the relationship between the state conditions at the start and finish: its pre-condition and post-condition. If the subprogram is called when the system state satisfies its pre-condition, then the effect of the call is to make the transition to the state determined by the post-condition. The parameters of the subprogram may be involved in its pre-condition and post-condition, depending on their modes (**in**, **out** or **in out**). The pre-condition may not involve **out** parameters; the post-condition may, however, involve **in** parameters.

Consider a call of a procedure without parameters:

```
PR1;
```

The claim for this procedure will define a pre-condition and a post-condition. Whenever it is called, the pre-condition should hold, or the behaviour is not determined. (An exception might be raised.) After successful execution of such a call statement, the post-condition will hold. If there are any parameters, the formal parameters may be involved in the claim for the procedure; the corresponding actual parameters must be substituted for them in the corresponding state conditions before and after the procedure call.

An alternative approach is to work backwards from the post-condition at the end of a sequence of statements, deriving the prior condition that must hold in order for the statements to achieve that condition. This is known as 'hoisting' the condition, since in normal layout of the text it raises the position of the predicate to a higher line.

Here again it is important that there is no confusion from aliasing: the subprogram body must guarantee that it makes no change to any variable in the caller's scope other than those mentioned in its claim. This is why certain Ada constructs are prohibited in safety-related packages.

The state conditions facilitate verification of sequentially executable parts of a program, by delimiting segments that can be checked independently. Each segment starts from one of the check-points (typically (a), (c) or (g)), and finishes at the next break-point, having executed the intervening statements in order. Simple statements (assignment and procedure/entry calls) are ready for verification in terms of their declarations and claims. Delay statements and abort statements do not affect the system state of the task containing them, and so are not relevant to this analysis. Accept and select statements similarly do not affect the system state of the task containing them, but relate the state of one task with that of another.

9.3 Defensive programming

An algorithm, when first written, implicitly assumes certain properties about its input parameters and the other variables it depends on. Defensive programming is a style in which such assumptions are made explicit, and innocuous actions taken when the assumptions turn out to be wrong.

Thus if PRE is the predicate that is assumed to hold on entry to a subprogram (for it to work properly), and POST is the predicate that is claimed to hold when the algorithm completes (if it does), we can make the program defensive by building into the algorithm a check that PRE actually does hold, with an alternative action (avoiding danger) if it does not. The pre-condition of the defended algorithm is then TRUE, and its post-condition is

POST or DANGER_AVOIDED

(where DANGER_AVOIDED is the predicate that holds on completion if **not** PRE holds on entry). Exceptions in Ada are based on this idea.

Issues to be considered in designing programs defensively are what level of detail to defend and what kinds of alternative action to take. Although the issues are logically distinct, the pragmatic solution is to work backwards from the second to the first. The fact that a pre-condition does not hold may be detected within the body of the algorithm: although we state the assumption at the beginning, it is feasible to check it there only in simple cases. (Thus in matrix inversion, the assumption is that the matrix is non-singular. Discovering whether the assumption holds comes naturally in the middle of the algorithm, when the value of the discriminant has been calculated.)

Useful alternative actions, to be taken when the normal assumption does not hold, might be to close down the plant, send an alarm signal to the operator, open escape valves, start up stand-by equipment, or activate isolation procedures. The procedures to control these could be written as exception handlers, at a position in the program such that when the exception-handling actions have been completed (including all logging and abnormality reporting), normal activities are resumed.

Where there is no useful alternative action, the current action cannot be completed and the pre-condition of the enclosing algorithm is now known to be false. This is the Ada rule for propagating exceptions.

The specification of the formal parameters of a subprogram implies some pre-conditions (for example when an input parameter is specified as a subtype) but there may be further assumptions, such as relationships between one input parameter and another. The type matching rules of Ada will ensure that actual parameter values are of the right type, but a CONSTRAINT_ERROR will be raised if any does not conform to its specified subtype. Relationships between parameters and/or external variables need explicit checking, raising an exception if the check fails.

The above discussion is presented using the concepts of Ada exceptions; however, there are arguments for not using exceptions in safety-critical software (see Section 8.3), based on distrust of the generated code. To avoid exceptions, the equivalent testing has to be done explicitly using **if** statements. To avoid CON-STRAINT_ERROR exceptions being raised, there must be no subtypes in the package, and each constrained input parameter must have an individual check to ensure that it satisfies the pre-condition. (The difficulty with the exception-free style of defensive programming is that the alternative actions must be closely built in with the checks.)

If exceptions *are* used, it is important to make sure that testing (Chapter 14) covers them, including all the handlers and checks on assumptions.

Defensive programming is always relative. Each alternative action has its own assumed pre-conditions, and no matter how hard we try, there are always assumptions we make tacitly. The greatest danger is in the assumptions about the real-world environment which are true during the development period and initial operational use of the system, but which for completely unconnected reasons become false later. The difference between an automaton and a responsible person is the reaction to such a situation: awareness of it, and ability to cope with it. It is unreasonable to expect an automaton to cope with an unplanned situation of which it has no means of becoming aware. By deploying an automaton in a safety-critical role, we are taking the responsibility for the continuing validity of its assumptions.

9.4 Timing

No software can by itself satisfy timing constraints, since its performance depends ultimately on the speed of the computer executing it. The important distinction that can be made is between those actions that take place (if successful) in a bounded time, and those for which the time can not be bounded. This is another pervasive property of software: the boundedness of its execution time. If an action contains an unbounded construct, then any other action that calls it must also be considered to be unbounded.

There are five basic constructs in Ada that can lead to unbounded timing:

(a)   a **select** without a **delay** or **else** clause;
(b)   an **accept** outside a **select** statement;
(c)   an **entry call** outside a **select** statement;
(d)   a **loop** without a **for** clause;
(e)   a **go to** statement.

Notice that the first two can only occur in passive tasks; they show how the timing of such tasks depends on the tasks that call them. They do not occur in active tasks (i.e. tasks without entries), and will consequently be restricted to category 2 packages.

An entry call may in principle take an unbounded time, since the passive task with which the rendezvous is sought may never become ready. For this reason, when timing is significant, each entry call should be enclosed within a **select** statement, accompanied by a **delay** or **else** part to define the alternative action if the called task cannot make the rendezvous.

A loop without a **for** clause cannot be guaranteed to terminate, so should be analysed to ensure that it does (by a **while** clause or **exit** in a normal loop or a **terminate** in a task). A loop invariant, describing the intended state of the system at each iteration of the loop, should be provided to assist in such checking. The analysis will have to show that as well as maintaining the invariant, repetitions of the loop will eventually satisfy the exit condition. This may be by establishing a bound on some variable that tightens with the loop iterations, towards the completion condition.

A **go to** statement, even when severely constrained by the rules of Ada, can imply timing problems. We can distinguish between forward and backward jumps, depending on the textual position of the destination label in relation to the **go to** statement. The timing problem only arises with backward jumps, which make implied loops. A state condition, describing the intended state of the system at the destination label, should be provided to assist in such checking. The analysis will have to derive the state from the label through all intermediate statements on the path that leads to the **go to**, and derive the conditions for that path to be executed. The analysis must show the following two properties of the program:

(a)   **if** the path is executed, then the state condition is satisfied when execution reaches the **go to** statement; and

(b)   the condition for the path to be executed will eventually not hold, so that the implied loop terminates.

Any program unit (normally a subprogram or task) that contains such a construct or calls such a unit must be analysed if its timing is critical. To assist in this analysis, each unit should be marked if it contains an unbounded construct, so that units calling it can be identified and checked.

In addition to the analysis of the program units containing unbounded constructs, the actual timing of the bounded constructs in certain units may be important. As a general rule, it is desirable to have targets for the performance of each subprogram, which will depend on the performance of all the subprograms and elementary statements it contains, with multipliers for loops. In a typical program structure with layered packages, it must be expected that the time-scales of the packages increase significantly with the height of the layer: higher-layer packages, whose bodies make use of lower-layer packages, inevitably must take longer to execute.

The specific timing for individual actions may vary depending on data values and scheduling, and must be checked by execution in the target environment. This is discussed further in Chapters 13 and 14.

9.5 Context and specifications

For a system involving input–output with mechanical or potentially dangerous devices, the package structure should correspond to the control loops involving sensors and effectors between the target computer and the plant. The design practice recommended here is to devise a package to handle the device, with visible facilities to manipulate the device in safe ways, and internal checks in the package body to protect the device and its surroundings, with the raw (unprotected) input–output hidden.

The principal considerations that the designers must bear in mind while making this software are the effects of timing, unreliability and operational problems relating to safety. There may be limits of movement for a computer controlled device, and it may have physical inertia which affects its ability to respond to control signals from the computer. Timing refers to the latency periods between the environment or plant being in a particular state, the sensors detecting it, the software taking note of the state (in interlocks), a driver sending a control signal to an effector and the effector causing the state of the plant to change. Usually the last of these is the most time-consuming, but the earlier ones must not be forgotten in the detailed design of interlocks.

Unreliability must also be considered at all stages – the possibility of malfunction by a sensor or effector, communication loss between peripherals and computers, loss or malfunction of processing in a controlling computer, or (ultimately) a residual error in the software.

Operational problems arise when human–computer interaction is involved in the safety system, as human behaviour includes further failure modes arising from misunderstanding, perversity and malice.

In order to show the detailed design of a safety-critical control loop, we present first a simple situation: that of a device which has only two modes of operation, for normal operation and maintenance. The context for safe use of such a device is:

```
package SAFE_CONTEXT is        — for use in one task only

    type MODE is (NORMAL, MAINTENANCE);
    procedure SET_MODE(M: MODE);
    function MODE_IS return MODE;   — the most recent SET_MODE

    DANGER_AVERTED: exception;   — requested operation not safe

end SAFE_CONTEXT;
```

We presume that the device can carry out a single operation, which is visible for use in the rest of the program. This is specified as:

```
package SAFE_DEVICE is

    procedure OPERATE;   — carries out operation if safe

end SAFE_DEVICE;
```

9.5.1 Package body

The essential structure of the package body is:

```
package body SAFE_DEVICE is

    package RAW_DEVICE is

        procedure OPERATE;

    end RAW_DEVICE;
```

```
package body RAW_DEVICE is separate;

function SAFE_TO_OPERATE return BOOLEAN
    is separate;

procedure OPERATE is separate;
```
    end SAFE_DEVICE;

Notice the double insulation in the above structure. The outer package, SAFE_DEVICE, makes the procedure SAFE_DEVICE.OPERATE visible to the rest of the program; but inside its body, not visible externally, is the inner package RAW_DEVICE (which contains the unprotected and externally invisible procedure RAW_DEVICE.OPERATE) and the interlock predicate SAFE_TO_OPERATE.

The expansion of the various subunits follows. Central to this structure is the Boolean function SAFE_TO_OPERATE, which determines whether the operation should be carried out when it is requested. To show the structure of this function, we give a rudimentary form in Section 10.6 below, assuming that there are no parameters for the operation. We presume that the operation is deemed to be safe if the sensor detects that there is no susceptible subject (victim) currently liable to harm by the requested action, or the system is being maintained, and independent guards are used to ensure safety.

The procedure OPERATE is also given in a rudimentary form, with no parameters. In practice, there would be several possible operations on the device, some with parameters.

The analysis presented here should be carried out for each operation that is potentially dangerous. (We do not expand CONFIRM_AUTHORISATION here, as it would be specific to the particular case, and does not introduce any matters of principle.)

9.5.2 Context body

The body of the context package contains the facilities that are not directly dangerous, but are essential to ensure the safety of the potentially dangerous facilities of the raw device.

```
package body SAFE_CONTEXT is

    procedure CONFIRM_AUTHORISATION;

    CURRENT_MODE : MODE := NORMAL;

    procedure SET_MODE(M: MODE) is
    begin
        if M = MAINTENANCE then
            CONFIRM_AUTHORISATION;
        end if;
        CURRENT_MODE := M;
    end SET_MODE;

    function MODE_IS return MODE is
    begin
        return CURRENT_MODE;
```

```
    end MODE_IS;

    procedure CONFIRM_AUTHORISATION is separate;

  end SAFE_CONTEXT;
```

The text inside this package and all its subunits must be completely and rigorously checked. The structure of this design limits to the minimum those parts of the program needing special attention to verify their correctness (and to justify the trust that is placed in them), as explained in Part III. By treating input/output devices in this way, their logical and representational aspects are clearly distinguished. This opens the way (after physical design) for analyses to be carried out to show that the sequences of statements correctly provide the required control and data to the effectors, taking account of all the circumstances.

10

Physical design

THE PHYSICAL DESIGN of safety-related software (eventually formulated in executable Ada statements with explicit data constructs) comprises the drivers for the controlled devices in the plant (both the hazardous effectors and the guards), the sensors, and the interlocks between them. Of these, the input–output drivers are normally logically simple (depending on their physical characteristics) and the interlocks as complex as the safety logic requires. In addition, when system availability is relevant, the physical design must include alternative executable components to take account of run-time failures.

The most important semantic aspect of design for safety is the relationship between the state of the system and the safety or danger of each controlled device. The need to know that it is safe to operate a device is fundamental to safe operation, and the way in which this information is obtained must be absolutely foolproof. There are various different circumstances to consider: the safety may be instantaneously determinable from the inputs at specific sensors, or it may be some combination (instantaneously determinable) of sensor data and internally stored values. In more complicated cases, safety may depend on some timing relationship between the sensor data, or even between data obtained from distinct sensors in different computers communicating over data-links. The most difficult case is when safety depends on the coordination of actions in distinct computers communicating over data-links.

The state of the plant is determined by sensory signals that are sampled at discrete intervals; the sampling interval must be sufficiently short for the circumstances. The detailed design of the software involves planning the algorithms for the interlocks and the device control. The main information about the semantics of the safety conditions has to be obtained from analysis of the plant controlled by the sensor. This is closely tied to those features identified in the requirements and explained in Chapter 6.

When a desired change involves input–output (as do the raw input and output operations on which safety depends), we have to define the information to be transferred into or out of the computer, and define the partner for the communication. It is good design practice here to separate the physical input–output (for transmission to and from the partner) from the change of representation that is involved (e.g. binary numbers for internal use to sequences of decimal digits externally). The two subproblems, then, are to carry out the internal change of representation and to transmit a value across an interface between the target computer and the plant with its environment. The program to change the representation has to be validated by proving that the two representations concerned preserve the value of the data involved. The program to perform the transmission has to be validated by proving that it communicates with the right partner.

The general sequence of operations to assure safety is as follows:

- apply guard (wait for guard to become effective);
- check interlock;
- perform action (wait for plant to become safe);
- check interlock;
- remove guard.

The sequence may be simplified in particular cases, for example when a guard is not necessary. On the other hand, it may be more difficult than it appears if the computer controlling the guard differs from that handling the interlocked operation, or if the plant does not have a safe state. Each of the steps in the sequence may fail, and if this could lead to danger, positive confirmation must be obtained, with substitute steps to be carried out if necessary.

These issues are discussed in the following sections illustrating the problems in systems of differing characteristics: simple electrical systems (where effects are virtually immediate, so latency can be ignored), inertial systems (including those with electrical reluctance, as well as mechanical systems, where timing delays in effects can be significant), communication systems (including distributed control, where failure as well as delay must be considered), and man–machine systems (which must get the right balance of responsibility between those involved).

This chapter covers details of input–output handling (Section 10.1) with particular attention to hardware/software interfaces (Section 10.2). Information about the interfaces must be fully documented for the DO-178A software design document. The detailed design of unprotected output devices (Section 10.3) is followed by corresponding treatment of sensors (Section 10.4) used in the interlocking logic (Section 10.5). We present a general discussion on interlock function bodies (Section 10.6) followed by particular details specific to important categories of device (Section 10.7). Finally, Section 10.8 illustrates the use of Ada in some techniques for improving the availability of the system.

10.1 Input–output handling

Input–output handling is ultimately responsible for the actions of the plant that might be dangerous, so all the attention and analyses that have been given to the system design so far now come to fruition. The work has to be done for each kind of critical output device (both effectors and guards), and each kind of sensor used in interlocks.

The handlers may be in category 1 packages, when they need to use representation specifications and/or machine code to access the devices; according to the other rules given in Section 9.1, they should then not contain any of the following constructs:

- normal task entries;
- passive tasks (i.e. those without accept statements);
- unsafe programming;
- access types;
- aliasing;
- **go to** statements.

However, the device specifics may be contained in a deeper package, in which case the higher-level handler can use category 3 facilities.

10.1.1 Critical outputs

The outputs from T to U have been identified (see Section 5.1: 'Identifying the potential dangers'), and categorised as safe or potentially dangerous. The specification of the device-handling package (such as RAW_DEVICE in Section 9.5) will have identified the actions that U can be made to do, and any parameters needed. The detailed design consists of sketching the bodies of the corresponding subprograms, as illustrated in Section 10.3 on 'Unprotected output', paying particular attention to local types needed for device addressing and device control. The algorithms will normally be very simple, needing a suitable (constant) bit-pattern to be applied to the control register.

10.1.2 Sensor inputs

The inputs from U to T that are involved in safety interlocks have been identified (in Section 5.3, 'Criteria for safe operation'), and package specifications introduced (in Chapter 8, 'Structural design'). We must now make package bodies to control the sensors and deliver status values. This may well involve new types, and possibly output controls to put sensors into appropriate states for reading the conditions of U and V. The package will export (make visible) the function that reads the sensor.

10.2 Interface details

The final information that must be formalised for the critical modules concerns the details of the input–output devices, describing their status, control and data transfer register addresses. These are expressed in Ada as representation specifications for the interfaces to the relevant hardware devices.

10.2.1 Device addresses

Each device has some unique identification by which the computer communicates with it: as an address in some special range in systems with memory-mapped architecture, or as a special kind of address in other architectures. This could need a type definition or use of package SYSTEM. Replicated devices will probably have systematically allocated device addresses.

10.2.2 Device control and status

Each device has a bit-pattern used to control its actions, and each input device has a specific layout of bits delivered when it is read (with their meanings in terms of the external information sensed). These all need to be specified, with the particular values for the parameters or control options given as enumeration representation clauses and/or record representation clauses.

The way to specify this in Ada is to define a type for each kind of control/status register, as a record with the constituent fields identified and a representation clause to define the layout of the fields in the machine word. Then define a particular variable of the appropriate type for each interface register of each device connected, giving the memory-mapped address of the register as its address clause. Similarly, define any data buffer register for the device. Define constants of the control/status type for each of the actions that the device can carry out.

The documentation of this information is required in DO-178A document 3 (Design Description Document) under the heading of 'Descriptions of data and control interfaces between software partitions and between software and hardware'. The document should refer both to the Ada text and the hardware specification document from which the representation clause is derived.

10.3 Unprotected output

Each output device should be controlled by a distinct package, written as a subunit of an interlock-protected package. To illustrate the structure, we presume that the input–output devices are memory mapped, as on an M68000, with the device control register at address 777464 octal, and the operation taking place when the integer value 1 is written to that register:

```
package PHYSICAL_DEVICE is — category 1
    type DEVICE_CONTROL is — e.g.
        new INTEGER range 0 . . 1 ;
    GO : constant DEVICE_CONTROL := — e.g.
        1;
end PHYSICAL_DEVICE;
```

```
with PHYSICAL_DEVICE;
separate (SAFE_DEVICE)
package body RAW_DEVICE is

    THIS_DEVICE: PHYSICAL_DEVICE.DEVICE_CONTROL;
    for THIS_DEVICE use at — e.g.
        8#777464#;

    procedure OPERATE is
    begin
        THIS_DEVICE := PHYSICAL_DEVICE.GO;
    end OPERATE;

end RAW_DEVICE;
```

The physical device package specifies the format and contents of the device control register. The body given here for a raw device specifies the I/O address of the control register to which some value is written to make the device carry out its operation.

10.4 Sensors

A similar but simpler structure is needed for each significant input device, which could be a source of discriminatory information for interlocks:

```
package SENSOR is

    function VICTIM_PRESENT return BOOLEAN;

end SENSOR;
```

It is desirable (as mentioned in Section 5.3) that each significant sensor be used in a specific interlock; in which case the sensor package should be embedded as a subunit (for further protection) inside the interlock unit, SAFE_TO_OPERATE.

Because malfunction of a sensor is a significant possibility to be considered, it is unwise to rely on the reading of a single device. One easy technique is to use a complementary pair of microswitches to detect a binary state in the plant: one normally open, and the other normally closed. Thus the reading is made both positively and negatively, and the 'stuck-at' failure modes of the microswitches are detectable.

If the two sensors give the same reading, there is an indication of a sensor failure. (The indication is not absolute, however, because of the timing slew between them: when the plant state changes, the two microswitches will not change exactly simultaneously, but one will lag slightly behind the other. Consequently a delay must be allowed after a match, before the sensor failure is confirmed.)

For example, the control system for an airlock needs to know when each door is open or closed. Two microswitches are installed at each extremity of each door; they indicate positively and negatively whether the door is at the extremity. We show the program for the sensors at one extremity of a single door; in practice this structure would be repeated many times, in distinct tasks.

```
package CHECKED_SENSOR is  — category 1

    type AT_EXTREMITY is new BOOLEAN;

    function DETECT return AT_EXTREMITY;
        — claim: the returned value is the door state
        —           at call time or up to 0.1 sec later.

    SENSOR_FAILURE: exception;
        — claim: raised if the sensors are inconsistent

end CHECKED_SENSOR;

package body CHECKED_SENSOR is
        — for use only in the task for the specific sensor

    type MICROSWITCH is new BOOLEAN;

    POSITIVE, NEGATIVE : MICROSWITCH;
    for POSITIVE use at 16#FFE0#;
    — TRUE when detected AT_EXTREMITY = TRUE
    for NEGATIVE use at 16#FFE1#;
    — TRUE when detected AT_EXTREMITY = FALSE

    function DETECT return AT_EXTREMITY is
    begin
        if POSITIVE = NEGATIVE then
            delay 0.1;
            if POSITIVE = NEGATIVE then
                raise SENSOR_FAILURE:
            end if;
        end if;
        return AT_EXTREMITY (BOOLEAN (POSITIVE) );
    end DETECT;

end CHECKED_SENSOR;
```

Note that this package body (like all device handling package bodies) is written for use in a single task, according to the recommendation of Section 8.4. It presumes that there is nothing else for the sensor task to do if the microswitches are in the skew condition, so that nothing is lost by having the explicit delay inside the DETECT function body. The delay of 0.1 seconds is presumed to be sufficient to cover the time difference between the two microswitch transitions.

10.5 Interlocking

We describe two ways in which interlocks may be organised, which we call 'passive' and 'active' interlocking, depending on the status of the interlock in the tasking structure of the program. The difference between the two methods arises when a request to operate is made when it is not safe to carry out the request. The first style allows the requesting task to continue, using the exception mechanism to report that

the requested action could not be carried out at the time; the second style holds up
the requesting task until it is safe to carry out the requested operation.

10.5.1 Passive interlocking

With the first style, we have a structure as follows (for each critical output
operation):

```
with SAFE_CONTEXT;
separate (SAFE_DEVICE)
procedure OPERATE is

begin
    if SAFE_TO_OPERATE then
        RAW_DEVICE.OPERATE;
    else
        raise SAFE_CONTEXT.DANGER_AVERTED;
    end if;
end OPERATE;
```

The above structure presumes that only one task may initiate actions by each device.
If there is the possibility that several tasks may asynchronously request an action by
the same device, there should be some higher-level sequencing, or the following
method of active interlocking should be used.

10.5.2 Active interlocking

In this (more complicated) style, the outer structure of SAFE_DEVICE is the same,
but there is another task defined in the package body that is stimulated by the active
interlock.

```
task CONTROL is
    entry OPERATE:
    entry STIMULUS;
        -- claim: STIMULUS is called whenever
        --         there is a change to plant status that
                   could affect SAFE_TO_OPERATE
end CONTROL;

procedure OPERATE renames CONTROL.OPERATE;

task body CONTROL is
begin
    loop
      select
          accept OPERATE do
              while not SAFE_TO_OPERATE loop
                  accept STIMULUS;
              end loop;
              RAW_DEVICE.OPERATE;
```

```
          end OPERATE;
      or
          accept STIMULUS;
      end select;
    end loop;
 end CONTROL;
```

The technique presumes that any operation requested will eventually be safe, and the calling task should be made to wait until that is so. The STIMULUS entry triggers a re-evaluation of the test for the requested action being safe to carry out, which may arise from polling or an interrupt. This implies sampling the state of the plant at discrete intervals; the sampling interval must be sufficiently short for the circumstances: the latencies and response times of the devices concerned.

Note that a guard on an accept statement will *not* give the necessary protection. This is because the guard is evaluated significantly before the rendezvous takes place, and the state may change while the accepting task is awaiting an entry call to the open accept statement. Even though the system is safe when the guard is evaluated, it may become dangerous before the rendezvous.

10.6 Interlock function bodies

Central to the structure is the Boolean function SAFE_TO_OPERATE, which determines whether the operation should be carried out when it is requested. The interlocks that ensure safe operation have been identified (in Section 5.2, 'Classification of danger'), and corresponding predicate specifications defined in package SAFE_DEVICE (in Section 9.5, 'Context and specifications'), as illustrated by the subunit SAFE_TO_OPERATE. We now write the function body for each of these, formulating the interlock criterion, and making use of the sensor inputs identified above.

To show the structure of this function, we presume that the operation is deemed to be safe if the sensor detects that there is no susceptible subject (a 'victim') currently liable to harm by the requested action, or the system is being maintained, and independent guards are used to ensure safety.

The inputs from U to T that are involved in safety-interlocks have been identified (in Section 5.3, 'Criteria for safe operation'), and package specifications introduced (in Section 10.4, 'Sensors'). We must now make package bodies to control the sensors and deliver status values. This may well involve new types, and possibly output controls to put sensors into appropriate states for reading the conditions of U and V. The package will make visible the sensor reading function for use in the interlocks.

Thus a typical structure for a simple interlock function body will be

```
with SAFE_CONTEXT, SENSOR;
separate (SAFE_DEVICE)
```

```
function SAFE_TO_OPERATE return BOOLEAN is
begin
    return— e.g.
        (SAFE_CONTEXT.MODE_IS = MAINTENANCE)
        or else
        not SENSOR.VICTIM_PRESENT;
end SAFE_TO_OPERATE;
```

More complicated interlocks are needed to deal with timing and mutual interlocking in systems with inertia or distribution of control, and with particular situations such as power supply sensing and emergency shut-down. These are described in the following section.

10.7 Device specifics

Particular consideration must be given to the control loops in the plant, taking account of specific characteristics of the devices concerned. Several topics are common to many systems and deserve general discussion: the problems of identification of replicated devices, inertia in the controlled plant, and protocol handling in distributed control systems. In addition, there are likely to be special considerations at power supply on/off events, and for emergency shut-down.

10.7.1 Device identification

Most control systems include multiple copies of each kind of sensor and effector. We have already referred to replicated sensors in Section 10.4, and note that multiple effectors would be used to control (for example) the doors in an air-lock or the valves in a chemical plant. The safety of such a plant depends on the proper identification of these devices: associating the starboard heat-sensor with the fire extinguisher for that engine. Particular attention must be given to the installation and maintenance procedures, to avoid misconnection (which could not be detected by software). If each device is wired separately to the control computers, some positive means of identification must be designed in, to permit checking of the complete feedback loop. If the devices are connected to a ring, each device will have an electronic identification in its connector, which makes it inherently less liable to misidentification.

10.7.2 Inertia checks

Most physical devices have inertia, which means that they do not respond immediately to control signals. There might be mechanical inertia, as with heavy moving machinery (which does not stop immediately a brake is applied), or thermal inertia (where the temperature does not come down as soon as a cooling fan is started), or electrical inertia (where high voltage or charge takes a significant time to decay). The common property of such a constituent (for the plant) is that potentially dangerous situations persist after the controlling computer has sought to make it safe. The danger continues in spite of the safety control.

The control system might be able to sense when the hazardous device has become safe, or it might rely on dead reckoning to give sufficient time for the danger to pass. During such a period, a guard must prevent access by any possible victim to the dangerous area until the situation is really safe, as indicated by sensors or timeout.

In any case, the possibility of malfunction must be considered: a sensor may be faulty, or the dynamics of the inertia may be influenced by other activities.

Fail-safe checks for sensors can be carried out by correlation between diverse devices and with the controller for the plant. A sensor check in conjunction with a timer gives a check on any pre-calculated decay time for the inertia. The guard for a device with inertia should therefore be sensitive to the time at which the signal is sent to make it safe, the expected elapsed time before it is effective, and the sensor that confirms when a safe state is reached.

10.7.3 Protocol checks

Whenever the control loop involves communication between one computer and another, there is a need for messages to be passed between them, and a protocol to define the proper message structures, sequences and interpretations. Part of the protocol must cover the possibility of the messages being distorted or lost during transmission. Protocol checks must be included in such a system to ensure that messages are reliably communicated when the medium is intrinsically unreliable.

The technique for detecting distorted messages is by incorporation of redundancy in each message: typically a checksum calculated from the whole contents of the message, using an algorithm that is sensitive to the kinds of distortion that might occur. If an error occurs during transmission of the message, the checksum recalculated at the receiving end is different from that transmitted, and a recovery procedure can be instigated.

The technique for dealing with lost messages (which also detects duplicated messages) is to include a sequence number (cyclically, using a fixed field in every message) that is checked by the recipient.

Recovery of a distorted or missing message is usually achieved by retransmission. There are basically two approaches: positive and negative acknowledgement. In the positive acknowledgement approach, each message (or sequence of messages) is acknowledged by its recipient when it has arrived safely, and the transmitter repeats any message that has been sent but not acknowledged. The negative acknowledgement approach is for the recipient to notify the transmitter of any messages it has not received properly, presuming that it knows they should have been sent. Both techniques rely on the possibility of communication in both directions, with a 'reverse channel' from the message receiver to the transmitter. Thus unreliability of transmission is replaced by extending the time taken to transfer the message reliably.

Above the level of the transport protocol, an important interlocking technique is the use of handshakes to reach agreement on the state of the system at the ends of a communication link: guarded/unguarded; safe/dangerous; going safe/going dangerous. This is essential when the sensor is remote from the corresponding effector.

For a distributed interlock, there must be a scheme to protect the controlled device in case the interlock becomes inoperative (for example if the communication medium fails). The danger to the interlock from distribution is the same as if the sensor detecting the safety state for the effector is inactive.

A scheme for mutually locking the guard and interlock in a distributed system can be developed using a handshake between them. Assume that the potentially dangerous effector is controlled by one computer (which includes the interlock function SAFE_TO_OPERATE and certain sensors), while the guard to protect against danger from that effector is controlled by a different computer. The computer handling the guard will have a state indicating whether the guard is applied.

Mutual locking means that the dangerous device and the guard are controlled in a way that each takes account of the state of the other, indicated by messages sent between the two computers. To achieve the handshake, the computers concerned must exchange messages about their respective states (which implies a time delay). The combined state of the system can be illustrated in Table 10.1.

Table 10.1 Mutual locking

		Guard applied	
		Yes	No
Device locked out	Yes	OK	OK
	No	OK	Danger

Bearing in mind the transfer time delay for messages, each end does not know the instantaneous state of the other, so the transitions in this state space must take place in two steps, through the *safe* intermediate state in which both the guard and the interlock prevent the device from acting (rather than the *dangerous* intermediate state in which neither holds).

The criteria to apply are:

- *Guard opens only when device is locked out;*
- *Interlock permits device to act only when guard is locked in.*

Thus both guard and dangerous effector need interlocks, and both interlocks depend on the state of the other. To prevent deadlock, the external initiative must be able to request actions only of the dangerous device, not explicitly of the guard. When the action is requested, the controller must first put up the guard, and then (after it is in position) operate the device; when the device action has completed, it must lower the guard.

10.7.4 Power supply

At changes to the power supply to the computer (switch-on, restoration following a failure, supply interruption and resumption) and on switching between manual and automatic control modes, the same interlocking principles should be applied to ensure that internal data are coherent and that any necessary resetting of the system is carried out. The HSE Guide points out the importance of this, requiring that the program can only be entered at a point where it is safe to do so. (There is no way of infringing this rule with the discipline imposed by Ada and the present program structure.)

10.7.5 Emergency shut-down

Emergency shut-down systems need to be tested; this involves simulating fault conditions to check that the system responds correctly to them, but without activating a real shut-down. Thus the safety functions must be 'muted' during the on-line tests of the emergency system. The maximum time allowable in the muted condition for a specific safety function must be determined as part of the design. The interlock must include a check to detect periods longer than this during operation, and to take appropriate action (including possibly a real shut-down) if the period is exceeded.

10.8 Resilience

Availability of the control system may be necessary for it to ensure the safety of the plant. Even with correct software, there remains the certainty of random failures occurring in the supporting hardware (processors, memory, communication links and particularly the input–output peripherals). The possibility of faulty sensors has been mentioned in Section 10.4, and failures in communication in Section 10.7.2. Here we (briefly) refer to the role of Ada in handling faults in the main computer hardware.

The topic of defensive programming has been discussed in Section 9.3, from the logical point of view: ensuring that every assumption about the run-time situation is explicit and checked before any potentially dangerous action is taken that depends on it. Achieving resilient performance applies the same principles to the whole control system (of target computer and its transducers). The philosophical approach of Ada with regard to potential failure is again illuminating.

Any action might fail. The designer must have acknowledged this in the structural design of the control system, and must provide sufficient redundancy in the equipment so that the total failure rate is acceptably low. The HSE Guide in its Table 5 (HSE Guide, Vol 2, page 44) gives figures for the failure rates and failure mode ratios to be expected in various kinds of electronic device, including the following:

> Proportion of failures detected by
>   external watchdog (alone):   90%
>   extensive self-checking programs *and* external watchdog: 98%

When a number of redundant channels are used, the resulting failure rate is related to that of a single channel by what is called the β-factor, with typical values of 10 per cent for identical systems and 1 per cent for diverse systems (within a factor of 3 up or down). Guidance on performing the calculations for PES hardware reliability are given in the HSE Guide (paragraphs 173–223) and its Appendix 3.

What this really means is that there must be built-in test software (BITS) to detect the hardware failures, and arrange for appropriate substitutes from the redundant equipment to be brought into operation when a failure has been detected. The software may also be used to diagnose a reported failure, to assist the maintenance engineer in repairing it, and to check it out before it is reaccepted into operational service.

Thus software has to be treated as an 'added value' to the hardware, rather than a distinct entity. Each failure mode in the hardware must be covered by software detection and recovery, which must be included in the subsystems identified in Section 8.1. Each subsystem (including the recovery process) itself has a possibility of failure. Thus, in a well-designed system, the probabilities of failure reduce as the size of the subsystem increases, up to the whole control system.

The software used for fault detection and recovery is itself dependent on the availability of the underlying hardware, so must be monitored by a simple autonomous device: a watch-dog. If the watch-dog detects that a computer is not working, the reporting and recovery must be done by other active units of the control system (which could be the same software being executed on a different computer).

Sometimes the recovery consists of trying the operation again (when the failure is 'soft' or transient); sometimes it consists of using different hardware from a set of units that can substitute for one another. The detection and recovery should be linked to monitoring to record the occurrence of failures and permit diagnosis.

It is worth noting that the number of 'spares' of hardware units must be finite, so that when an alternative is brought into use, the system inevitably becomes less resilient until the faulty unit has been repaired and replaced. However, software can be considered to have an infinite number of 'spares', as new copies can be loaded into main store from backing store without limit. (Of course, every one of them will contain the same design errors, as will the replicated hardware units.)

A failure mode analysis of the system will therefore consist of a hierarchical set of recovery actions, each covering a set of failures in simpler (and more frequent) actions. The probabilities of failure of the elementary hardware actions have to be combined to estimate the probabilities of failure of each higher action, up to complete system failure. This then must satisfy the requirements for reliability explained in Section 5.4.

PART III   CONFIRMATION

11

Checking principles

PART III of this book is written separately because the activities involved are of a different *kind* from those of Parts I and II, not because they come later in the development process. Checking is an integral part of software development, and takes place throughout the process, not as a separate activity afterwards, to confirm that the design is adequate for its purpose. Checking activities (verification, validation and testing) must occur concurrently with software creation. The developer performs checks (including automatic checks from compile-time onwards and tests on all pieces of software from individual modules through all stages of integration), and an independent organisation may validate the results by further checking. System validation provides confirmation that the total system complies with its requirements.

Confirmation does not change any of the information about the software concerned, but generates new information about it (which is logically derived from the original). If the process of confirmation shows up any defects, then the construction described in Part II must be reworked in the light of the new understanding arising from the detection of the defect, and the amended software reconfirmed. Confirmation is solely concerned with generating auxiliary information *about* the software that has been constructed, in the context of the target computer and plant; it is this information which is central to the confidence that will justify its operational use in a safety-related situation.

Part III comprises this and the following four chapters, which deal with different kinds of confirmation that have to be considered. In this chapter, we first discuss the general principles of checking designs (Section 11.1). The nature of confidence in Section 11.2 and safety analysis is considered in Section 11.3, which leads to a scheme for assuring software quality (Section 11.4). Verification and validation (Section 11.5) summarise the checking obligations, however carried out. Finally, Section 11.6 explains the use of software tools in combination with human intelligence.

11.1 General checking principles

Any design, not only one expressed in software, is a human artefact, and is therefore susceptible to errors of human fallibility. The greater the complexity of a design, the more it must be checked in suitable ways to ensure that the errors are within acceptable bounds. There are three fundamental principles that underlie the checking of software: independence, variety and persistence. The checks must be carried out by minds other than those of the original designer(s), by a rich variety of different processes, and they must be carried out progressively throughout the design processes, with means of ensuring that checks once made are not invalidated by subsequent development of the design. All three principles apply throughout the life of the software, the last being particularly important during its evolution in operational service.

11.1.1 Independent checks

Independent checking is necessary to guard against designer blind spots: a designer eventually becomes so familiar with a system that he can no longer view it unencumbered by his accumulated perception. Another viewpoint can show up errors. Among the important kinds of independent check are those by computers during development (applying extensive rules for consistency and conformity to language rules), checks by others in the development team (peer judgement), checks by others in the company outside the development team, checks by the company's quality assurance department, and checks by another company for verification and validation. Clearly, the cost increases with the independence, as more people have to become familiar with the details of the design and techniques involved.

The rules applied by the different checkers need not differ: the important characteristic is the fact that their viewpoint is distanced from that of the designers, and hence is less prone to bias. In practice, it is likely that detailed checks of closed parts (compilation units) are concerned with small-scale correctness, while the global checks deliberately search for faults that would not be detected automatically.

This part of the book is structured on the above basis, first considering the formal checks provided by an Ada compiler and other automatic processes (checking the static semantics), then moving outwards and more globally to intelligent inspection (using human awareness, going beyond formality by taking account of the context of use) and finally to dynamic analysis using conventional testing. Each stage involves searching for errors that are likely to remain after the previous checks, and by the absence of errors carefully sought, confirming that the plant will behave as intended in operational use.

11.1.2 Variety of checking

In Section 4.1 we pointed out the importance of identifying and distinguishing the positive and negative functionalities in critical areas, as part of the software requirements specification. The different techniques used to give assurances of the positive and negative properties contribute to the variety of checking.

Analytic checks and testing are complementary ways of establishing confidence in a software-based system, although neither is adequate by itself. DO-178A describes both kinds of activity as *verification*, meaning analysis and testing: checking for consistency at each stage of software development.

In general, each level of the design must be checked twice: once immediately after that level of design is completed (analytically, in relation to its requirements, at which time the acceptance tests are also formulated), and again when its components have been built (testing the integration of those components, in relation to the acceptance tests formulated earlier). These correspond to the two phases at each level in the STARTS V-diagram for the software life-cycle (see Figure 7.1). Analysis is carried out during the creative period of the system's life (i.e. the left side of the V-diagram), progressively covering smaller and smaller units as they are invented. Testing is carried out during the integration period of the system's life (the right side of the V-diagram), progressively covering larger and larger units as they are brought together.

Testing deals with one set of data values at a time, over all layers of software and

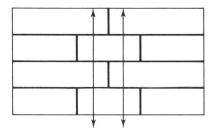

Representative samples confirm actions in those cases

Figure 11.1 Checking by test cases

hardware, illustrated in Figure 11.1 (based on the layered structure explained in Section 7.4.2 and Table 7.2). In any software, we implicitly presume that there is uniformity of behaviour in regions of the data space (see Figure 11.2), and that each

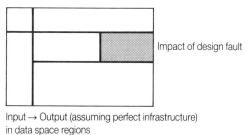

Input → Output (assuming perfect infrastructure)
in data space regions

Figure 11.2 Internal software failures

test case is typical of a range of data values among which the behaviour is uniform. Any error in the software exercised by data in that range would be shown to be defective by the test results (illustrated by the shaded region in Figure 11.2), unaffected by other data values. In contrast, analytical checks deal with one layer of software at a time, over a range of data values determined by the type of the data, illustrated in Figure 11.3. In any analysis, we implicitly presume that the underlying

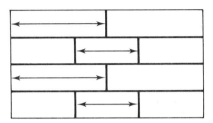

Exposes dependencies, data space structure and
adverse interactions

Figure 11.3 Logic checking

mechanisms are correct; similar analytic checks of the hardware confirm its correctness, assuming that the physical devices work properly.

We can think of these checks by testing and analysis as horizontal and vertical slices through the behaviour of the system, which mutually confirm one another's hypotheses: see Figure 11.4. The testing confirms that the mechanisms under each

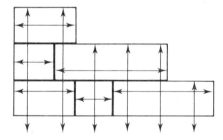

All critical units at each level in each region

Figure 11.4 Combined horizontal and vertical checks

layer are correct (in some cases), and the analysis identifies the regions of uniformity surrounding the data values used in the tests (in some layers) and thus confirms that the regions are complete (or locates untested regions).

By checking all critical units at each level in each region of data space, we have a horizontal and a vertical check of each part of the design.

11.1.3 Persistence of checking

Checking must not be by-passed when a design change is made during integration or subsequent development. This means that the software that has been once checked must be maintained under change control, so that when any subsequent change is authorised for any module, the checks to that module must be repeated as rigorously as first time round. The tests for each module must therefore also be held under change control, so that they are available for use in the event of a change.

The ultimate purpose of the checks is, in total, to provide the evidence that the system is safe, and to justify the confidence of the eventual users in it.

11.2 Confidence and reliability

As explained in Chapters 4 and 5, reliability requirements are conventionally expressed as an expected period of time before failure, with the connotation of progressive (stochastic) deterioration. Software does not behave like that. Section 4.5 has explained how we interpret the concept of expected time to failure in a software based system.

The various checks we describe produce a body of evidence concerning the properties of the target computer's behaviour, which gives confidence that its subsequent behaviour will be safe in all circumstances that might arise during operational use. But we have to assess this confidence, and put a figure of merit or probability on it. If there are any residual faults (and we must presume that there are), then they will appear when some combination of circumstances arises that was not covered by the tests or other checks. The time to failure is the time taken in the environment of operational use for such a situation to arise: not simply related to the software itself or the checking applied. The three-term formula explained in Section 4.5.1 summarises the contributors to the probability of failure.

The analysis of Section 4.5.1 applies for a single item of software, without considering its inner design. In practice, we use knowledge about the software design (and the development processes used) to estimate the confidence we can have in the software. The first two terms in the three-term formula contribute to the software quality: the rate of errors of *commission* in explicitly formulating the Ada text, and the rate of *omission* of coverage by the checks applied, so that initial errors are not detected and corrected before operational use.

If we imagine all the input data channels to the target computer as spanning a state space, each particular input constitutes a point in this space, and the operational use of the system is described by the points in the state space that actually occur, which will be contained in a set of regions. (There are other dimensions of the state space corresponding to internal data values, but for the present purpose we consider the projection onto the space spanned by the input channels.) Some regions of the space are frequently occupied by input values; others rarely. Thus we can ascribe probabilities to the regions of state space, dependent on the operational use and not on the software. A fault in the software will affect data points in an associated (but unknown) region.

For each region of the state space R, there will be certain distinct parts of the program that become active (in addition to parts that are active for the larger enclosing regions). If the probability of a fault existing in the part of the program dealing with that particular region is Pf_R, and the probability of the operational data input being in that region is Po_R, then the probability Px of a failure occurring is the combination of these two probabilities, summed over all regions:

$$Px = \Sigma_R \, Pf_R \times Po_R$$

Thus the confidence in the software comes from three sources: the complete partitioning of the state space into a set of regions R; an estimate of the probabilities Pf_R based on the quality of the software; and estimates of the probabilities Po_R based on knowledge of the operational pattern of usage.

In practice, it is the partitioning into regions that is the most difficult. With a program in Ada, the structure of the packages in the program allows us to estimate this. Static analysis establishes the extent of each region, within which the behaviour of the software is uniform (always correct or always faulty). Tests aim to include at least one data point in each region, in order to demonstrate that Pf for that region is zero. The region implies a neighbourhood of each test data point, such that the result of the test for the data point applies to all the region, assuming the design to be well-conditioned (see Bougé, 1983).

However, after tests with a set Q of data points (intended to cover all regions) have shown that Pf_Q are all zero, the residual probability of failure is the combination of the probabilities concerning regions that were not envisaged in Q:

$$Px = \Sigma_{(R-Q)} \, Pf_R \times Po_R$$

Pessimistically, we must assume that the Pf_R in these regions are non-zero and contain the same density of faults as the other regions did *before* testing. The density of faults detected in each package must be measured during the integration period of the software development, as this gives the fundamental data for the quality of the software (see Section 4.4). The residual failure rate is therefore estimated by:

$$Px \simeq \Sigma_{(R-Q)} \, Pf_Q \times Po_R$$

Thus the most important issue for the analysis of a program is the identification of *all* the regions in the data space, taking account of plant state, operational mode and relevant history. Most packages comprise a number of subprograms, which are tested individually to cover the state spaces they expect. We must be concerned with the state space of the plant as a whole, but particularly those regions whose criticality Risk Factors are 1 or 2.

11.3 Safety integrity analysis

The HSE Guide requires the safety-related system to be analysed to ensure that the required level of safety integrity (see Section 5.5) has been achieved, according to the criteria set for the particular plant. This means investigating all possible influences that could affect the ability of the plant to perform its required functions in the desired manner under all the relevant conditions and on the occasions when it is required so to perform. There are basicaly two steps: (a) identify all the influences; and (b) delimit the functions, conditions and occasions in which the performance could be affected. Hardware failures are explicitly to be included in the safety integrity analysis, for example communication between subsystems in a distributed control system.

With regard to the software, the HSE Guide recognises that the safety integrity cannot be quantified, but can only be considered qualitatively. The above two steps are the investigations of the configuration and the quality of the safety-related system. (The HSE Guide gives an example in which there are two independent channels contributing to safety: one programmed in BASIC, the other a Programmable Logic Controller, in which the real program is independent of the application, with parameters defining the particular protection logic used.)

The qualitative method of analysis given in the HSE Guide uses lists of questions covering the requirements, hardware, software, operations, maintenance and common-cause failures. Each question is formulated to take an answer 'yes', 'no' or 'not applicable', where the 'yes' answer is the good one. The analysis is completed by summarising the percentage of questions to which each answer is given: values around 80 per cent of 'yes' answers may be required for the safety of a petro-chemical plant. (Note that this way of summarising the answers gives equal weight to all the questions. This is not absolutely justified, but it is a basis for comparison, and establishes a common framework of assessment for all safety-related systems.) Each of the 'no' answers should be investigated further in order to determine how serious it is.

The questions in the HSE check-lists are mainly unaffected by the decision to program in Ada, but some of the software questions can be further amplified in this case, either by giving a direct answer now, or by showing how the question is to be interpreted for software in Ada. Each check-list has a number, and each question has a number which starts with the check-list number. We give the specific Ada-related questions below, with appropriate comments.

HSE CHECKLIST 10A: SOFTWARE SPECIFICATION

(ADA PROGRAM UNIT SEMANTICS)

10A.4 'Is use made of a formal specification language or some other means of ensuring a precise and unambiguous specification?' The example in the HSE Guide shows that pseudo-code is considered adequate to answer this question 'yes', so the recommended style of using claims would also be satisfactory.

10A.9 'Are automated tools used as an aid to the development of the software specification in (i) documentation; (ii) consistency checking?' An Ada compiler would count such a tool, treating the annotated package specifications as the documentation of the software, and noting the automatic consistency checking between compilation units.

HSE CHECKLIST 11A: SOFTWARE DESIGN

(ADA PROGRAM UNIT SPECIFICATIONS)

11A.4 'Is use made of a formal, structural program design language or some other means of ensuring a clear and unambiguous statement of functions to be coded?' Ada satisfies this.

11A.5 'Is use made of a suitable graphical representation of programme [sic] flow control (e.g. flow chart) and program$_{me}$ data flow or other means of assuring that the program$_{me}$ operation is clear and easily understood?' With Ada it would be normal to rely on the 'other means' in the question – specifically the readability of Ada and the use of claims.

11A.6 'Are there guidelines for constraining the control flow of the program$_{me}$ by the use of acceptable flow control structures?' The question does not define which flow control structures are 'acceptable'; the design rules given in this book (about the use of **go to** and exceptions) satisfy the question.

11A.7 'Are automated tools used as an aid to design in regard to (i) documentation; (ii) control flow analysis; (iii) data flow analysis; (iv) information flow analysis; (v) semantic analysis?' An Ada-specific editor would satisfy point (i), and the SPARK examiner would satisfy the others.

11A.8 'Are there guidelines for the design of data structures?' Some are given in ARINC Paper 613 (see Appendix A), but there is little relevance to safety. The guidance to avoid access types could be considered as satisfying this question, but it is not clear what purpose the guidelines are intended to serve.

11A.15 'If a concurrent processing philosophy has been adopted rather than sequential task execution: (i) has the need for this been established; (ii) have suitable concurrent processing methods been adopted; (iii) has the use of interrupts been kept to a minimum?' The issue of the use of Ada tasks in the program is discussed in Chapter 8. Suitable concurrent processing methods are provided by Ada run-time environments. Minimisation of interrupts depends on the timing analysis, to determine whether polling is an acceptable alternative.

11A.16 '(i) Are separate software modules used to implement the safety-related functions; (ii) Is the data used by them protected as far as possible from write access by other modules?' The recommended structural design satisfies the first point. The scope rules of Ada ensure that the second is satisfied.

11A.18 'Does the software contain adequate error detection facilities allied to error containment, recovery or safe shutdown procedures?' The style of defensive programming explained in Section 9.3, possibly with Ada exceptions, satisfies this.

11A.19 'Are safety critical areas of the software identified?' This point underlies the categorisation of packages described in Section 8.2.

HSE CHECKLIST 12A: SOFTWARE CODING

(ADA PROGRAM UNITS WHICH ARE PROPER BODIES)

12A.9 'Is an appropriate high-level programming language used where speed considerations allow?' Ada is currently the most appropriate such language.

12A.10 '(i) Is a well established compiler/assembler used; (ii) Does it have a good error detection capability; (iii) Is it certified to recognise standards?' A validated Ada compiler is assured to be sufficiently well established to satisfy the validation tests, which include tests of the error detection capability, and certify that it conforms to the standard definition of Ada.

12A.11 'Does the programming language: (i) encourage the use of small and manageable modules; (ii) allow access to certain data to be restricted to defined modules; (iii) permit operations to be carried out on variables of the expected type; (iv) allow the definition of variable type sub-ranges?' Ada strongly satisfies these.

12A.12 'Is the code written in a form which helps comprehension by (i) adequate use of comments; (ii) sectioning of functions or modules etc.; (iii) the consistent use of acceptable control flow structures; (iv) the use of different levels of indenture for associated statements?' Ada satisfies this by its concern for readability, although the necessity to use comments (in any language) must be regarded as a weakness: information that cannot be formalised in the programming language itself is not so strongly checked for consistency.

12A.13 'Are automated tools used as an aid to development in regard to (i) documentation; (ii) control flow analysis; (iii) data flow analysis; (iv) information flow analysis; (v) semantic analysis?' (Note the similarity of this question to question 11A.7, illustrating the fact that design and development are not really distinct steps in software engineering.) Depending on the interpretation of 'documentation', the first point could be satisfied by an Ada compiler (treating a package specification as its documentation) or the SPARK examiner (treating the annotations as documentation). The SPARK examiner would satisfy the others.

12A.14 'Are there guidelines for limiting the size of program modules to avoid over-complexity?' The design rules to facilitate verification avoid overcomplexity, but not explictly by limiting size. General guidelines (not specific to safety) limit the size of individual compilation units, e.g. to 200 lines.

12A.15 'Are safety critical areas within the code identified?' (This is like question 11A.19, again confirming the similarity of design and development.) The recommended categorisation of program units would satisfy this.

HSE CHECKLIST 13A: SOFTWARE TEST

13A.10 'Is each software module tested individually as fully as possible before incorporation onto the full program?' This will be satisfied if the recommendations in Chapter 14 are followed.

13A.11 '(i) Are there specified criteria for the coverage of tests (for example, is each control flow path through the program tested to ensure that each statement is executed at least once); (ii) If not, is the coverage of the tests known; (iii) Are test results analysed to reveal any areas of the software which show an unexpectedly high rate of failure in test; (iv) If so, are the reasons for the high rate of failure established?' The recommendations of Chapter 14 deal with the coverage of the tests. The points about an expected rate of failure seem to imply possible acceptability of a safety-related system in which tests have exposed failures. The coverage analysis should show that these cannot lead to danger.

13A.12 'Have arithmetic functions been tested with the sets of input values which give the maximum and minimum computed results to ensure that no overflow conditions are reached?' This would be satisfied by extreme-value testing (Section 14.2: data on boundary values) and Ada exception detection for range constraints.

11.4 Quality assurance

Software Quality Assurance is not a well-understood practice, as software quality is still more a wish than a reality (in spite of the analysis we have given in Section 4.4). Methods of quality assurance in other branches of engineering are mainly concerned with limiting the imperfections of replication of an ideal design, rather than looking for imperfections in a design that can be perfectly replicated. The fact that software quality means quality of design is recognised by the attention given to checking the procedures of software production rather than the software products themselves. A Software QA department is likely to be concerned principally with ensuring that various kinds of checking and test are carried out, properly reported, and linked with corrective actions taken to eliminate whatever faults are found. Quality Assurance is associated with Configuration Management (CM); DO-178A permits the Software QA plan to be separate or combined with the Software CM plan.

Current software quality assurance procedures (e.g. IEEE Std 730–1984) combine the persistence principle with independence. The QA ensures that suitable independent attention has been given to each item of software, and that the results of the attention are applied properly. Current software configuration management planning (e.g. IEEE Std 828–1983) deals with configuration item identification, grouping and change control. The CM ensures that all items are adequately identified in an evolving context, and that no changes are made without proper authorisation.

General-purpose QA plans do not identify the stages at which checks should be made: that is left to individual projects. With the interpretation of quality (of software) that we have introduced in Chapter 4, the QA becomes focussed on the kinds of error that might pass the checks undetected. The analysis of quality levels presumes that the program text is examined systematically for certain classes of error, and may be sampled for other kinds. Each software unit has a specific purpose, which the checks must take into account. Since each kind of sampling check might miss some errors, the level of assurance is principally based on the systematic checking applied. This principle underlies the recommendations for checking in Def Stan 00–55 (see Appendix D).

For software developed according to the present approach, we can be distinctly more specific. As explained in Section 11.1, each item of software should be checked (in complementary ways) at two distinct times, related to the software development plan. The first is on completion of the design (of the unit at each level); the second is on completion of the integration of that unit at that level (by combination of smaller units that have already been checked). Different checking criteria are relevant at the two stages. The first is purely a logical and functionality check; the second is an implementation and performance check (as well as a confirmation of the functionality). Checklists for use at each stage at each level are given in later chapters.

For Risk Factors 1 and 2 functions, testing documentation (test plans, procedures, and results – document 11) should be recorded and retained under configuration control. In addition, for Risk Factor 1 functions, an audit should be carried out to confirm that all necessary tasks have been completed. All problems resulting from the testing process should be logged, and corrective actions tracked.

For Requirements coverage analysis, the document must identify the test cases which are essential to demonstrate that the software complies adequately with each software requirement (individually and by interaction). In addition, since software functional partitioning is employed, the means of partitioning must be verified to the same level as that required for the most critical software elements. Interpreting these principles to the quality analysis of Ada programs, we treat packages in accordance with their criticality category. The Software Safety Assessor (see Appendix D) must be convinced that the analyses and checks have been carried out adequately.

11.5 Verification and validation

Verification and validation (usually abbreviated to 'V&V') refers to the complete range of checks that must be performed on a system, in order to give adequate confidence in its suitability for its intended purpose. This range might include a rigorous set of functional tests, some performance tests (for ordinary and stressful situations), and reliability tests. The IEEE definitions are as follows:

● **verification**: (1) The process of evaluating a system or component to determine whether the products of a given development phase satisfy the conditions imposed at the start of that phase; (2) formal proof of program correctness.

● **validation**: the process of evaluating a system or component during or at the end of the development process to determine whether it satisfies specified requirements.

Although the definitions are similar, the precise distinction between the terms is not always drawn; in looser terminology, the verification aspect normally refers to completely objective checking of conformity to some well-defined specification, while the validation aspect normally refers to a somewhat subjective assessment of likely suitability in the intended environment, whatever has been officially specified in the development contract.

As has been pointed out in Chapter 4, there is no guarantee that specifications are error-free. As well as confirming that the software is correct with respect to its specification, it is necessary to check that the two together are appropriate for the intended use of the system. In the case of a safety-related system, this would mean checking that the potential hazards are made sufficiently improbable.

The difference in principle between V(erification) and V(alidation) is less important than the independent examination of the software that the process entails. For critical software (whether safety or security are involved), a V&V contract is often set up with a company other than that responsible for the software production, in order to provide an independent and comprehensive check that confidence is justified. In this case, the process is sometimes described as IV&V: Independent Verification and Validation.

11.5.1 Impact of Ada

The role of a V&V contractor with regard to safety-critical software written in Ada includes re-compiling all the delivered software on a different Ada compiler (to confirm that all the rules of the language are kept), and checking the logic of the critical software (using formal methods where appropriate). The inspection must confirm that residual problems are identified and bounded (by study of particular aspects of the program.)

The significance of using Ada structure is that it allows the V&V contractor to check the sets of operations applicable to each data type for completeness and adequate coverage. (Thus there should be operations to create, access, and modify items of each data type, and possibly to delete such items.)

If the guidelines given in Part II have been followed, each package will fall into a particular safety category, and significant packages will contain an explicit claim about what they are intended to be or do. The verifier, by intelligent inspection and the use of automatic tools, should confirm that the claims are met.

11.5.2 Verification of claims

Any claim that a system is fit for its intended purpose must include the following:

- complete identification of the system concerned;
- statement of the intended purpose of the system;
- demonstration that all individual parts of the software have been tested;
- evidence of the overall accomplishment of the system;
- reasoning that links statements of the software produced with the requirements.

The verification of such a claim must inspect all the information provided to ensure that it is complete, and that the logic is sound.

Each category 1 unit should be independently, rigorously and (as far as possible) formally verified to ensure that the claim is met. Such packages should not include any other complicating features, both to facilitate the analysis and to avoid any further risk that might arise from the translation from the linguistic semantics of the Ada program into the executable binary code. For software implementing critical functions (Risk Factor 1), the whole process must be audited for completeness, with tests traced back to the requirement, deviations from standards justified, and problems tracked from detection to cure. Risk Factor 2 software must adhere to agreed standards and have predicted results.

11.5.3 Verification that recommended criteria have been met

Where particular criteria are set for safety-related software, it is important to verify that they are met in the software produced, and all infringements of the criteria are identified and justified.

Thus the acceptability criteria (e.g. target error rates) should be agreed as a constraint in the initial requirements. The development procedure should include production of documents to show that the criteria are met, with complete audit trails. The verification should be carried out by qualified people independent of the developers.

11.5.4 Software accomplishment summary

In general, for software with Risk Factor 1 (i.e. packages upon which a critical function depends), the results of each verification process should be recorded and retained as evidence for safety assurance. All problems resulting from each verification process should be logged, and the corrective action tracked. A cross-reference list (traceability matrix) should link each step to the following one in the development process, to ensure that the verification has properly covered them all.

```
system requirements =>
    software requirements =>
        software design =>
            software implementation
```

An audit should be performed to confirm that all the tasks have been completed, and a report written and retained. Any deviations from the project's software design standards (recorded in document 12) must be noted and justified.

For software with Risk Factor 2, a summary description of the verification process is required, with all problems logged and corrective action tracked. The developer should provide a Statement of Compliance, normally in the Accomplishment Summary document.

For software with Risk Factor 3, no safety assurance is required: what must be verified is determined by the acceptance criteria laid down in the contract.

11.6 Use of software tools

A software tool can be used to check a piece of software according to well-defined rules and explicit information. Such a check is of course formal, as it takes no account of the interpretation of the rules or the significance of the software in its operational context. Many formal checks can be applied: as many as rules can be formulated. We discuss specific checks in the next chapter, but the principles here.

As has been mentioned in Section 7.7, software tools may themselves be defective (but their failure modes are different from those of human mathematicians or logicians). The technique of diversity, including the use of a different Ada compiler by the V&V agency, provides the cross-checking on which confidence relies. The rules of Ada permit a number of variations between valid compilers (defined in the Ada Langage Reference Manual, Appendix F: Implementation-Dependent Characteristics), and it is important that any use of them be explicit. Recompilation on a different compiler is a (partial) check for such 'dialect' dependencies.

11.6.1 Implications of using software tools for checking

Broadly we can categorise the formal checks that can be applied into two: those that make use of only the Ada program text, and those that need additional information. The former include checks for the appropriate use of Ada constructs, and may derive information about the Ada text for subsequent inspection (e.g. the distinct data regions that should be tested, the existence of uninitialised variables, or the use of representation specifications). The latter can apply stronger checks formally, when the additional information expresses intentions that the program ought to satisfy (e.g. lists of the outer variables on which a fragment of program depends, and the dependency relations of the results). These are intermediate steps to formal program proof.

Formal proof of a program (with respect to a specification) means a logical demonstration that the program satisfies its specification, without reference to its intended meaning or interpretation. Thus a package in SPARK or in Ada annotated in Asphodel (to define the specification) would be formally proved by giving the logical steps which show that the specification is implied by the program text. This demonstration must be completely logical, so may be carried out by a human logician or an automaton. The steps are usually so many and tedious that it is preferable to use an automaton to carry out the logic, with a human to guide it and determine the strategy.

Techniques for formalising the semantics of an Ada package specification have been introduced in Section 7.6 and developed in Chapters 8 and 9. Formal specification and formal proof are mandatory for safety-critical software elements, and application-dependent for high integrity elements. For Ada programs, this implies providing additional information about the claimed properties (as explained in Section 9.2) and formally analysing all category 1 packages and selected category 2 packages. These are explained in Chapter 12.

11.6.2 Using unreliable checking tools

As pointed out in Sections 4.5.3 and 7.7, we must be able to build a system that is more reliable than any of its constituents, by incorporating internal checking and redundancy. In the case of software tools, this principle means that we must be aware of the possibility of defects in every software tool we use, and must include checks that confirm the tools as well as the checks (using the tools) that confirm the created software. Following the categorisation of tools explained in Section 7.7, we concentrate here on possible defects in *analysers*, which derive information from the sources to expose some (supposed) logical deductions.

If an analyser is defective, it will either report as an error a situation that is actually innocuous, or (seriously) fail to report a situation that actually is defective. The former case can be handled by intelligent inspection, and is not intrinsically harmful. The latter case would be significant only if a single tool was being used to discover all errors; but in practice, no tool is expected to discover all kinds of error, so the fact that a particular tool does not discover a particular error will be covered by general variety of the checking procedures.

It is, however, well worth while applying every checking tool to the software under development at an early stage, when it is highly likely to contain many defects. It is also worth applying each checking tool to a software unit containing a small deliberate fault (of the kind the tool is supposed to detect). The kinds of defect that the tool detects can thus be checked, and the experience used to confirm the intended power of the tool before it is used 'in anger' on the (supposedly) final software.

The configuration records of the software should record which checks have been applied to each software unit, and the same technique used with software tools as with batches of test data: when a defect is discovered after the initial software has been checked, it is important to discover why the newly discovered defect was not detected earlier. This may expose defects in the checking tools, which would have passed other errors of the same kind.

12

Formal checks

FORMAL TECHNIQUES are fundamental to computer-based systems, as all information handling in a computer is formal, being based entirely on its form (ultimately as bit-patterns) regardless of any intended meaning or interpretation. Formal analyses may be carried out by a person (with logical/mathematical skills) or by an automaton. Extensive software tools already exist, and more are being developed, to carry out formal checks on software in Ada. These have significant advantages, but also some drawbacks, in comparison with other kinds of check. In general, a check carried out by an automaton (for that is the best way to think of automatic checks using software tools) is an exhaustive application of the individual checks deemed appropriate by the human inventor of the software tool. It thus eliminates the risk of unintentional or resource-imposed omission or incomplete coverage that is common in human checking, but loses the application of natural intelligence to any individual peculiarities of the software under test.

Checks based on static analysis of the program text also have benefits and shortcomings in relation to tests of the dynamic behaviour of the system under particular conditions, whether carried out automatically or by intelligent inspection; they presume a perfect execution of the program in terms of the semantics defined by the language, thus assuming a perfect compiler, linker, run-time executive, library routines, processor, memory and peripheral hardware. Testing, on the other hand, does not rely on such assumptions. We return to this point in Chapter 13, since the issue is even more significant in that context. Checks based on static analysis can show the *absence* of particular features, in either all units or a selection of them. Testing can only show the *presence* of particular features.

Formal proof of a program (with respect to its specification) means a logical demonstration that the program satisfies its specification, without reference to its intended meaning or interpretation. Thus a package in SPARK or in Ada annotated in Asphodel would be formally proved by giving the logical steps to show that the specification holds from the program text. This demonstration must be completely logical, so may be carried out by a human logician or an automaton. The steps are usually so many and tedious that it is preferable to use an automaton to carry out the logic, with a human to guide it and determine the strategy.

In this chapter, we discuss (in Section 12.1) the checks made by an Ada compiler (which show that a compiler is much more important as a software tool for checking than just for code generation), and other checking based on the Ada program text by itself, both small-scale (i.e. within compilation units: syntactic checking, in Section 12.2) and large-scale: dependency between program units (Section 12.3). The subsequent sections describe formal checks that require additional information as well as the Ada text: claims (Section 12.4), and static semantic analysis (Section 12.5). In each case, to emphasise the need of the checker to be aware of the limitations of formal checks, we draw attention to the kinds of defect that the check would not detect. At present there is little hard information about the likely incidence rate of such defects, so it is important for the checking agency to measure the observed rates as an indication of the density to be expected in operational use.

12.1 Compile-time checking

All programming languages (including Ada) are formal, so that inferences can be made about programs in them by analysing the texts in source language. Every time a unit of an Ada program is compiled, it is checked extensively by the compiler. This establishes a coherent syntactic framework, so that the significant information is well-formed and clearly delimited.

The essential checks made at this stage are the disjunction of identifiers and the internal consistency of specifications/declarations with use. Package specifications in Ada are formal, and Ada compilers check that the body corresponding to each is consistent with it; however the information contained in an Ada package specification is limited to the declarations of its constituents, with no formal specification of its claimed or intended sematics. The disjunction of identifiers is the beginning of analysis, providing the nomenclature specific to the target system. Even with its rules of overloading, Ada ensures that an identifier declared as a data type is used only in positions where a data type is appropriate, and an identifier declared as an exception is used only where an exception might be raised. Thus the compiler checks that there is a consistent categorisation of the identifiers in the program, which provides a good check that there is a consistent nomenclature.

Even more important is the compile-time check for consistency within categories concerning data objects (variables and constants) and operations (procedures, functions and operators), taking account of renaming and overloading. These checks ensure that there exists an interpretation for each name, expression, assignment, procedure call and entry call in the program (but not necessarily that the chosen interpretation is the one intended).

Certain aspects of completeness are checked at compile-time: the set of subprograms specified for a package must all be included (at least as stubs) in the package body, and all the entries in a task must be matched by accept statements in its body. Completeness of the whole program, in terms of the library units and subunits involved, is also checked automatically by the linker associated with an Ada compiler before a program can be executed.

The above automatic checks are obtained by the designer during the development phases of a project. There are further benefits to be obtained from compiling each unit again independently on a different Ada compiler.

The benefits to be gained from the independent recompilations by the V&V contractor are (i) confirmation that the designer has not inadvertently made use of non-portable features (allowed in Ada through package SYSTEM); (ii) confirmation that any compiler restrictions have not adversely affected the design (since each implementation may have distinct limits, as defined in Appendix F of the Ada Reference Manual); and (iii) confirmation that the packages identified in the context clause are under proper version control. These may be particularly important if the program is written for a 'restricted target', i.e. a computer without the full facilities required for the validation of the compiler.

Matters on which no automatic checks are possible include consistency of achievement with intention, and completeness of functionality. Errors that would not be automatically detected by a compiler include confusion between identifiers or symbols in the same category, particularly between those referring to the same data type. Thus it would not detect a confusion between '+' and '−' or between two variable names declared to be of the same type. Because of the latter possibility, it is recommended that identifiers should never differ by just a single character. In the case of function designators (with overloading), the characters cannot be made very distinct, since Ada defines which symbols can be used. Recognising this limit of compile-time checking draws attention to the importance of subsequent checks that can discriminate between the functions concerned.

Software can never be checked for performance, independently of a target execution environment. In particular, for the present work there are no automatic checks on any matters specifically related to safety.

This is not to belittle the checks applied by a compiler: unless a text is well-formed, no implications at all can be derived from it, so further analysis would be futile.

12.2 Syntactic checks

Other significant checks can be made automatically on an Ada program, by the use of an appropriate software tool (which could be a simple editor). These distinguish the parts of that program responsible for system safety, and are particularly important for safety integrity analysis during program integration. As package bodies are completed, they are integrated into the program according to the normal rules of Ada. Special attention has to be given to the safety-critical parts, which we now explain. The residual source of danger in an Ada program written according to these guidelines arises from the software/hardware interaction. The checks described here are related to the categorisation of packages explained in Sections 8.2 and 9.1.

12.2.1 Actual input–output

Representation specifications for data object addresses are uncontrolled by the rules of the Ada programming language: any data object may have an address specified, with no obligation that addresses be disjoint. It is important, therefore, to check explicitly that input–output addresses are not misused. Ada cannot check that representation specifications are given correctly, or that they are restricted to specific parts of the program (category 1 packages).

It is therefore necessary to carry out a comprehensive check of the complete program to locate all representation specifications and analyse them in an integrated way. The program in Ada expresses the logical structure of the system, which has no significance for representations.

The most important check to apply is on the device address specifications. The address of each input–output device should be distinct and in a distinct package. This can be checked by preparing a list of all address specifications sorted by address, identifying the package and relevant variable (object) name.

A simple check is to establish whether a compilation unit does or does not include address specifications or machine code, and compare this with the category of the package. Those packages that do not include an address specification or machine code cannot directly control input–output and thus cannot be direct sources of danger. But those that do contain such a construct must be marked as category 1 so that they are fully checked.

For each type of device there should also be a control and status word format such as DEVICE_CONTROL in the sections on Structural Design and Device Control and Status. The use of packages declaring these should be checked for congruity with the categorisation of the devices into device types.

Category 1 compilation units that do include address specifications or machine code must be checked to establish which addresses (or address ranges) they cover. The devices in the target system will have specific addresses: this check provides a focus of attention on the software that relates to actions referring to the addresses of hazardous devices or related sensors (by selecting out the software referring only to innocuous input–output).

12.2.2 Package use

Context clauses for the use of packaged facilities are also uncontrolled by the rules of Ada: any compilation unit may begin with a context clause referring to other library units. The key structural protection for safety requires that packages dealing with hazardous devices are not misused.

Such packages, identified as described above, can in principle be used anywhere; their actual usage can be tracked into the rest of the software by searching for the occurrence of the package names in other context clauses. The technique (of double insulation), advocated in this book ensures that all such packages are subunits rather than library units and are thus automatically constrained in usage by the rules of Ada. However, the check on context clauses is worth bearing in mind for general use and as a check that all dangerous output *is* doubly insulated.

12.2.3 Timing implications

In Section 9.4 we listed the five basic constructs in Ada that can lead to unbounded timing. Since these can have adverse effects on the real-time behaviour of control software executing on the same computer, it is necessary to examine them throughout the program, regardless of package category. The design rules given in Section 9.1 would limit the selective accept to passive tasks in category 2 packages, but the other constructs could occur in category 3 packages. The syntactic check can locate all occurrences of such constructs, to focus the attention of the human analyst on the specific parts of the program and give confidence that none have been inadvertently overlooked.

12.2.4 Data isolation

The principle of categorisation is to ensure that category 3 packages cannot affect the safety checks in category 1 packages; the intermediate role of category 2 packages can be picked out by similar syntactic checks (for tasks with entry declarations, any kind of unsafe programming, or exception declarations without handlers).

12.2.5 Task termination and other residual weak points

The residual weaknesses of Ada are discussed in Section 13.4 below; each can be recognised by some syntactic construct in the program (e.g. **abort**).

12.2.6 Summary

Thus in order to select out the packages needing special checking (by intelligent inspection or further automatic checks) the syntactic checks are to detect the following:

● representation specifications, i.e **for** in a declarative part, and within these address clauses, i.e. **use at**;
   also representation clauses, i.e. **use** aggregate, or use record;
● context clauses, i.e. **with** referring to a critical package name;
● constructs with unbounded timing implications;
● other constructs acceptable only in category 2 packages;
● constructs that indicate residual weaknesses in Ada (see Section 13.4).

Packages that are not selected by these criteria need only a weaker check to confirm that they will not adversely affect the packages that might cause real harm. For example, use of real arithmetic (by data types derived from **delta** or **digits**) should be detected, and its use confined to category 3 packages where the possible internal danger arising from the approximations involved is investigated.

None of these syntactic checks are absolute: they do not indicate whether the program is or is not safe; they simply draw attention to particular parts that must be further analysed.

12.3 Dependency between program units

The principal analysis of an Ada program for safety is of its structure: the relationships between its program units and compilation units.

The context clause (i.e. the **with** lists of unit names at the head of the compilation unit) shows which other units it depends on. These dependency relationships define the structure of the program.

If a package specification has a context clause, the dependency shows impurity in the design: incomplete separation of concepts in the formulation of the program. Each such dependency needs further analysis to confirm that the impurity is not dangerous. It is less serious if the referenced package has no body (since this avoids elaboration-order dependency). There is no situation where a package with a body should be needed in the context clause for another package specification. Examples of this situation arise when a set of application-dependent types are declared in one package, and subprograms for manipulating objects of these types are specified in a distinct package. Provided that the types are not involved in the safety or protection control loops, such impurity is acceptable (although it may be undesirable for other reasons). Similarly in a distributed system, the communication between computers at the higher protocol levels may be expressed by having a common set of message types in one package used in each computer, with manipulation procedures for the messages in multiple packages in the separate computers.

If a package body (or subprogram body) has a context clause, the dependency shows layering in the design, and has an important bearing on the risk factor associated with the package or subprogram concerned. Two checks should be carried out, to confirm (a) partial ordering of the layers and (b) downward awareness of criticality.

The partial ordering of the layers check is needed to avoid circularity of dependencies: i.e. two packages mutually dependent on one another, or several packages forming a ring. While such relationships are not prohibited by the rules of Ada they imply another kind of design impurity, with the possibility of elaboration complications that are best avoided. This check is crucial for establishing the safety structure of the software.

Downwards awareness of criticality is directly related to safety: if package A depends on package B, then B must be at least as safe as A. In general, the criticality risk factor of each package must be no less than that of the packages depending on it. The header of each package should state its criticality risk factor, ready for checking during the layering check. The criticality risk factor should be expressed in a uniform way, so that a general-purpose software tool for recognising patterns (such as 'grep' in Unix) can extract the information and contribute to a formal check.

To investigate these relationships, it is necessary to form the *transitive closure* of the dependencies between the packages. Again, this analysis is in principle formal, but if tools to carry it out are not available, it has to be done by human brain power. Further discussion of dependency analyses is therefore deferred to Section 13.4.

12.4 Claim checking

The claim made for a program unit may be checked formally when the activity is entirely internal to the computer (but not when it involves external activities, which of course are the potentially dangerous ones).

Category 1 units should be independently, rigorously and (as far as possible) formally verified to ensure that the claim of each is met. Such packages should not include any other complicating features, both to facilitate the analysis and to avoid any further risk that might arise from the translation from the linguistic semantics of the Ada program into the executable binary code. Category 2 units should be independently checked statically to ensure that their claims are met, subject to all dependent packages working correctly in accordance with their claims.

The following technique of Analytic Walkthrough has been developed for carrying out a claim check using human logical skills, as a short-term solution before automata are available to do it. While humans *can* act as automata, they are not very good in that capacity, and the risks of mistake are much higher than with a real automaton. (This section could arguably belong to the next chapter, on intelligent inspection, but is placed here because the intention is to check the claim formally.)

The author of the program unit and one or two others analyse it, recording any discrepancies between the actual effects and those intended. They do not make any changes at the time.

The Analytic Walkthrough is a quality check on a program unit (both specification and design) after it has been debugged and tested. The steps in the analysis are as follows:

1.   Identify critical points.
2.   Characterise the state at each critical point.
3.   Check the statements in each segment of program (sequence of statements between consecutive critical points).
4.   Track state changes through each segment.
5.   Report and classify all anomalies.

Stage 1 Establishes significant positions in the program unit, between which there are transitions controlled by simple segments of the program. This should have been done as part of the design. On this basis, a state transition diagram can be drawn.

Stage 2 Characterises the state of the system at these positions, defined in terms of the concepts, variables and parameters accessible at the position. This is also a design activity, which has been described in Section 9.2.

Stage 3 Confirms that the statements in each segment are compatible with the state conditions before and after the segment. This is a formal check of individual statements. Tools are available for identifying the variables used and the variables changed (i.e. the information flow).

Stage 4 Checks that the sequence of statements in the segment has the effect of changing the state in the way intended. This is a formal check of sequential statements. Tools are already available for establishing the dependency relations between the variables involved, and for checking for consistency between the sequence of statements and the intended change.

Stage 5 Allows consequent actions to be determined, and measurements to be gathered. Measurement of software attributes is formal (but not well-supported by tools at present). The action to be taken on detected anomalies requires human attention.

12.4.1. Critical point identification

We have explained in Section 9.2 that rigorous analysis requires the program to contain assertions at certain well-defined positions. We distinguished there between check-points and break-points; here we treat them both together, as *critical* points.

Critical points are positions in the program (usually at semicolons) where any of the following hold. The critical points should have been marked (during the logical design of the software, covered in Chapter 9) by annotating the program:

    0.   Entry to subprogram body
    F.   Final end of subprogram (implied if last statement is **return**)

Between statements in any of the following situations (which may sometimes coincide), numbered consecutively through the initial program text (and extended if necessary, out of textual order, as a result of subsequent modifications):

(a)   before each **if, case** or **select** statement;
(b)   after each such statement, i.e. **end if, end case** or **end select**;
(c)   before each **loop**;
(d)   at beginning of the body within each basic loop (where the loop invariant will be defined);
(e)   after each basic loop, i.e. **end loop**;
(f)   after each **return** statement (this gives the final state for this path through the subprogram);
(g)   at each «label»;
(h)   at each **exception** handler.

12.4.2. State characterisation

At each critical point, the assertion should define the state that the system should be in. This will depend on the values of global variables, parameters and local variables. It may also depend on system-wide concepts. The state condition should use mathematical formulae (relations) where appropriate, but not assignments. The condition may include *universal quantifiers*, namely 'all' or 'any' when appropriate (where 'all' means every one of a set; 'any' means at least one of a set, but which one is not determined).

The condition at each critical point is defined in the same way, but those at certain points have special names. The condition assumed on entry to any subprogram is called its 'pre-condition'; the condition intended to hold on exit from a subprogram (by whichever way the subprogram finishes) is called its 'post-condition'; and the condition that is supposed to hold at the same point in every repetition of a loop is called its 'loop invariant'. In general, for each segment, there is a condition at its beginning and another condition at its finish; we call these the conditions 'before' and 'after' the segment. Note that, in consecutive execution, the condition 'after' one segment is exactly the same as that 'before' the following segment (but different variables in the state may be significant). The same principle, with suitable variations, relates the conditions 'before' an **if** statement and 'before' each branch that it controls. The rules are explained in Section 12.4.4 on state tracking given below.

12.4.3. Checks on statements in segment

- Check all variables mentioned in the segment:
  - each variable used must be
    - mentioned in starting state condition
    - *or* assigned earlier in the segment
  - each variable assigned must be
    - mentioned in state condition reached
    - *or* used subsequently in the segment
- Check each **if** or **case** statement:
  - each variable in the expression must be mentioned in the starting state condition
- Check each **for** or **while** clause controlling a loop:
  - each variable in the controlling expressions:
    - those other than the **for** index must be mentioned in the starting state condition
    - the index in a **for** clause must be not mentioned in the starting state condition.

12.4.4. State tracking through a segment

Starting with the state condition at the start of the segment, derive the condition at each semicolon. Check the final derived state as explained below.

- In a segment starting after an **if** or **case** prefix:
    Note the more restricted state condition at the start of each branch: the
        condition before the prefix combined with the discriminating expression
- In a segment beginning the body of a loop:
    check that the initial state satisfies the loop invariant
- At each assignment statement,
    derive the state after the assignment
        by combining the properties of the variables in the expression
- At each subprogram call,
    check the state on entry: with parameters substituted, it must be
        compatible with the expectations of the subprogram;
    derive the state after the call
        by substituting the parameters in the exit condition of the
        subprogram
- At the end of the segment (in general),
    note the final derived state;
    check that it implies the stated condition after the segment
- At the end of a segment ending with a **return** statement:
    check that the derived state implies the post-condition of the subprogram
- After a loop:
    check that the loop invariant and the negation of any **while** clause *or* any
        exit statement implies the state after the loop
- At the end of the last (or only) segment of a loop body:
    check that the derived state implies the loop invariant

12.4.5. Reporting

Record all the details to monitor quality, measure error density and keep track of trends.

For each observation, note the check that was not as it should have been and decide whether the defect impacts the program or the specification (possibly both). Note how it should be tested when corrected.

For claim checking by intelligent inspection, the forms given as Figures 12.1–12.4 may be used:

- Record of program unit analysis
- Subprogram specification
- Subprogram internal states
- Record of subprogram analysis

Record of program unit analysis

Program unit name .... Version number ....

Date of analysis .... Build/make file ....

People involved:

        author ....
        scribe ....
        other ....

Number of subprograms
        specific to program unit .... total ....
                          ratio ....%

In the above subprograms:

Number of lines:

...... + ... + ... + ... + ... + ... + ... + ...

      = ...

Number of critical points:

...... + ... + ... + ... + ... + ... + ... + ...

      = ...

Number of segments:

...... + ... + ... + ... + ... + ... + ... + ...

      = ...

Number of observations:

...... + ... + ... + ... + ... + ... + ... + ...

      = ...

Ratios:

        obs/lines ...... %
        lines/seg ......
        CP/subprog ......
(counting subprograms in this program unit only)

Figure 12.1 Form for recording program unit analysis

```
┌──────────────────────────────────────────────────────────────┐
│                                                              │
│                    Subprogram specification                  │
│                                                              │
│                                                              │
│     Subprogram heading (name and parameters) ...............  │
│     Version number ......                                    │
│                                                              │
│     Non-local variables used          Read    Updated    Written │
│                                                              │
│                                                              │
│                                                              │
│                                                              │
│     Pre-condition (assumed state on entry)                   │
│     involving initial values of parameters and non-local variables read or updated │
│                                                              │
│                                                              │
│                                                              │
│                                                              │
│     Post-condition (intended state on exit)                  │
│     involving final values of parameters and global variables updated or written │
│                                                              │
│                                                              │
│                                                              │
│                                                              │
│     Dependencies (global constants and other subprograms used) │
│                                                              │
│                                                              │
└──────────────────────────────────────────────────────────────┘
```

Figure 12.2 Form for subprogram specification

12.5 Semantic analysis

One way of verifying that an Ada compilation unit has particular semantic properties is to investigate it with a static semantic analyser. The SPADE (Southampton Program Analysis Development Environment) is a collection of software tools for performing the semantic analysis of programs, initially for programs written in Pascal but now extended to handle a subset of Ada. The SPADE tools have been written explicitly for the purpose of ensuring that software is 'safe', but based on a somewhat different conception of safety than pervades this book (see Section 1.3). It is important to appreciate that 'safe' in the SPADE context does not refer to physical safety, but to the logical safety of relying on any claim made for it; an Ada unit that is unsafe in the SPADE sense is not necessarily unsafe as a driver of a dangerous device, but SPADE does not have enough evidence to certify its semantics.

The SPADE subset of Ada, called SPARK (SPADE Ada Kernel) contains most of the features that would be needed for the doubly insulated packages explained in Part II of this book; the principal omission being the representation clauses. The SPARK examiner is an analysis tool that gives help during the development and final verification of safety-related Ada programs. It consists of a number of components (like SPADE) which analyse the topology and semantics of programs. Topological analyses expose relationships between constituents; they include investigations of the access (usage) relationships between algorithms and their data,

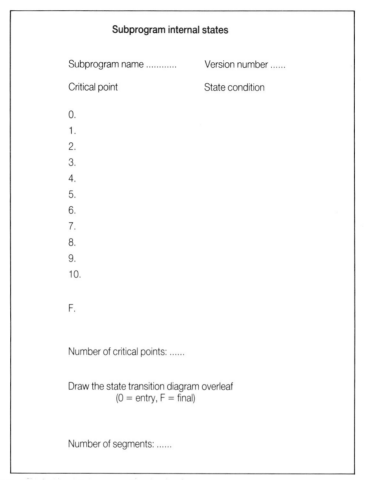

Figure 12.3 Form for subprogram internal states

and the dependency relationships between outputs of subprograms and their inputs. Semantic analyses identify effects achieved under various conditions, and the conditions under which particular paths in the program are executed; they expose the transformations made to the visible data in consequence. Programs may also be executed symbolically, using formulae instead of specific values for variables, so that the behaviour over a region of the state-space is expressed generically (in contrast to spot-checking in conventional testing).

MALPAS (Malvern Program Analysis Suite) is a similar analysis tool, which was also written originally to analyse programs written in Pascal. It has also been extended to apply to Ada programs. The MALPAS analyses (Pierce and Webb, 1989) cover sequential execution, data flow and information flow, data dependency and conformance with semantic specifications.

Record of subprogram analysis

Subprogram name ....   Version ......

Date of analysis ....

People involved:
　　　author ....
　　　scribe ....
　　　other ....

Number of lines ....
Number of crit pts ....   CP/lines .... %
Number of segments ....   segs/CP .... %

Observation   Impact

Number of observations ......   obs/lines ...... %

Number of program obs ......   pr.obs/seg ...... %

Number of specif^n obs ......   sp.obs/CP ...... %

Figure 12.4 Form for recording subprogram analysis

From the point of view of static analysis and these tools, any output is not safe. A safe program performs no output, and can therefore cause no danger.

Formal semantic analysis does not cover representation clauses and machine code for inut–output, since no software tool can verify any claims made concerning the representations and the real hardware. For this reason, it is necessary to give special attention to checking these during the integration testing: see Chapter 14.

13

Intelligent inspection

ANOTHER HUMAN MIND, distinct from that of the designer, can locate many flaws in a design (as explained in Section 11.1.1). The main problem is that the inspector, properly seeing a different way of designing the system, is tempted to be constructively critical, and thus to suggest changes to the software that do not solely eliminate mistakes. This is not necessarily bad, but it makes the responsibility of the inspector clear: there are likely to be many ways of designing satisfactory packages, of which the designer has chosen one. It is not the role of the inspector to select a different one (whatever its merits) but, rather, to identify the potential safety risks in the design that has been chosen.

This search for potential problems must not be restricted to the formal program text, but must encompass the whole context of intended use (applying the principle in Section 11.1.2): the adequacy of the interlocks and guards, as well as the stated intention of each operation provided by the critical packages. There are opportunities for formal notations other than Ada to be used to express intentions, against which appropriate parts of the Ada program can be checked.

Inspection is so important for safety systems that organisations are structured to facilitate it (as has been mentioned in Section 2.3). Verification and Validation (known as 'V&V') is often the specific responsibility of a distinct company or group, which is independent from the design organisation. The activities may include testing as well as inspection, extending the initials to 'V,V&T' (described in this book as 'checking'). This chapter concentrates on the review activities, leaving testing until Chapter 14.

The highest-level inspection is of the software requirements, which must be reviewed against the system requirements (Section 13.1). There are likely to be many levels of design review (Section 13.2) and, ultimately, many modules needing code review (Section 13.3). These are rather general reviews for correctness, not particularly specific for safety, but the dependency analysis (Section 13.4) is an important large-scale check of the dependency between packages; this must be inspected to ensure safety integrity. The known weak points in Ada, which must be inspected carefully in a safety-related system, are explained in Section 13.5, followed by notes on the review of input–output device handlers (Section 13.6), which are the ultimate places where software affects safety or danger.

13.1 Software requirements review

Verification of software requirements (against system requirements) is intended to show the adequacy of the coverage and to ensure that the software developers understand the system requirements. (DO-178A Section 6.2.2.2 covers this topic.) It involves comparing and checking documents 1 and 2 (system requirements and software requirements).

The specific points to be shown are as follows:

(a)   completeness and adequacy of both the system requirements and the software requirements;
(b)   partitioning criteria for functionality between hardware and software, with adequacy of the interfaces between them;
(c)   comprehensive definition of the software requirements.

This presumes that some system requirements are to be met by software; the investigation must verify the completeness and adequacy of all of these requirements (a). In particular, it must confirm that those system requirements to be met by software (c) are properly defined, and have adequate interfaces (b) to the hardware. The check against the system requirements must confirm that the system resources are adequate to support the software, and give the response times and reliability required.

The information prescribed for DO-178A document 2 only partly supports this verification: much of the material that is required to be in document 2 is not directly mentioned in the verification criteria.

Thus, although DO-178A describes this as verification of software requirements against system requirements, the specific points checked are more those of the system requirements (document 1) than of the software requirements (as defined in document 2). The real purpose of this work, from the DO-178A viewpoint, is to review the system requirements (document 1) in order to make the context for the software requirements clear, and implicitly to confirm revisions made as a result of formulating the software requirements.

13.2 Design review

Verification of the detailed software design (including the test plans) against the software requirements checks the documentation for completeness and consistency. To ensure that the design is testable, the associated test criteria must be reviewed with the design.

The verification must show that the requirements have been correctly satisfied by the detailed design, that the design standards (document 12) have been followed, and that the algorithms are suitable (i.e. representative of the engineering design within accepted tolerances of accuracy and stability). In addition to these criteria laid down in DO-178A, the verification should confirm that the representations for the data types concerned are adequate mappings of the properties of the real-world objects they denote.

Ada package specifications, subprogram specifications and task specifications define the syntax of the respective constituents, but not their semantics (and certainly not their performance or availability). We have discussed in Section 9.2 how to describe the semantics by the use of claims. The notation used to express claims must be recorded as part of the documentation of the software, so that the V&V contractor can use the claims as the basis for the design review.

An important element of intelligent inspection concerns the pattern of operations provided in each package. The identifiers chosen by the designer are strong influences on the inspector, indicating the designer's intention for each constituent. (This can be appreciated by considering the difficulties of inspecting a program in which all the identifiers are arbitrary, as they are when the Ada text has been generated from another source, or when the natural language used by the designer is foreign to the inspector.) The identifier is the convenient short-hand chosen by the designer to express the purpose of each element in the program, whether data object or action; the inspector must investigate the program by looking in both directions from each identifier: inwards ('Does the implementation of the object or action support an interpretation suggested by the identifier?') and outwards ('Is the identifier open to multiple interpretations that could be a source of confusion or danger either now or during modification at some time in the future?'). The inspector must also consider the contexts containing sets of identifiers (such as enumeration types and subprograms in a package): do the identifiers in each set form a proper partitioning, complete and disjoint, of some coherent aspect of the target system?

As well as locating difficulties of possible misinterpretation, omission or partial duplication, the inspector should also be alert to problems that can arise in program structure due to interlocks and guards being handled at an inappropriate level: again, problems that are avoided by double insulation, but needing human checks to ensure that the logical relationships do protect potential victims from danger by hazardous devices.

Throughout this work, the inspector must be aware not only of the program as it is now, but of how it might evolve as subsequent errors are detected and changes made. The persistence principle (see Section 11.1.3 above) is more difficult to apply with human checks than with automatic ones, so the responsibility of the checker is correspondingly greater.

Every facility provided by a package must be considered as potentially usable by any other package, not just by the packages that currently reference it. The human inspector must take account of the full generality expressed in the software, not relying on artificial limits of current use.

The means of partitioning must be verified with the same rigour as that required for the most critical software elements, considering particularly

● execution sequences and timing;

- data flow and the possibility of data corruption;
- hardware actions affecting the integrity (i.e. software functional partitioning).

The Design Description (Document 3 of DO-178A) covers:

(a)   [description of] the program structure (design trees) and partitioning;
(b)   data flow [description or diagram];
(c)   program control flow [description or diagram];
(d)   data and control interfaces between software partitions and between software and hardware;
(e)   algorithms;
(f)   timing specifications;
(g)   memory organisation and sizing [information];
(h)   program interrupts.

DO-178A permits this information to be contained in the program source listing – but apparently not as formal program text, presuming that the programming language could not express the program structure.

13.2.1 Verification of program design in Ada

By treating Ada as a Program Design Language (not just an Algorithm Design Language, which is what most styles known as PDLs really are), the process of verification of executable parts can be facilitated and regulated.

A program in Ada is partitioned into packages (statically) and tasks (dynamically). The program structure is determined by the context clauses on the compilation units, which covers item (a) of the Design Description Document mentioned above. The package specifications satisfy requirement (d). The package bodies satisfy requirements (c) and (e). Memory organisation is determined by the declaration of data objects in the compilation units, according to the conventions of the compiler; this covers part of requirement (g). The program interrupts are given as address representations on entries to task bodies, for requirement (h). So the additional information to be included beyond the Ada text is the data flow and resource usage (timing specifications and memory sizing).

Ada package specifications, subprogram specifications and task specifications define the syntax of the respective constituents, but not their semantics (and certainly not their performance). Additional notations for expressing the semantics have been mentioned in Section 9.2; the semantic specification is necessary for the V&V contractor to check the respective bodies and the coverage given by the sets of test data.

If timing is critical for safety, the relevant statements must be analysed in their fully executable form – including all subprograms called and machine instructions executed. This is clearly non-portable, but specific to a particular target environment. The performance of the control sequence involved must take account of all possible interruptions and higher priority tasks, as explained in Wirth's classic paper 'Towards a discipline of real-time programming' (Wirth, 1977). Testing can give an indication of performance (as explained in Section 14.5), but can give no assurance that performance criteria will be met in operational use.

An important style of verification is based on the discipline of proving programs correct, adjusted for practical use with Ada (i.e. by intelligent inspection). This style is suitable for support by software tools as has been explained in Section 12.3, but such tools must still be supplemented by natural intelligence.

13.2.2 Relating program design in Ada to functional specification

Within the overall program structure, there will be levels of abstraction, ranging from user-significant concepts through various intermediate levels to the fundamental machine level. The relationships between the Ada packages, through their context clauses, exposes the structure. (Suppose package A deals with entities at a certain level, and the package body of A uses other packages B and C; then B and C are at a lower level than A. Ada discourages circularity in such references.)

Thus there will be user-significant packages in the designed program, and more packages at lower levels. The top-level packages will contain data types and operations for entities that are meaningful to the user, and these should be *complete*. The V&V analysis, by intelligent inspection, can confirm that all the necessary attributes and operations are included.

The designs of the bodies for these operations show how they are planned to be implemented, and in particular what operations are assumed at a more basic level. The same analysis can be applied in turn to the next level of packages, but this time it is not the user-significant concepts that are relevant, but rather those chosen by the higher-level designer as the most appropriate. Their functionality is also likely to be expressed informally, and the V&V contractor should check for adequate coverage and completeness, as well as confirming proper version control and consistency.

13.2.3 Concept definition

During structural software design (Section 8.1), the application and infrastructure concepts were named and formulated as package specifications for appropriate data types. The designer should have explicitly stated the characteristics of the concepts with their intended relationships, together with the operations or manipulations that involve them. For each of these, the verification consists of demonstrating that the given program design will cause the intended relationships to be maintained, assuming correct lower-level design.

The concepts defined are in package specifications, for which there should be claims or assertions about the intended (time-independent) relationships:

(a)   type of each attribute;

(b)   relationships between characteristics of the same concept;
(c)   relationships between characteristics of distinct concepts;
(d)   change in relationship required for each operation.

The verification consists of demonstrating that the given program design achieves the intended relationships. Part of this assurance is given automatically by the rules of Ada (i.e. checked by compilation). The parts needing intelligent inspection, and the relationships concerned, are:

- data types 'not defined yet' (a);
- variant records for disjoint attributes (b);
- data structures for related concepts (c);
- the initialisation part of each package (b), (c);
- each subprogram involving the data type as an *in out* parameter (d);
- each subprogram involving the data type as an *out* parameter or function result (b), (d).

Note that the last two checks above require state assertions (see below).

There must be at least one subprogram in one of the last two categories for each defined data type. (This provides a completeness check: the package cannot be complete unless there is some way of delivering the values of variables of the data type.)

13.2.4 Guide for reviewing a subsystem design

Consider the information produced in the creative phase (see Chapter 8) in reverse order from its creation. If the designer takes part in the review, the role must be limited to showing the reviewer where the information is documented. All supplementary information, including interpretation of the documented information, must be treated as part of totality reviewed. The review must check for adequacy, necessity and sufficiency. A checklist of questions for the review is given in Table 13.1.

13.3 Code review

There is an argument (Tooby, 1986) that it is inappropriate to refer to text in Ada as 'code' since that word implies unintelligibility rather than precision, and Ada was designed with readability as one of the prime requirements. However, there is a common usage of the term which can be used: the formally defined text, which must be reviewed as part of the confirmation process. Verification of module implementation, as defined in DO-178A, confirms that the program written for each module properly expresses the design as specified, and also meets all 'coding' standards. It is intended to show that the program text which produces an error-free compilation or assembly is consistent with the applicable standards and software

Table 13.1 Guide for reviewing a subsystem design

1 *Quality*
Are all necessary target attributes included?
Does each attribute appear achievable?

2 *Faults*
Are all possible faults included?
Is the condition for each fault clearly stated?

3 *Data types*
Are all relevant kinds of data included?
Is each input and output sensible and necessary?
Is each kind of locally shared data necessary and sufficient?
Is each kind of data that is created in this subsystem clearly stated?

4 *Operations*
Are all relevant operations included?
Are all the identified kinds of data used?
Is there an operation to produce each kind of created data?
If there are several operations to produce data of the same kind, are they all necessary?
Are the failure modes of the operation clearly stated?
Is the condition for success of each such operation clearly stated?

design documents, and presumes that those documents have already been reviewed and approved.

Interpreting this principle for programs in Ada, we must show that each compilation unit produces an error-free compilation and is consistent with the applicable standards and software design documents. (The reference to other standards is still necessary with Ada, although to a lesser extent than with earlier languages.)

Much of the work that had to be done in Code Review in earlier languages (e.g. by code walkthroughs, with checklists of individual error types), is done automatically by an Ada compiler (particularly relating package bodies to their specifications, and checking for consistency of use of all entities with their declarations), so the review can focus on significant semantic issues, identifiable weaknesses or insecurities in the Ada program, checking that the executable parts of the program cause the required changes to the state of the system.

The automatic checks of an Ada program have been described in Chapter 12 above; the further checks for intelligent inspection of executable sequences of statements in Ada are described below, particularly for the program units relevant to safety: the device handlers, interlocks and guards.

13.3.1 Alias check

As was pointed out in Section 9.1.2, checking is distinctly more difficult if there is the possibility of the same variable having more than one name by which it may be accessed. The design rules of Section 9.1 prohibited aliasing in category 1 packages, and we consider them undesirable in category 2 packages. It is therefore necessary to check the category 1 and 2 packages for any aliasing in them. The relevant rules are given in Section 9.1.2. If there is aliasing in a category 2 package, an explicit comment should be made to draw attention to the fact during subsequent checking.

13.3.2 Verification of executable code

The lowest-level Ada modules are distinguished by the absence of any context clause from their package bodies. They may (depending on the program design) be subunits, again with no separate context clauses, but dependent on declarations in their parent.

The category 1 modules can be compiled independently by the V&V contractor, and (unless the modules include representation clauses) tested by using their package specifications to generate the black box test cases. This is particularly important in the case of critical modules related to safety or security. When the module contains a representation clause, logical testing can be carried out by compiling a modified version of the module with the representation clauses commented out.

For the critical modules, a rigorous check can only be applied if there is a claim or formal functional specification of the intended effects, which our design rules have required for category 1 packages. The functional specification of a subprogram would identify the following:

●   all constraints on inputs;
●   all constraints on outputs;
●   all relationships between inputs and outputs;
●   all invariants among values of variables accessed (which apply whenever the variables are not being manipulated internally).

Formal analysis of the Ada subprogram bodies can be carried out by the use of software tools, as explained in Chapter 12, or by intelligent inspection.

Intelligent inspection must check for any misuse of aliasing, and establish the state conditions at each semicolon between statements in each subprogram body. The rigorous check is satisfied if these state conditions:

(a)   on entry to the subprogram match the input constraints and invariants;
(b)   on exit from the subprogram match the output constraints and invariants;
(c)   before and after each statement, differ only in ways determined by the semantics of the statement;
(d)   before and after the whole subprogram, match the specified input–output relationship.

Some automatic tools are currently available to carry out such rigorous checking (e.g. SPADE, see Chapter 12), but the rules given here can be used as a guide for personal use if tools are not available, and the lower level of confidence is acceptable.

13.3.3 Rigorous analysis of executable parts

As has been explained in Section 9.2, the critical points in the executable parts of the program can be separated into certain well-defined 'check-points', and other 'break-points' at which it is necessary to provide the justification that the appropriate assertions are satisfied. The break-points are at the ends of sequences of normal statements, at which the effect of the statements is determined symbolically, where the sequence of execution may break from the textual order and continue from a defined check-point. The assertions to be checked at the break-points should include the pre-conditions, post-conditions and invariants of the specification, as explained in Section 12.4.2.

At the specific points in the executable parts of program units (which we called check-points in Section 9.2), the designer should have explicitly described the intended state of the system or subsystems concerned, in terms of the current concepts. At other distinct points (which we called break-points), the verifier must demonstrate that the given program design will cause the system or subsystem to reach that intended state, assuming that the initial state and the lower-level designs are correct. Each of these points is in effect a semicolon in the Ada sequence of statements (or the keyword marking the start or finish of the sequence).

The check-points, at which there should be assertions of the intended system state, are as follows:

(a)   at the beginning of each subprogram body or **accept** statement;
(b)   at the end of each subprogram body, package initialisation or **accept** statement;
(c)   at the beginning of each **loop**, before the loop statement starts;
(d)   at the end (after completion) of each loop;
(e)   at the end of each **if, case** or **select** statement;
(f)   at each declared **exception**;
(g)   at each «label».

All the assertions should be expressed in terms of concepts established in the context of the subprogram: all Ada identifiers used within them should be in scope. An operation that changes the state in some disjoint part of the system (e.g. an output operation, or a manipulation of a variable of a private type) may not be capable of being expressed in such terms. (The Euclid language recognises the possibility that an action might be 'unspeakable' in this sense, when the change in internal state cannot be directly observed outside the abstraction.) For example, pushing a new value onto a stack has no immediate visible effect outside the stack handler. Nevertheless, there is an effect on the future behaviour, which the assertion should express.

The break-points (at which the sequence of execution may break from the textual sequence of statement) are where the verification must be done; there is an obligation to check that the state reached at the break-point satisfies the assertion at the logically associated check-point. The break-points and corresponding checks (referring to the above list) are:

(i) after the last normal statement within each subprogram body, exception handler and package body initialisation part (check b);
(ii) after the last normal statement within each **accept** statement (check b);
(iii) after each **return** statement (check b);
(iv) after each **raise** statement for an external exception or an anonymous **raise** statement in an exception handler (check b);
(v) after the last normal statement of each **loop** body (check d);
(vi) after each **exit** statement (check d);
(vii) after each **raise** statement for an internal exception (check f);
(viii) after each **go to** statement (check g);
(ix) after each normal statement preceding a label (check g).

Note that this focusses the verification activity onto textual sequences of simple statements (assignment and procedure/entry calls) starting from one of the check-points (typically (a), (c) and (g)). Delay statements and abort statements do not affect the system state of the task containing them, so are not relevant to this analysis. The analysis of task interactions must be considered further, by intelligent inspection, bearing in mind the potential weaknesses that might remain, as explained in Section 13.5.

13.3.4 Ill-conditioning

A particular kind of fault in an algorithm that must be sought by intelligent inspection is a break in the continuity of numerical approximations. This has been described as *ill-conditioning* by Gordon (1990). When an algorithm is used to handle a function with mathematical singularities, the treatment at the boundaries of different approximations must be shown to be sufficiently continuous. For example, the function

$$\sin(x)/x$$

is continuous across $x = 0$, even though a direct interpretation would lead to a calculation of zero divided by zero. The algorithm has to be written so that for small values of x the function is evaluated by a power series such as

$$1 - x^2/3! + x^4/5! \ldots$$

The choice of the critical values of x at which the different formula is used depends on the trade-off with the precision needed and the accuracy of the power series used.

An *ill-conditioned* algorithm is one in which a mathematical singularity is not taken into account in such a way, so that the execution of the algorithm will behave wildly for some data values and possibly give severely inaccurate results or overflow. Test of such an algorithm will not necessarily catch the ill-conditioning, which typically is exposed for a small range of data values. Intelligent inspection must be used to identify the possibility of ill-conditioning, checking that the formula is continuously valid throughout the range of the variables concerned, so that suitable boundary-value test cases can be set up to check that the algorithm gives sufficient continuity of the numerical approximations.

13.4 Dependency analysis

The checks on dependency between units can be carried out manually or automatically: each package must be shown to be in a higher layer than all on which it depends, and the safety criticality factors must be propagated downwards.

To carry out the checks manually, start by recording the names of all the library units in the program. In most cases, the library units are package declarations; they may also be subprogram declarations, subprogram bodies, generic declarations or generic instantiations. For the library units that are declarations, there may be corresponding library unit bodies, which must also be taken into account. List (for each library unit and library unit body) the other units mentioned in the context clause at the head of the compilation unit. The process iterates over this list, progressively removing items until all have been treated.

First, mark each unit that has no context clause on either declaration or body as layer '0'; cross them off the list and cross out all occurrences of their names in the residual context clauses. This will reduce the number of residual dependencies among the compilation units, so that some now have all their dependencies crossed off. The units that now have all their listed units crossed out are layer '1'.

The same process identifies the units in successively higher layers: mark the units in each layer when their dependencies are crossed off.

If there is any circularity in the dependency relationships, there will be a stage when every unit is dependent on another: when no packages have all their units crossed off. Conversely, termination of the process confirms that the dependencies are partially ordered.

To complete the check, refer back to the source program, with a list showing the layer containing each package or other library unit. Check each compilation unit, to confirm that the layer it is in is higher than the layers containing all the units in its context clauses.

Finally, check the safety criticality factors of all the units, and confirm that the safety criticality factor (Risk Factor) of each unit is not higher than that of any of the units in its context clauses.

This check is illustrated in Figure 13.1, based on the 'brick wall' diagram of layered software structure of Section 7.4.2 and Table 7.2. Any critical module such as that labelled C in Figure 13.1 depends on other modules (probably software and

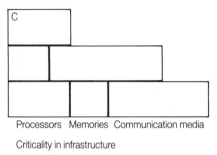

Criticality in infrastructure

Figure 13.1 Pervasive criticality

eventually hardware); all those modules of infrastructure are implicitly critical, and must be identified by the dependency analysis.

13.5 Residual weaknesses in design in Ada

The strength of a program design in Ada stems from the comprehensive consistency checks provided automatically by the compiler: the human designer is not allowed the luxury of deferring critical decisions or of following several incompatible paths at the same time. (This does not exclude the possibility of exploring several designs to discover the best: it simply ensures that they are *visibly* distinct.)

The residual weaknesses are those aspects of the design that are not automatically checked by a compiler that enforces the rules of the language. These aspects are those the V&V contractor will concentrate on – and be the more effective from having a clear focus of attention.

A comprehensive review of 'insecurities' in Ada has been carried out (Wichmann, 1989), discussed in Section 8.3. The specific features concerned for safety verification are (i) intercommunication between distinct computers; (ii) input–output, and the use of representation clauses, (iii) exception handling, (iv) task termination, and (v) mutual exclusion (and shared variables). We discuss each below.

13.5.1 Weaknesses at intercommunication

Since Ada deals with the program in a single computer, there is no check for consistency between programs in distinct computers. (Current research is addressing this problem, but there are no satisfactory solutions yet.) In particular, whenever messages are sent between computers, there is no automatic check of type-compatibility or of proper sequencing. Thus the whole issue of intercommunication protocols is beyond the scope of Ada checking, and must be investigated using other methods by the V&V contractor. Specifically, the protocol must be specified and checked. The program (i.e. relevant packages in Ada) can be checked as a correct implementation of the protocol, and the rules of Ada used to ensure that all communication is carried out by means of the operations in the proper package.

13.5.2 Weaknesses in input–output

Low-level packages that drive peripheral devices to carry out input–output operations will use representation clauses to reach specific addresses, with specific record structures, bit-maps and representation codes. While Ada allows these to be specified, there are no automatic checks on them, for consistency, completeness or repetition.

The information in representation clauses depends critically on properties of the target computer, particularly on details that computer manufacturers seem cautious about exposing, so the independent check by the V&V contractor will be particularly valuable.

Ada does not prevent several distinct driver tasks from using the same physical address (since the hardware may necessitate this), and a valuable V&V check is to look for repetitions among the addresses given throughout the whole program (not limited to individual packages). A simple tool could be developed to produce the information needed for this check.

A further check at the input–output level concerns safety: where output devices have the potential to be harmful, the package that allows the rest of the program to use them should include the safety interlocks. A raw device handler should always be encapsulated inside a protective package.

Similar principles would be applied when information has to be encrypted for transmission over insecure communication channels.

13.5.3 Weaknesses in exception handling

While Ada recognises that any action in a program might fail, the designer has the responsibility for deciding the level of abstraction at which the failure is handled, so that appropriate repair and recovery can be carried out.

The design expressed in Ada will identify the exceptions that are recognised at each level, listing them in the packages with the data types whose operations may be defective.

The basic Ada rule is that an exception is propagated upwards until it is handled: consequently a failure at some level where there is no handler amounts to failure at higher levels, up to that containing a handler. The usual nesting scope rules apply to the exception names as to all others, so exceptions can be raised deeply within packages in the context of the declarations.

A possible program error is therefore to have an exception declared, and handlers in some but not all of the subprograms declared at the same level. If the exception is raised in a deep subsidiary procedure that happens to have been called by a subprogram that does *not* have a handler, then propagation will continue upwards to the enclosing task or main program. This might occur for predefined exceptions such as STORAGE_ERROR. If dynamic storage allocation is used (even allocation of storage for variables in the body of a subprogram), the possibility of this exception must be considered. It is better, however, to design safety-related programs with static storage allocation to avoid the possibility altogether.

The V&V check should relate all exception handling to the relevant declaration and handlers (across packages, taking account of context clauses), and ensure that the protection is complete. In particular, there should be a check that the top level of every task and main program has a handler for **others** as a catch-all. The top-level exception handler is not so much a safety check as a warning mechanism. Without it, the task or main program could be abandoned silently.

13.5.4 Weaknesses in task termination

Ada tasks are allowed to abort one another and voluntarily to terminate themselves, as well as to reach a natural end. The program designer will have to make particular choices as to the use and disposition of tasks, with no automatic checks for coherence.

The scope rules ensure that only tasks within the same computer can abort one another, so one task is assured of survival. Tasks containing a **select terminate** construct have a clean end, but any execution of **abort** can leave the referenced task with variables in an inconsistent state, and any structure containing a task with **loop select** without **select terminate** will never reach completion. All these problems can be detected by the V&V contractor examining the task termination relationships in the program.

13.5.5 Weaknesses concerning mutual exclusion

Ada provides the mechanism for mutual exclusion (by selective entries in a passive task), but also permits re-entrant use of procedures in a package. It is the designer's responsibility to specify mutual exclusion (as opposed to re-entrance) when necessary; there are no compiler checks.

If the facilities of a package are only used by one task, there is no problem. The V&V contractor will therefore locate any use of a package by more than one task at a time, and investigate such usage carefully to determine whether the operations interact (e.g. by using shared variables). The same principle will be applied to any variables or procedures in the same declarative part as the task declarations, since these also may be improperly accessed without mutual exclusion.

13.5.6 Other Ada features

Certain other Ada features need particular attention because they may impact on the complete behaviour of the target computer, thus influencing the safety of the plant it controls. In addition to representation specifications (which are central to the present approach) and certain task interactions, these are the facilities introduced in particular sensitive packages, namely LOW_LEVEL_IO, SYSTEM, UNCHECKED_ CONVERSION, UNCHECKED_DEALLOCATION (or application-specific packages making use of their features), and of course MACHINE_CODE.

In addition, where timing is important, the software must be checked for adequate performance. As explained in Section 9.4, certain Ada constructs can lead to unbounded (i.e. context dependent) timing, as well as the general dependence on the speed of the target computer. The timing for control loops relevant to safety must be analysed in terms of data values and task interactions, taking account of any unbounded constructs that might be present.

Apart from the timing constraints, the structure and checks advocated in the present approach give sufficient protection to ensure that any of the above category 3 constructs **outside** the double insulation (of category 2 and category 1 constructs) will fail-safe rather than fail-to-danger. The proscribed features should not be used directly or indirectly *inside* the double insulation other than as advocated by the given design rules. In other words, keep the checks and controls simple.

13.6 Review of input–output

The residual source of danger in an Ada program written according to these guidelines arises from the software/hardware interaction. Ada cannot check that representation specifications are given correctly, or that they are restricted to specific parts of the program.

It is therefore necessary to carry out a comprehensive syntactic check of the complete program to ensure that the elements in each package satisfy the design rules. In particular, the checks must locate all representation specifications and analyse them in an integrated way. The program in Ada expresses the logical structure of the system, which has no significance for representations.

It is particularly important to verify those packages that handle application-specific devices. The general 'concept definition' guidelines given in Section 8.1 should allow the verifier to focus clearly on these; in addition, for safety-critical output devices the verifier must confirm that the designer has specified the following:

(a) the circumstances under which it is safe to operate the device;
(b) the safe closed-down condition of the device.

The most important check to apply is on the device address specifications. The address of each input–output device should be distinct and in a distinct package. This can be checked by preparing a list of all address specifications sorted by address, identifying the package and device name.

For each type of device there should also be a control and status word format, such as DEVICE_CONTROL in the sections on 'Structural Design and Device Control & Status'. The use of packages declaring these should be checked for congruity with the categorisation of the devices into device types.

The verification consists of checking the data structures and representations for control registers, and the operations on the device. The verifier should:

(i)   confirm bit-pattern interpretations in control registers, by reference to the hardware specification;

(ii) confirm addressses for access to control registers, by reference to the configuration specification;

(iii) check that device operations can only take place when it is safe to do so (by rule (a));

(iv) Check that safe close-down and safe operation are the only operations possible (rules (a) and (b)).

It should be always borne in mind that logic is not the prime influence on I–O device checking, because the attributes are highly specific and application-dependent, usually put together in rather *ad hoc* ways.

The verifier has to rely on the information provided about the device by its supplier, which must be cross-checked against information from other sources, e.g. tests carried out on the actual device (as discussed in Chapter 14).

14

Testing

NOTWITHSTANDING ALL THE CHECKS of the software provided by automata and intelligent inspectors (accompanied by the use of formal methods where inferences can be formally derived from the program text), testing is essential to produce evidence that the software causes the target computers and plant to behave as intended. The real world of the plant is not formal, and the input–output devices perform operations whose formal descriptions must be checked. This chapter addresses two problems: how an Ada program should be tested in general, and what special steps should be taken for safety-related systems. (Perhaps the more general matters could have been left out, but given the present dearth of experience on testing Ada programs for embedded-computer systems, it was decided that the material would be useful to readers.)

Tests exercise the binary code and the hardware that executes it, thus confirming the code generated by the Ada compiler, the run-time system and the underlying computer and its peripherals. These dynamic checks complement the static semantic analyses described in the preceding chapters. Testing has to cover both the algorithms and the data representations. Traditional analyses have concentrated on testing the algorithms, without explicit attention to the mappings between abstract data and their representations. Data typing is a central concept in Ada, and the adequacy of the mapping (e.g. variants for compound types, range for scalar types, precision for numerical types, size for dynamic types) must be tested.

The fault incidence rate depends fundamentally on three separate influences: the source language (which limits the faults that can be articulated); the checking strategy (which determines the probability of residual defects); and the operational utilisation of the system (since an error will show when the input data stimulate a residual fault in the program that was not detected by previous testing or operational use). The intrinsic limitations of testing are discussed in Section 14.1, with notes on various testing strategies. Fault seeding is useful at the end of conventional testing to estimate the number of errors remaining undetected, but it cannot relate them to operational utilisation. Mutation testing is valuable for estimating the effectiveness of test data as representative of the input data space. Random data testing has the advantage that different samples from the data space avoid any bias by the tester about operational use, and give rarely occurring data equal probabilities of being tested. Different information can be inferred from deterministic and probabilistic testing. By analysing the tests with respect to the requirements at each level of design (i.e. performing a requirements coverage analysis), we can relate each test case to the software requirements it confirms (individually and in combinations), and thus identify which test cases are essential to demonstrate that the software adequately complies with the requirements.

Safety is a negative property – so testing can confirm the presence of interlocks and guards, but cannot confirm the absence of danger. A suitable module testing strategy is to plan tests for all the operations which each device is capable of performing (the potentially dangerous ones as well as the safe ones) and all the modes of operation available (typically a normal mode and a maintenance mode, when external guards are used to keep victims out of danger). Testing must cover the individual program units that drive each input–output device related to safety (and the others as well, for full confidence in the program), particularly the combinations that give interlocked protection.

DO-178A (see Appendix C) gives comprehensive guidance on the tests that are needed, the testing documentation that should be recorded, and the associated procedures, depending on the software Risk Factor. Applying the principles of DO-178A to Ada programs, we discuss module tests (Section 14.2) for compilation units (usually packages), and the relationship between software components and their operational environment (Section 14.3). Module integration tests (Section 14.4) check complete coherent sets of software components, and hardware/software integration tests (Section 14.5) treat an Ada program in an environment which contains the plant peripherals (with control loops and replicated devices), including the performance of the system controlled by the software (as this can only be determined by testing, to confirm (or amend) what could only be estimated in the design. Testing documentation (Section 14.6) should be kept permanently (under configuration control), and we summarise the requirements. The test plans, procedures, results and all problem reports from the testing process and the corrective actions must be tracked for Risk Factors 1 and 2. An audit must be performed to assess the completion of these tasks for Risk Factor 1 software.

14.1 Limitations of software testing

Testing can never prove that software is correct. Instead, it gives us confidence in the software tested by a double negative process: we try diligently to find faults, and (hopefully) fail to discover any. The confidence is only justified if the search is thorough. A fault that causes problems five days or five years later was there all the time: only our tests were not sufficiently thorough to find it.

The fault incidence rate depends significantly on the operational utilisation of the system, not only on the distribution of defects, since an error will show when the input data stimulated a residual fault in the program that was not detected by previous testing or operational use.

14.1.1 Sampling and exhaustive testing

Exhaustive testing (of all possible values or bit-patterns) is not feasible with most software – sampling is necessary. But this is different from sampling for an opinion poll: we are not trying to establish the 'typical' situation, but to examine the most extreme possibilities that might arise. The theory of sampling for testing is based on continuity hypotheses: the test process assumes (implicitly, if not explicitly) that each test case is representative of a (possibly infinite) set of neighbouring cases. Imagine the multi-dimensional space of all the possible input data (including any relevant external variables) to the software under test. Each test case corresponds to a point in this space. The sampling assumes that in the neighbourhood of each such point there is a region such that all points in the region pass or fail the test together. In other words, the assumption is that any underlying error in the software will affect cases in a contiguous region of the data-space, and that the program will work correctly for data in similar contiguous regions. Successful sampling depends on the insight of the tester in knowing what kinds of error can occur, and how the software partitions the data-space.

The major problem with sampling is judging the extent of sampling needed to provide adequate confidence. This is not the same as the number of tests or the number of test cases. (Ten tests of the same thing give no additional information for software; ten test cases may span a certain region of the data-space, another ten may be in the same region and thus give no additional information.) The guidance for testing is a combination of theoretical analysis, knowledge of programming failure modes, and pragmatic experience.

It is desirable that test data be prepared by people who are not involved in the design, to avoid unintentional oversight of possibilities. This also acts as a pressure to ensure that the design is described sufficiently well for another person to use it. However, there is a practical difficulty with independent test preparation: the need to understand the partitioning of the data-space. The kinds of error that can occur, and hence the partitioning of the data-space, depend on the way the program has been designed (and the skill of the programmer). The programmer both understands this structure better than anyone else, and is also predisposed to turn a blind eye to its defects.

Where the importance of testing justifies the effort, the solution is to have two people prepare different tests: one using the specification (normally not the programmer) and the other using the design (normally the programmer). The different tests produced from the two viewpoints are explained in the following two sections.

14.1.2 Requirements-based (black box) testing

Black box testing is simplest. This treats the software under test as completely indivisible, defined only by its specification and claim. The test cases and the number of cases to be tried are derived entirely from the Ada package (or subprogram) specification, by considering the structure of the specification as the criterion for partitioning the data space. The tests can be prepared before the body of the package has been written. Thus for black box testing:

1. Analyse the specification to identify all the input data (variables, parameters, etc.) with their types.
2. Analyse the specification to partition the data-space *as much as* the specification permits.
3. Take the number of partitions as the number of test cases.
4. Invent one test data set (of all input data items) for each partition.
5. Analyse the specification to determine what the result should be (or what post-condition it should satisfy) for each test data set.

(All of the above can be done in parallel with the design.)

6. Test the software with each test data set.
7. Compare the results.
8. Preserve the test data sets as a basis for future use in regression testing.

The test data sets for step 4 above may be chosen arbitrarily, by intelligent inspection in simple cases, but a random or pseudo-random selection is acceptable (which must of course be frozen for each particular test case so that it can be repeated). Random data testing has the advantage that different samples from the data space avoid any bias by the tester about operational use, and give rarely-occurring data equal probabilities of being tested.

Rather than using test data sets *within* each partition, some authors recommend boundary testing, in which the test data are deliberately chosen to be at the edges of each region rather than inside it. This complicates the analysis and requires more tests (since there are more boundaries than regions), but addresses the issues of ill-conditioning and wrong boundary association (which are well-known kinds of error to arise).

The process of preparing the test data and expected test results (rather than carrying out the actual test) indicates any ill-conditioning in the algorithm, where the behaviour near a boundary changes dramatically (e.g the tan function across the value $\pi/2$). Mutation testing (explained in Section 14.5 below) is another way of detecting boundary errors.

Black box testing gives confidence not only in the software but in the specification from which it was derived: the above analysis (which is quite different from that carried out by the designer) exposes any weaknesses or ambiguities in the specification itself. This should normally be the minimum level of testing applied to any software, but is rarely sufficient. (Imagine the risk of a fault remaining in the software if one of the above regions of the data space has not been tested.)

14.1.3 Structure-based (white box or glass box) testing

White box testing, or program (algorithm) structure testing, is more thorough. This takes account of the structure of the algorithm under test, typically thinking of it as a directed graph or flow-chart where nodes correspond to individual actions, and arcs correspond to the order in which they are performed. An action may be of arbitrary complexity (tested separately). A path is a contiguous sequence of arcs and its length is the number of arcs in the sequence. The flow graph may contain loops, so there may be paths of infinite length. There are several degrees of white box testing, depending on the lengths of paths in the flow graph. The coverage of a test set may be expressed as a Test Exploration Ratio, being the proportion of paths of the particular length that are actually covered in the tests. TERn refers to paths of length n arcs. TERn = 1 means that all paths of length n are tested. (If a program contains paths that cannot be executed for any possible data, the structure of the program should be reconsidered.)

Node-testing means testing all nodes in the graph, in other words all individual actions (basic blocks, sequences of non-control statements). It amounts to testing all paths of length 0, so TER0 = 1. The test data sets are organized to test each action at least once. One test data set may touch several nodes, so the number of test cases is roughly the number of nodes divided by the minimum length of the flow graph.

Arc-testing means testing all paths of length one, in other words all sequences from one node to another. The number of test cases needed to achieve TER1 = 1 is the width of the flow graph. This needs roughly the same number of test cases as for TER0, but more careful analysis to prepare suitable data. It is distinctly more powerful than node-testing.

Testing paths of length 2 is not worthwhile, but testing paths of length 3 (TER3 = 1 if all such paths are tested) has been found in practice to expose significant errors in the design of loops. For example, this covers the case when a loop body is executed, repeated, and the exit from the loop is taken to the following segment.

An alternative way of covering paths is by *basis path testing*. The *basis* of a flow-chart is a minimal set of finite paths from start to finish such that all arcs are included in the set. The set of paths in the basis has the following properties (McCabe, 1982): (a) no one path in the set can be duplicated by a linear combination using only the other paths in the set; and (b) all paths through the graph can be represented as a linear combination of the paths in the set. The number of paths in the basis can be calculated from the structure of the flow-chart. For basis testing we make a test case for each path in the basis. (Walsh, 1979, has shown that testing paths extra to the basis set is not as productive and efficient for locating errors.) The procedure is very similar to that for black box testing:

1.   Analyse the designed algorithm to establish the flow-graph.
2.   Analyse the flow-graph to determine the basis.
3.   Take the number of paths in the basis as the number of test cases.
4.   Invent one test data set for each path in the basis.

5.   Analyse the specification to determine what the result should be (or what post-condition it should satisfy) for each test data set.
6.   Test the software with each test data set.
7.   Compare the results.
8.   Preserve the test data sets for future use, in regression testing.

White box testing should be planned for each software unit when it has been designed, at least to the level of arc testing (TER1 = 1), but if there is any need for greater confidence, by basis testing or to a high value of TER3. The planned tests should be carried out when the body of the unit has been implemented, and all its dependent units have been adequately tested.

This intensity of testing is difficult in general, but less so in practice for safety-related systems if design rules are used to keep the structures simple. For example, with the structures we have introduced in Part II, the individual packages UNSAFE_DEVICE and SENSOR should be tested for *all paths* from beginning to end. They should contain no loops, so there should be no question of an impossibly large or infinite number of paths. The subprograms in each package should be tested separately, each with all values of enumeration-valued parameters. No compromise should be needed for fully comprehensive unit testing.

14.1.4 Mutation testing

Mutation testing is valuable for estimating the effectiveness of test data as representative of the input data space. It is even more thorough, being based on analysing the test data set as well as the program under test, to discover whether the tests in the set are capable of detecting particular variations in the program. It can be thought of as a special case of the 'bug-insertion' technique.

In practice, most programmers are trying to produce the right program, and compilers can detect many clerical and superficial faults (particularly with a high-level programming language such as Ada). Mutation testing looks for the errors that can easily be made but not detected by a compiler, and asks whether the test data set will detect them. Examples have already been mentioned in Section 12.2, such as substitution of + for −, or of < for >: single character changes that are syntactically equivalent. Single character insertions or deletions are also important, particularly >= exchanged for >, etc. (This is one reason why identifiers should not differ by a single character, although the restriction on operator symbols for overloaded functions conflicts with this ideal.)

In mutation testing, the source text of the program is changed by one of the above substitutions and then executed using the original test data set. The results are compared with the results obtained with the original program. If they are the same the mutation is not distinguished by the test data set, and either the change is insignificant (which suggests a simplification of the program design) or the test data set is deficient (which suggests that additional cases are needed to test the program comprehensively).

14.1.5 Regression testing

Software produced by integrating several units is susceptible to different kinds of error: misuse of facilities as versions are developed. When a major unit depends on one or more minor units, at least the black box test data for the major unit should be applied to recheck it when any minor unit is changed. This is the case when an Ada package body has a context clause. The rules of Ada handle the situation when the specification of a minor unit is changed, but the tests should be repeated after a minor body has been changed, even if the specification is the same. Before major milestones, the white box tests should all be reapplied.

The history of success or failure with the major unit tests shows how well the changes to the minor units are stabilising. In general, a small number of faults in non-critical parts of the software are often deemed acceptable in order to release the program for further integration as part of an even larger unit. The project manager must exercise judgement on the relative risks of the residual errors and further delay to eliminate them. When the software seems to be stable, it can be used elsewhere, while further investigation of the residual errors continues and eventually leads to authorised changes.

Analysing the number of residual errors that are detected, as a function of version number, shows the degree of stability of the software being developed, giving an estimate of the number of yet-to-be-detected faults. Fault seeding (for example by mutation testing) may be used at the end of conventional testing to estimate the number of errors remaining undetected, but it cannot relate them to operational utilisation.

14.2 Module testing

Module tests show that each module performs its intended functions and only those. We have introduced the idea of a *claim* to express what the program unit is intended to be or do, and discussed its use in static semantic analysis. Now we use it as the reference for dynamic testing. Every module must be tested, from the lowest device driver to the main procedure that initiates all the rest.

The tests for an individual module comprise logic tests and computation tests; they confirm the structural and functional correctness of the design as implemented in the module. Each subprogram (except those at the lowest level) may call on other subprograms to carry out individual actions. At first, each module is considered individually, presuming that all its constituent actions work as they are intended. This assumption is investigated by module integration testing, taking progressively larger combinations. At any stage during testing, it may become apparent that the test set is deficient, and that additional test cases are needed to cover some aspect of the software. Coverage analysis is intended to ensure that the test cases are sufficiently comprehensive.

14.2.1 Computation tests

The computation testing confirms the adequacy of representations, particularly numerical accuracy (linearity, resolution, etc.) of real types (fixed and floating point) in numerical algorithms, by showing correct behaviour (according to the claim) with the following:

- data within bounds;
- data out of bounds (which should raise an exception);
- data on boundary values;
- data at discontinuities in the algorithm (i.e. at critical values in **if** or **case** statements).

For an Ada package, computation testing can mainly be treated as 'black box' testing, derived from the software requirements after the package specification and claim are formulated during the design process. At this stage, the tests are formulated to confirm the above properties. The fourth of the above categories checks the software against ill-conditioning: ensuring smooth transitions across boundaries in data-space. Each requirement must have an associated test or tests.

14.2.2 Logic tests

In contrast, logic testing implies 'white box' analysis of each constituent subprogram, deriving tests from the software design itself. Module logic testing seeks to demonstrate the correct implementation of the claimed behaviour and to confirm the absence of unintended behaviour, including the following:

- loop termination (and maintenance of loop invariants);
- decision logic (proper combinations of the intended variables);
- data input (individually and in combinations);
- sensor functionality detection (implying input data validity).

These tests augment the requirements-based tests, checking implied features and providing protection from unintended functions in the software (which may exist, even though it passes all its requirements-based tests). These tests must be exercised to a degree commensurate with the risk factor.

14.2.3 Module integration tests

Further tests for modules, described in DO-178A under module integration tests, with notes in interpretation for Ada with the present design rules are as follows:

- linkage between modules: data and control flow (to confirm parameter modes **in, out** and **in out**); order, type and number of arguments in subprogram calls (comprehensively checked by the compiler with Ada); absence of spurious outputs from undesired changes to global data (defensive programming: checks of exception handling);

● timing behaviour (dependency on underlying layers);

● sequences of events including initialisation and changes to control flags and variables (particularly operational mode dependencies);

● correct resumption of interrupted sequences, when one of the modules being integrated is an interrupt handler (i.e Category 1 package, containing task with interrupt entry);

● separation of functions of different criticality categories (by inspection and dependency analysis).

In addition to these, tests specific to Ada should concentrate on constraint checking at subprogram calls, exception handling and generic instantiations.

To test an Ada package, it is necessary to set up a test-harness consisting of a main program with calls to the subprograms in the package and manipulations of any visible variables. A software tool exists to do this automatically, based on the Ada package specification. This can also drive the subprograms in the package from previously generated data, and compare the results with expected values. In principle it would be possible to generate pseudo-random data values (particularly for enumerated types), but without a formalism to express the intended semantics of the subprograms, it must be left to the human engineer to define what results are to be expected.

14.2.4 Dummy modules

When a module under test depends on other packages, there is a problem over the order of integration (see Section 14.4 below). Ideally, all the subsidiary modules should be tested before the module that depends on them. However, sometimes there will have been delays in a subsidiary, and it is urgent to start testing a higher-level module. One technique is to use a dummy module, with the same specification but a temporary substitute body delivering credible results for a limited set of data (i.e the data values with which it is called in the module under test). If this technique is used, it is important to keep all the module tests, and apply them again after the subsidiary module has been properly incorporated in place of the temporary version.

14.2.5 Test coverage analysis

Test definitions and coverage analyses (derived from the software development documents) are required by DO-178A for critical and essential functions. This means checking the test cases to discover which aspects of the requirements or software structure are confirmed by successful execution of each test.

● Requirements coverage analysis means identifying which test cases are asserted to demonstrate *adequate compliance with* each (*software*) *requirement*. (The analysis shows if any requirement is not covered by a test case.)

- Structural coverage analysis means identifying which test cases are asserted to demonstrate *execution* of each element of the software, which we interpret as sequence of statements in Ada. (The analysis shows if any software element is not covered by a test case.)

These are needed for software of Risk Factors 1 and 2.

14.3 Components and environments

The purpose of the scheme is to separate the testing of a system into (a) the testing of its components and (b) the testing of the environment within which the components are executed. When a system is intended to be extensible, its environment must be capable of containing components which do not at first exist. There must be a means of ensuring that when new components are introduced, the system will exhibit only the faults of those components. Applying this principle to the systems with the initial components that *do* exist, we see the point of the separation. By eliminating the testing of the components, we concentrate on testing the environment, and thus greatly reduce (and make finite) the amount of system testing needed.

14.3.1 Service interfaces

The components fit into the environment by making use of standard interfaces. The environment provides services that can be requested through these interfaces, analogous to the services provided in a communication system by the protocol handlers. (The analogy is particularly apt, because a communication system has to be designed to be resistant to faults, and part of the process of testing a protocol has to be the investigation of its behaviour under fault conditions. In the same way, a software system may be faulty: the testing of the environment must investigate the behaviour of the system under fault conditions, to ensure that any fault is handled properly, but otherwise it must ignore faults in the component and concentrate on the services provided by the environment.)

14.3.2 Software partitioning

Partitioning of software is important to ensure that no action of one function can cause another to fail. The verification process to assure this is significantly easier when the software is written in Ada, but still depends on the hardware supporting the execution of the software. If a task runs amok, it must not imperil the behaviour of any other task in the same processor. The action needed to assure safety in such a situation depends on the task concerned: in most cases, further action by the control system must be limited to a controlled shut-down of the plant, followed by a controlled restart. It would not be adequate simply to restart the software.

A method of assurance of effective partitioning is described by Helps (1986), based on reports and deductions from full software emulations which incorporate memory access monitoring. Accesses to all relevant memory bytes are recorded in order to assess the extent of the coverage provided by each test, and to show whether any unplanned access has been made to other parts of the memory. Two sets of tests are performed: one to cover each module and one to cover each process (i.e. Ada task). Since the tests cover all the requirements and structure of the software, the observation of no unintended access to instructions or data outside the unit under test confirms effective partitioning of the software.

By analysing the types of error which could remain undetected with this testing, Helps shows that partitioning breaches are highly unlikely, and thus justifies the assured inter-function software partitioning for safety-critical functions.

This technique was used with a non-modular programming language (i.e. pre-Ada software technology), and led Helps to conclude that it is easier to ensure the absence of undesirable functions in software than the presence of desirable ones. This observation is less applicable to software written in Ada, where partitioning is achieved by visibility constraints checked at compile time. However, Helps' technique bypasses any dependence on the correctness of the code-generator and link-loader, since it works directly on the executing binary code.

14.4 Software integration

It is important to separate the testing of *combinations* of modules from that of individual modules, particularly for modules that depend on other modules (as is the general case). If module A depends on modules X and Y, we must be able to distinguish defects in A from defects in the linkage between A and its subordinates. This requires careful planning, as there will be no way of executing A without something to fill the positions of X and Y. The way round the problem is to use subsidiary modules only in situations that have already been tested individually when first testing the senior module, before testing A generally. The module test for A is thus the integration test for A, X and Y. The essence of software integration is getting the modules together in an orderly way for progressive testing that permits discrimination between the various kinds of possible error.

In DO-178A, such tests are treated as a distinct category, but in practice (and in particular with programs in Ada), they are no different from other tests of a module when it happens to call others for some service. We have therefore described the topics to be considered in Section 14.2.3 above. However, the integration testing may expose some deficiencies in the original module test set, which we mention below.

14.4.1 Order of integration

Software integration calls for control of the order of integration of modules to form the complete program, with testing to confirm that the combinations have their intended properties. The integration and testing plan for the project must define the preferred order of combining modules (and any contingency plans for variations).

Software integration tests confirm interfaces and data accesses between modules. Ada ensures that interfaces are type-compatible and data accesses satisfy the visibility rules, which DO-178A expects to be covered by these tests. In an Ada program, integration testing concentrates on dependent library units and subunits.

14.4.2 Combining library units

In the case of dependent library units, we have the body of one package dependent on the specification of another, say:

```
package X is
    ——
end X;

with X;
package body A is
    ——
end A;
```

showing that A depends on X. (The specification of A may be compiled before or after that of X; and the body of X before or after that of A. These are the ordinary rules of Ada.) Here X must be tested first, then partial tests of A (using tested cases of X), and finally the full integration tests to show that A satisfies its claim.

14.4.3 Integrating subunits

In the case of subunits, the integration plan has to combine module testing with combination testing. Suppose a parent module P has a subunit (child) C. The body of P includes the specification of C, with a stub:

```
package body P is
    ——
    procedure C is separate;
    ——
end P;
```

and this must be written and compiled before the proper body of C:

```
separate (P)
procedure C is
    ——
end C;
```

where the declarations in P ahead of the specification of C are visible to it (and similarly for each subunit). As far as C is concerned, such declarations are 'global'. Note that any executable part of P has to follow the stubs, and is always invisible to the subunits. Only when all have been compiled can the combination be linked for testing (under a test harness for P). The module tests must then be arranged to test C individually (in the context defined in P), then the executable part of P *using cases of C that have already been tested and shown to be satisfactory*. Only then should the integration tests of P be carried out to show that it satisfies its claim.

14.4.4 Safety-critical units

As package bodies are completed, they are integrated into the program according to the normal rules of Ada. Special attention has to be given to the safety-critical parts, which we now explain.

The critical packages (handlers for safety-related devices) cannot be fully tested before integration in the target computer environment, which is discussed in the next section. For software integration, therefore, it may be appropriate to use temporary substitutes for them.

The category 2 packages, which ensure proper isolation of the safety-critical parts, are the focus of attention in software integration. Tests must be prepared to explore them extensively in order to ensure that their enforcement of isolation is effective.

The ordinary packages (category 3) must then be checked in combination with the category 2 packages, as they will include the calls for facilities that must be guarded by the isolation enforcers.

14.4.5 Deficiencies in the test set

Whenever a fault is found during the later stages of testing – module integration, software–hardware integration, or evolution during operational use – it must be treated as a potential indicator of a deficiency in the module tests, as well as indicating a software error to be corrected. Indeed, it is advisable to start the fault investigation by locating the test(s) that should have detected the situation at the earlier stages of testing, and so locate which module needs to be corrected. The first constructive action should be to formulate test(s) to detect the newly discovered situation, and apply these to the existing software for diagnostic purposes. (This strategy operates on the principle that the test set for the module is then known to have been defective; we put that defect right, then perform the module development with the test set as now amended.)

14.5 System integration

The planning of system integration is a significant aspect of software development, as has been explained in Chapter 7. A progressive sequence of hardware–software integration should be planned, with associated testing to ensure that the right software is installed and operates properly within its target hardware environment.

The emphasis of this book is that safety in not a property of software alone, but depends ultimately on the plant which is controlled by the target computers executing the software. Consequently, the system integration, when the software is exercised in the actual context of the plant, is a critical stage for safety assessment.

The integration of hardware and software must be planned to cover the relationship between the software S, the target computers T and all the plant sensors and effectors U. The checks must cover all constituents individually and in combination, including timing, memory, input–output and any interrupts. This analysis shows us that there are two functional aspects to be covered by the tests: the devices and the plant environment. In addition, system integration is the stage at which performance can be confirmed: the adequacy of the processor speed, memory size and communication bandwidths for the plant environment.

14.5.1 Device testing

Tests must verify that the hardware–software integration is correct, since this cannot be done by formal analysis. The test cases are created by considering what kinds of error in the software and in the plant are detectable, where behaviour could be recognised to be incorrect or undesired.

The test cases for these situations must be prepared in parallel with the physical software creation (Chapter 9) on the basis of the plant properties, using FMEA to identify all kinds of hardware error, transients or failure modes. They must also be aware of the risk of compiler-errors in low-level programming. The low-level features in Ada are virtually unchecked by the official compiler validation tests, which means that there is a high risk of bugs in this part of a compiler. (According to Wichmann, 1990, recent tests by the Software Engineering Institute in Pittsburgh have revealed that virtually no Ada compiler could handle some quite simple tests on pograms using UNCHECKED_CONVERSION.) The compiler must be treated as an 'unreliable tool' (Section 7.7) in this context.

In order to perform tests comprehensively, additional software is needed to control and monitor the activities. This must be developed as part of the physical design of the system, to give access to the control and data for sensors, effectors and interlock states.

In order to test for faults in the hardware–software interfaces (and confirm their specifications by representation clauses in the Ada program), each individual bit or field in the sense/control registers must be covered, as well as any known interactions. As was pointed out in Chapter 10, manufacturers' information about device specifics must be treated with scepticism, as it is not unknown for such information to be incorrect (or equivalently, for the equipment to be incorrect with regard to the manufacturer's specification). The deficiencies can not be detected by software, and any bits in the interface registers that interact in undocumented ways constitute a residual danger which must be explicitly investigated.

The devices may be connected to the computers as individual peripherals, but more often they will be multiplexed, with some register to select which is concerned on each operation. Because of the risk of faulty wiring connections between the target computer and the devices in the plant when there are replicated devices, tests must be carried out to confirm that each is properly identified. For sensors, it is likely that inputs from several will be needed to define the plant state (to guard against failure of an individual sensor, as explained in Section 10.4). For effectors, multiplexing is an even more significant feature to be tested, as their actions will be at different positions in the plant.

Where devices can stimulate the target computers by sending interrupts, the Ada program to handle each interrupt may be written as a task with the entry address specified in a representation clause (in a category 1 package, according to Sections 8.2 and 9.1). Such packages should therefore have been extensively checked by formal analysis and intelligent inspection before testing starts.

Using the analyses of safety and danger (Chapter 6) to identify all the devices and interactions, tests need to be carried out for all dangerous effectors (by checking out each device both raw and with the relevant interlock), and for all protective sensors (by checking out each device raw and with all interlocks which depend on that sensor). The state of the system (as dangerous or safe to carry out a particular action) must be confirmed for the critical situations identified in the analysis.

The software developed for the operational system will normally include built-in tests to detect faults and failures (permanent or transient), with appropriate software to handle recovery when required, in order to give the necessary resilience (Section 10.8). Separate tests must be carried out with artificially induced failures in the hardware, to ensure that the recovery is satisfactory. (One of the reasons against using Ada exceptions in safety-related software is distrust of the recovery actions: only by deliberate tests can these parts of the program be exercised.)

The first comprehensive check on software/hardware interaction occurs when the software S is loaded into the target computer T and made to control the plant U in laboratory conditions (i.e. not trusting that the interlocks work). This can be done for individual packages (with suitable test-beds) but must eventually be done again for the complete program.

The source of danger to look for at this stage is a mistake in the representation specifications for device control and status. For example, if a potentially dangerous device can be commanded to go up or down using

```
type DEVICE_CONTROL is (UP, DOWN);
```

with the representation specification

```
for DEVICE_CONTROL use
    (UP => 1, DOWN => 2);
```

instead of

```
for DEVICE_CONTROL use
    (UP => 0, DOWN => 1);
```

this will not be detected until the program is running with the actual device. It is most important to test the device control and status for the sensors that are used in the interlocks, as well as for the effectors. Manufacturers sometimes make omissions or mistakes in the specifications of hardware that they supply, particularly for interfaces, so these checks must be carried out comprehensively.

Thus a sketch test plan for hardware/software integration would cover the following, first in MAINTENANCE mode,

- for each effector: for each command: confirm operation;
- for each sensor: for each state: display the state;

then in NORMAL mode,

- for each sensor: for each state: display SAFE_TO_OPERATE;
- for each effector: for each command: confirm safety or DANGER_AVERTED.

This would precede (and possibly be part of) normal acceptance testing.

As explained in Sections 10.7.4 and 10.7.5, tests must be carried out to show that the system can properly handle start-up, input power transients and transient input loads, and deal with emergency shut-down. Again, the abnormal situations must be artificially induced for the purpose of testing. Tests are needed to confirm that operational mode transitions never lead to unidentified, undefined or unsafe conditions (e.g. from volatile memory). The kinds of situation to be tested include the following:

- power switch-on;
- power restoration following a failure;
- brief interruption and resumption of power supply;
- switching between manual and automatic control modes (if provided).

In all cases, tests must confirm that the program can only be entered at a point where it is safe to do so, and that the initialisation activity includes any necessary resetting of the system parameters.

14.5.2 Plant environment testing

This is essentially independent of the use of Ada for the software. DO-178A recommends a series of tests to verify that the plant behaviour determined by the software complies with the requirements in the target environment. These consist of the following:

- real-time simulation or testing (driving the integrated plant in real time);
- behaviour of feedback loops (control loop tests);
- resolution of contention for resources, e.g. bus access;

- monitoring to measure the process utilisation;
- introduction of design limit conditions;
- introduction of selected hardware failures.

The last two above test safety-related devices in their operational context, repeating some of the tests carried out on them in isolation. The automatic monitored or self-checking of the safety system must also be checked, to ensure proper functioning of all safety critical functions. The tests must be caried out in all operational states and transitions between states.

System validation tests (described in DO-178A as the final step in the software development cycle: Block V7) ensure that the system behaves as expected during all operational modes, including (deliberately induced) failure modes. Tests must exercise all feedback loops involving each item of safety-critial equipment in the plant, particularly when any equipment is replicated.

A general safety check should be carried out at this time, reviewing all the sources of danger identified in the requirements (as amended by the design work), and confirming the effectiveness of all interlocks associated with them.

14.5.3 Performance issues

No current method of software development addresses the problems of storage and timing constraints, or of traffic capacity in communication. This is beyond the realm of software and high-level languages (as can be recognised by considering different compilations of the same program on different computers). The designer has always to bear the performance in mind, but there is no formal way of expressing what is desired or intended, and certainly no way of ensuring that a given performance target can be achieved automatically by a given compiler and target computer. The features of Ada relevant to this have been identified in Section 9.4 and discussed in Section 13.5. The integration of the software with the hardware of the target computer is of central importance in performance testing.

Packages dealing with time-sensitive control loops will have been identified (Section 9.4). There will be execution time constraints on the performance of their executable parts, which must be checked by testing the modules concerned individually and in groups with operational data.

Each package body will require space for its code and local variables (possibly a variable amount if dynamic storage allocation is used). Each procedure body will require time for its execution, depending on the values of its parameters and non-local variables. The designer will have recorded the intended values and dependencies between these resource allocations; the V&V contractor must provide an independent check that the allocations are both internally consistent and reasonable for the state of the art in programming, compiler technology and the hardware to be used.

These issues may be investigated initially by using models of the target system, but eventually the software must be tested in an appropriate operating environment.

A representative target computer may be used first in a representative plant (perhaps simulated), but final acceptance tests must be carried out on the real target in the real plant.

14.6 Checklists for test plan review

Test plans will be prepared in association with the program design, and their coverage must be checked by intelligent inspection at key stages in the development. As well as general functionality criteria, the test plans must be checked for compatibility with the safety assertions that are identified as a result of the safety analysis of the requirements (Chapter 5). These fall into two broad groups: positive and negative.

Each positive assertion must be checked by an identified test, with a cross-reference to link the test with the safety assertion.

Each negative assertion must be confirmed by an analysis of the situations that the assertion claims will not happen, and an argument from the structure of the program in support of the assertion.

14.6.1 Checks at code review

The Ada text of each module must be reviewed after successful compilation of the package body, taking account of its safety category. The compiler will have applied many consistency checks; supplementary checks must confirm that the appropriate design rules have been applied. Formal checks are applicable at this stage, to confirm that all variables are defined before they are used, and that the intended relationships are achieved by the executable statements (for example by the analytical walkthrough procedure).

The safety assertions may be absolute (i.e. pertain to the correctness of the software, and are checked analytically before execution) or may refer to situations that might occur during execution; so they must be checked at run-time by the program itself.

The test cases should cover the specific functional intentions of the package, as identified by its claim and the claims of its constituent subprograms. For packages whose bodies depend on other packages, the tests must be organised for the planned sequence of testing, making sure that the tests are separated according to their dependency on the correct operation of the subsidiary packages.

In the case of category 1 packages, the considerations of Section 14.2 indicate additional properties to be covered by the test cases.

14.6.2 Checks at test achievement review

When the module has actually been tested, the number (and proportion) of tests that were successful must be recorded. It will be most unusual for all the tests to be successful at the first attempt, and they will probably expose some faults that had not been noticed before. The source of the fault may be in the module under test or in a subsidiary module being used in an unexpected way. The exposure of the fault may indicate that further tests are needed, as well as a repeat of the tests of all modules affected by the correction of the fault. As noted in Section 14.4.5, a test which exposes a fault during integration of the software must also be considered as possibly indicating a deficiency in the set of test cases applied.

14.6.3 Checks at integration review

When the hardware/software integration is completed, the final check to confirm that the software is right must confirm that all critical actions have been tested and that all critical tests have been executed successfully. The coverage analyses described in Section 14.2.5 will have identified all the relevant tests for software at Risk Factors 1 and 2. The partial ordering of the packages for criticality dependencies (Section 13.6) must be checked to confirm the proper partitioning of the software installed for operational use.

All the software should have been under change control since the beginning of module creation, providing proper identification of the software to be installed in each target computer. The last check is that the right software is installed.

15

Evidence for certification

AS EXPLAINED in Chapter 2, an automatic system which is concerned with safety is likely to be subject to legal constraints, requiring it to be licensed by a statutory authority. Authorities responsible for licensing such systems publish guidance for applicants, explaining the information they need before they will award a licence to operate the system. Authorities differ in the details of the information they need, but substantially agree on the principles: they require full consistency of the executable software with the safety analysis, and sufficient information about changes that have been made during development to be sure that the analyses apply to the software as delivered. The authorities recognise that software development is lengthy and error-prone, so they require evidence to show that the process has been properly controlled, that appropriate analyses have been carried out, and that the analyses apply (after all changes during development) to the delivered software.

DO-178A particularly emphasises the assurance activity, which demonstrates to the regulatory agency that the development and the subsequent verification (analysis and testing) have been carried out in a manner appropriate to the software risk factor. The evidence produced to provide this assurance may include assertions (by the developer) of compliance with published standards, reports by witnesses, historical records, and information generated by verification analyses such as cross-reference matrices and test coverage calculations. In general, a Statement of Compliance with a documented software development process is needed for all development steps in the case of Risk Factor 2. All documentation and results must be inspected for software of Risk Factor 1 (which requires formal documentation, maintenance, control and retrieval procedures). In addition, for Risk Factor 1 software, there must be analyses to assess the coverage of the design requirements from the software requirements, and of them from the system requirements. Section 15.1 below expands on this point.

The Software Safety Assessor has the responsibility under MoD Standard 00–55 of evaluating this evidence and confirming its adequacy. In general, evidence must be produced for each distinct unit of software (i.e. Ada compilation unit), depending on the risk factor of the software unit concerned. DO-178A does not call for any specific evidence about dependencies between software modules (because it does not recognise layering in the software: see Section 7.4). The analysis suggested in Section 13.6 is therefore supplementary evidence of the software accomplishment.

The claim that the system is fit for its intended purpose must be justified, and verified by qualified people independent of the developers, by at least the following:

- reasoning and evidence of the overall accomplishment, linking statements of the software produced with the requirements, and
- demonstration that all individual parts of the software have been tested.

Tests have to be verified as well as performed satisfactorily. Where particular criteria are set for safety-related software, it is important to verify that they are met in the software produced, and to ensure that all infringements of the criteria are identified and justified.

Thus the acceptability criteria (e.g. acceptable system error rates, with software detection and corrective actions) should be agreed as a constraint in the initial requirements. Documents have to be produced during the development procedure to show that these criteria are met, with complete audit trails.

15.1 Software accomplishment summary

The kinds of assurance that the software accomplishes its requirements (dependent on risk factor) are given by DO-178A as:

	Risk factor		
	1	2	3
RCA	y	y	n
SSCA	y	n	n
TD	y	y	n
TA	y	n	n

where:

- RCA (Requirements Coverage Analysis) is intended to identify the test case or cases which are asserted to demonstrate adequately that the software complies with every software requirement.
- SSCA (Software Structural Coverage Analysis) is intended to identify the test case or cases which are asserted to have executed each element of the software. DO-178A implicitly admits that this may not be complete, referring to 'the degree of structural coverage'. This has to be determined appropriately, taking account of all applicable sources of error, including support software. The accompanying test plan document must explain how that degree of coverage has been achieved, by an analysis of the test results.
- TD (Testing Documentation) includes all the test plans, procedures and results, recorded and retained under configuration control. It also includes the logs and tracking records of all problems discovered as a result of testing, and the associated corrective actions.
- TA (Testing Audit) comprises a further check to assess the completion of all tasks arising from testing.

For software implementing critical functions (Risk Factor 1), DO-178A lays down that the whole process must be audited for completeness, with tests traced back to the requirement, deviations from standards justified, and problems tracked from detection to cure. For Ada packages with Risk Factor 1 (i.e. those upon which a critical function depends), this means that the results of each verification process must be recorded and retained as evidence for the assurance. All problems resulting from each verification process must be logged, and the corrective action tracked. A cross-reference list (traceability matrix) should link each step in the chain from system requirements to the package's implementation to ensure that the verification has properly covered them all (see Figure 15.1). An audit must be performed to

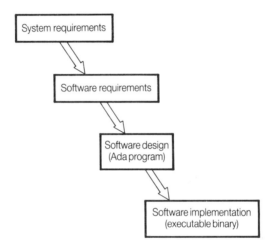

Figure 15.1 Justification chain

confirm that all the tasks have been completed, and a satisfactory report written and retained. Deviations from document 12 must be noted and justified.

DO-178A requires that Risk Factor 2 software must adhere to agreed standards and have predicted results. This means that for the packages with Risk Factor 2, a summary description of the verification process is required, with all problems logged and all corrective actions tracked. A Statement of Compliance must be provided by the developer, normally in the Accomplishment Summary document.

For the packages with Risk Factor 3, no assurance is required.

16

Conclusion

OF COURSE there are matters to do with safety that are beyond programming, but there is no doubt that software is a major area of concern to safety system designers and assessors. In particular, the actual analyses of the correctness of program texts cannot yet be automatically assured, and the ultimate correctness of operation of the effectors (irrespective of circumstances) depends on the correctness of the representation information (i.e. addresses of device registers and format of bit-patterns in them). Needless to say, writing the program in a high-level language gives no assurance that the compiler, run-time system and underlying computer hardware function correctly. Tests must confirm that these are satisfactory.

In this analysis we started by considering immediate direct dangers; we then showed that similar analyses can be carried out for indirect danger (arising from the *absence* of some explicit control) and for deferred danger (when inertia in the plant causes danger to persist after the relevant control has turned the dangerous device off).

No satisfactory model of the software production process yet exists as a basis for predictions about the possible errors in a design, and any estimates of residual error rates are based on extrapolation and assumptions about the process which are inherently uncheckable, since they arise because of imperfect foresight. Consequently, only the highest standards of professional competence supported by extensive computer assistance can give sufficient confidence in software for safety-critical systems. However, the encapsulation features of Ada provide a key mechanism for making operations executable only when the interlock permits, thus ensuring that any residual mistakes elsewhere in the program can never have dangerous effects.

A number of techniques have been identified for use in high integrity computing systems, with various degrees of insistence, depending on the criticality of the system. For a programmed system, the software is relevant to safety only as far as it is responsible for determining the behaviour of the dangerous devices in that system. If a system is designed in such a way that software is likely to be critical to safety, then the broad goal is to treat the software safety risk in the context of the system safety risk, so that it is *identified* and *minimised*, to such an extent that it is *acceptable*.

Ultimately, every computer-based system used to ensure safety must be analysed in its entirety, because safety is a property not just of the software, but of the system as a whole.

Appendix A
Guidance for using the Ada programming language in avionic systems

THIS APPENDIX is based on ARINC Report 613, which was adopted by the Airlines Electronic Engineering Committee on October 14, 1987, and published by Aeronautical Radio, Inc (ARINC). ARINC is a corporation in which the United States scheduled airlines are the principal stockholders. ARINC sponsors the Airlines Electronic Engineering Committee (AEEC), composed of airline technical personnel. The AEEC formulates standards for technical equipment and systems for airlines.

The major parts of this report are reproduced here with the permission of ARINC. The symbol '——' indicates places where there is more material in the ARINC Report, but which is not reproduced here.

A.1 Introduction

A.1.1 Purpose of this document

This document is intended to provide guidance on the use of the Ada programming language in commercial avionics applications. It is intended to provide guidelines to the airlines, airframe manufacturers, flight simulator manufacturers, avionics suppliers, and compiler vendors.

It is the desire of the airline community to reduce the cost and economic risk associated with avionics software systems. As a means to achieve this it is recommended that the Ada programming language be used as the standard High-Order Language (HOL) in avionics equipment design.

A.1.2 Intended audience

This document is intended for the following individuals who may be concerned with the use of the Ada language:

(a) Engineering Managers
(b) System Design Managers
(c) Software Development Engineers
(d) Software Maintenance Engineers

(e)   Support Software Developers (i.e. compiler vendors)

A.1.3 Scope

The scope of this document is limited to commercial avionics software; it addresses the use of the Ada programming language in the development, testing, and maintenance of digital avionics for the commercial aviation industry. This environment includes application of the Ada language in on-board processors on aircraft, and in ground-based systems such as test equipment and simulators.

———

A.2 Purpose of the Ada language

A.2.1 Introduction

The purpose of using the Ada language in commercial avionics software development is to reduce the cost of avionics systems over the entire life-cycle. Cost reduction is based on reducing software development effort and post-development software changes. This can be achieved by the following methods:

- Use of a modern HOL incorporating the latest software engineering constructs.
- Standardisation on a single HOL (benefits resulting from standardisation are contingent upon industry-wide acceptance of the Ada language and should therefore not be considered in a current cost/benefit analysis).
- Application of engineering methodology to software development.

The application of these methods should result in the following benefits:

1.   Increased understandability:
        create readable code;
        allow easy isolation of data structures and algorithms.
2.   Increased reliability:
        reduce errors in software design and development;
        simplify exception handling;
3.   Increased modifiability:
        control changes more easily;
        introduce changes without increasing complexity;
        capture design structure clearly and consistently.
4.   Increased efficiency:
        employ available resources (time and space) in an optimal fashion.
5.   Increased resusability:
        greater consideration given to adaptability, commonality, and interface
           requirements.

6.   Reduced training needs:
          utilize single HOL;
          utilize common tools.
7.   Reduced schedule or technical risk.

A.2.2 Ada language domain for commercial avionics systems

Avionics software is generally large, complex, subject to frequent revisions throughout its life-cycle and required to be highly reliable. Under these circumstances it is not surprising that the normal effort associated with software development is more intense for avionics systems.

Although the Ada language was originally designed for embedded system applications, not all elements are equally important for avionics software. Some elements of the language may lead to complications during test, may increase certification concerns, or may be inefficiently implemented by some compilers. Accordingly, this document concentrates on an avionics domain of the Ada language.

In this domain, certain features of the language have not been included due to potential for increased testing complexity, more difficult certification, and inefficient implementation by certain compilers. By delineating this specific Ada domain, the intent is to:

● Inform the Ada language user about relevant problems, concerns, and recommendations.
● Define a set of optional features which should be implemented on the compiler selected by the Ada Language user.
● Suggest to compiler vendors those features of the Ada language which should be implemented in a manner which produces the most efficient runtime code.

This document provides guidance on specific Ada language features for one or more of the following reasons:

1.   The features are commonly used in avionics software.
2.   They have a specific preferred implementation.
3.   They should be supported by the selected compiler.
4.   They should be used only after a careful cost–benefit analysis.
5.   They are inappropriate for avionics equipment.

In general, specific features may not be recommended due to certification questions or the lack of effective implementation by some compilers. While certification issues may continue to be in question in the future, it is likely that compiler implementations will improve. Accordingly, it is expected that compiler maturation may render some of these recommendations obsolete.

It is not the intent of this document to recommend that compiler vendors implement a subset of the Ada language. The word 'domain' was specifically chosen to avoid the implications of "subset". See Section A.17 for more information on this domain.

A.3 Design recommendations

A.3.1 Introduction

The primary goal of software engineering is to produce programs that are reliable, testable, portable, reusable, modifiable, efficient and understandable. The Ada language supports this goal by promoting modern software engineering design, modularity, and built-in checking features.

A.3.2 Design principles

A major concern in designing software is handling its complexity. The use of correct software design principles is essential to the development of complex software. Such principles are abstraction, information hiding and modularity. The Ada language is an integrated language which has interrelated features which support each other. In order to use the Ada language effectively, the user should understand the language as a whole.

A.3.2.1 Abstraction   Abstraction is the extraction of the essential features of a problem. In software design, real-world objects are modelled by abstract representation of the objects in a program design language. The Ada language provides a rich set of constructs for implementing abstractions that accurately model real-world objects. The Ada typing facility can implement more complex or abstract objects. Generic units and overloading can also be used to express abstract algorithms.

A.3.2.2 Information hiding   In the abstraction process, non-essential details are suppressed. These are typically details on how abstract objects are implemented in a program. To reduce side effects, access to such information should be limited. When Ada packages are combined with private data types, abstract data types can be created.

A.3.2.3 Modularity   Good software engineering practice suggests that Ada language programs should be partitioned into numerous modules of reasonable size to reduce complex programs to manageable units. Accordingly, it is recommended that the source code for each module comprise an individual compilation unit, and each compilation unit should reside in a separate text file. The entities in the modules will depend on the design approach; top down design, data structured design, object-oriented design, etc.

There are several advantages to this approach.

1.   When source code is segregated into a number of small files rather than a few large ones, software maintenance is simplified. Sections of code requiring modification are easily identifiable and the corresponding text can usually be edited and manipulated more efficiently. In addition, subsequent recompilations are completed in less time because large amounts of unchanged code are not needlessly recompiled.

2.   There is flexibility in managing code that has been created by the Ada language separate compilation facility and program library features.

3.   It promotes and facilitates good software configuration management practices.

COMMENTARY

Software designers should be aware that modular design implies that there are variables defined at the highest hierarchical level which should not be misconstrued as global variables.

Data transfer between compilation units should be explicitly defined in the specification, rather than be universally accessible, as in the case of global variables.

A.3.3 Data abstraction using types

A type (reference LRM 3.3), is used to define a set of values and a set of allowable operations. The Ada language's strong typing facility is a powerful feature for creating data objects and enforcing allowable operations. Following the type definition, an object is declared to be a variable of a specific type.

———

A.3.4 Activity abstraction

———

A.3.5 Encapsulation

A.3.5.1 Packages   The Ada package is a comprehensive construct for collecting program units into modules. Packages may also contain a named collection of data declarations or a set of related subprograms or tasks. In addition, they are used to implement abstract data types and generic units.

A.3.5.2 Tasks   Tasking should be used for, among other reasons, modelling concurrency. Tasks may be encapsulated in an Ada package to provide services for clients of the package. Using tasking, abstract data types can be implemented which may run concurrently with other objects. See Section A.10 for more information on tasking.

A.3.5.3 Private types Abstract data types should be implemented within packages using the private type or limited private type declarations. Private types hide the structure of the abstract objects from users. For limited private types, only operations defined by subprograms within the package (and implicitly declared operations like equivalence) are permitted on the object. This provides a high degree of protection from side effects. An example object is a stack, where PUSH and POP are the allowable operations, but the internal structure of the stack is inaccessible to the user.

A.3.6 Portability issues

The Ada language was designed such that underlying hardware and various support software would be transparent to the users of the language. In the language definition however, many explicit and subtle implementation dependencies have been identified. Several of the dependencies may result in unanticipated performance of programs transferred between various system implementations. Users of multiple support systems should be aware of potential dissimilarities in:

1. the order of range constraint expression evaluations;
2. the order of index expression evaluations;
3. the order of index constraint expression evaluations;
4. the order of index component expression evaluations;
5. the order of slice expression evaluations;
6. the order of record component expression evaluations;
7. the order of evaluation of operands in expressions;
8. rules for aggregate storage;
9. rules for rounding of values in real to integer conversions
10. parameter passing mechanisms and evaluation conventions;
11. implementation of shared variables;
12. rules and algorithms for data packing.

A.3.7 Efficiency issues

The use of the Ada language in avionics applications imposes stringent demands on efficiency. The penalty for using less than optimal tools may result in the excessive use of memory space, which would increase recurring hardware costs. Also, increases in program execution time may impact system performance.

If a compiler produces an unacceptable amount of object code or produces code with an execution speed which is inadequate, judicious use of another language (high-order or assembly) may be necessary. It is suggested that, in any case, the entire application be initially coded using the Ada language to prove the design. Run-time analysis will indicate which modules should be recoded in another language for efficiency. The original Ada source code should then serve as documentation. (See Sections A.9, A.10 and A.17.)

A.4 Format recommendations

A.5 Code recommendations

A.5.1 Introduction

Often there is a variety of designs which could satisfy the operational requirements of an application. This section identifies some of the areas where the Ada language provides options, and recommends preferred approaches.

A.5.2 Control flow

The Ada language provides a rich set of control flow structures (reference LRM 5.0). These constructs can be subdivided into the categories of selection and iteration. Composition of these constructs provides the programmer with a variety of methods of controlling program execution.

A.5.3 Numerical precision

Programs should not use the default accuracy of types such as FLOAT, but should use **digits** specifications to provide the necessary degree of accuracy. In a similar manner, **delta** should be used for fixed point types, and ranges should be used for INTEGER types. The LRM defines mapping from constants into model numbers (LRM Section 4.5.7), and this should be checked where accuracy is important. Note that in some cases it is possible that the relational operators may not have their expected operations when applied to floating point types.

Convergence should be controlled by using attributes rather than explicit constants. For example, assuming the series A(1), A(2), A(3),. . .,A(MAX) converges with all the non-negative terms the summing loop:

```
 .  .  .
type F is digits 7;
A: array (1 .  . MAX) of F; — not in ARINC 613
```

```
SUM: F;  — not in ARINC 613
begin    — not in ARINC 613
SUM := 0.0;
for INDEX in 1 . . MAX loop
    exit when A(INDEX) <= SUM * F'EPSILON;
    SUM := SUM + A(INDEX);
end loop;
```

This method will converge under any implementation.

Cautionary footnote:— not in ARINC 613

The above statement presumes that the terms are accumulated one at a time: the resulting convergence may be mathematically spurious. In any work involving series, the convergence and the truncation error should be determined mathematically before formulating the algorithm. In general, it is better to accumulate the terms in *increasing* order of magnitude, rather than in *decreasing* order (as here). (I.C. Pyle)

A.5.4 Storage management

Most embedded software applications execute according to a timed schedule. Events which could interfere with that schedule should be recognised, and either accommodated or avoided. One such event is free storage reclamation, more commonly referred to as garbage collection. Garbage collection can occur, if selected, at irregular intervals and can consume considerable time. It may occur when dynamically allocated objects (those created with certain usages of the **new** primitive, including tasks) are used. In certain compiler implementations, it may also be required when unconstrained types are used. These objects receive storage from a pool of available memory called 'the heap'. When a dynamically allocated task terminates, this storage is released but may not be immediately returned to the heap. Instead, when the heap is depleted, the previously released storage is recovered through the process of garbage collection. Due to the nature of embedded applications, it is recommended that dynamically allocated objects, including tasks, are not used.

A number of operations can be done in the Ada language to reduce these uncertainties. First, the total amount of storage for a collection of objects can be roughly estimated and specified at compile-time. Ada code can also be structured so that storage reclamation is limited to the moment at which the object becomes inaccessible. In addition, some control over when deallocation takes place can be exercised through use of pragma CONTROLLED. (See Section A7.2).

A.5.5 Resource allocation

The designer of embedded system software may need to explicitly specify the allocation of memory and processing resources for the application. Such resources may include:

1.   Space to be allocated for particular tasks (e.g. task control blocks and stack size).
2.   Assignments of tasks to a particular processor or tightly coupled multi-processor systems.
3.   Assignment of data and code blocks of specific target memory blocks.

It should be possible to specify these allocations in the program with pragmas, or outside of the program, for instance, in commands to the program linker utility. The system designer should verify that the compiler selected supports these capabilities.

With regard to item 3, for embedded systems in particular, it is essential that:

●   The compiler be able to distinguish between blocks of static data and code, and data that will change during execution.
●   The linker/loader be able to direct these data and code blocks to specific memory sections of the target system.

A.5.6 Ada programming support environment

A.6 Test recommendations

A.6.1 Introduction

Software verification is the combination of analysis and test activities to prove the compliance of a design to a specific set of requirements. The analytical portion of the verification process should include the review of requirements, design and code. The verification testing may include module testing, module integration testing and hardware/software integration testing. Software validation is determined by the successful compliance of the verification activities. For airborne software, the verification process and associated assurance activities should be coordinated with the appropriate certification authorities as stated in the pertinent RTCA DO-178A document.

In general, the strong language features of the Ada language, such as typing, reduce the number of common errors detected at compile time and help simplify testing. Although the basic principles of software verification are similar to those employed in other programming languages, there are some considerations which are unique to the Ada language. These considerations are discussed in this section.

A.6.2 Analytical activities

Typically, analytical activities are the review of software requirements against system requirements, software design against requirements, and code against software design. The actual methods used in these processes are outside the scope of this document. However, the design and coding recommendations described in Sections A.3. and A.5. are intended to aid the analyses.

A.6.3 Testing activities

Testing activities involve the testing of software requirements and software design together, while ensuring adequate coverage of the tests. It is not the intent of this document to describe the methods and disciplines for testing, as these are applicable to most programming languages. However, the Ada language does introduce some additional considerations, and in particular, ensures adequate test coverage.

Requirements coverage analysis is considered to be outside the scope of this document. Structured coverage analysis, however, aims to identify the test case(s) which should execute each element of the software (see DO-178A). In this analysis 'each element' has traditionally been taken to mean each machine code instruction. For critical and essential software, a combination of black box and white box testing should be used to ensure complete coverage. For Ada test activities, the package specification can be used to derive the data for black box testing and the package body for white box testing. The following considerations apply to module testing and module integration testing. It is recognised that it may be difficult to test some modules in isolation because some of the routines from the run-time library may be required. This should not present a problem if the recommendations described in Section A.6.4 are adhered to.

The following recommendations should be considered during the verification process:

1. The underlying machine code may not be evident from the source code, and therefore tools such as trace emulators should be used in with the assembler/machine code listings to ensure full coverage. It is desirable that the compiler manufacturer provide a code generation strategy guide.
2. If code is optimized for production then it is necessary for that code to be used for system verification. It is essential that the compiler be validated for both optimized and non-optimized code. (See Section A.15.)
3. Full coverage analysis is difficult to ensure when using exception handling. The code to reach the exception handler (and the exception handler itself) can be tested successfully only in the event of an exception being raised, and in general, when such an error does occur, it may not be intended. Hence, it is recommended that exception handling be suppressed during development where possible. (See Section A.7.8.)
4. The use of non-determinist constructs such as tasking (Section A.10) and

access types in garbage collection (Sections A.3.3.7 and A.5.4) should be avoided. In either case, full coverage analysis (which can also be equated with predictability of execution) can be difficult to ensure.

5.   If generics are used, then knowledge of how they are elaborated (i.e. in-line code or procedure call) is necessary in order to plan how coverage can be demonstrated.

A.6.4 Verification of the run-time library

The local Run-Time Library (RTL) is linked to the user's application software to produce the complete system. Verification of this software should include the verification of the Run-Time System (RTS) to the same level of criticality as the application software. Since the RTL can be large in size and may not be developed by the supplier, it may not be practical for the supplier to perform the verification activities. Hence, the following recommendations are made.

1.   It should be the compiler manufacturer's responsibility to verify the RTL, using the guidelines of DO-178A, to the highest level of criticality.

2.   The activity should include the production of verification evidence, as described in DO-178A, in a form which can be presented to the certification authorities (either separately or included in the supplier's documentation).

3.   It is desired that a selectably loadable RTS be used in order to eliminate the need for the supplier to demonstrate that unwanted code cannot be executed.

4.   Modification of the RTL should be avoided where possible since this could affect the verification undertaken by the compiler manufacturer and, hence, may require that affected modules be reverified. The verification should not be affected by the addition of new modules, or replacement of existing modules to the RTL.

A.6.5 Testing tools

Customarily, during the test phase of avionics software development, two types of tools are employed; symbolic debuggers and test drivers (or test harnesses).

1.   Symbolic debuggers should be used to help detect and isolate errors primarily during module testing, module integration test and hardware/software integration testing. Such tools are usually supplied by the compiler manufacturer and it is essential that the tools can use symbolic information produced by the compiler. Also, source code listings (showing source code to assembler/machine code equivalence with addresses) and linker/loader listings are necessary for this test phase.

2.   Test harnesses should be used to produce verification evidence by submitting test data to the software under test (either individual modules or integrated modules) and comparing actual results with expected results. Test harnesses

may not be part of the Ada software and may have to be developed by the system supplier. If this is the case, then the compiler manufacturer should supply relevant information such as symbolic data from the compiler or should incorporate the symbolic debugger into a batch oriented system.

A.7 Pragmas

A.7.1 Introduction

Pragmas are used as a means to direct information to the compiler. This section discusses the Ada language compiler directives or pragmas (reference LRM 2.8) that are appropriate for commercial avionics software applications. The system designer should ensure that the selected compiler supports these pragmas.

> COMMENTARY
>
> Although the LRM defines a set of standard pragmas, a validated compiler is not required to implement them. All that is required of a validated compiler is that it recognize each pragma. Accordingly when selecting a compiler, it is important to note which pragmas are actually implemented. The pragmas listed below should be supported by the selected compiler. The system designer should check the pragma implementation restrictions to ensure that the pragmas support all needed options.
>
> For example, certain implementations may support the pragma SUPPRESS, but only with the ALL option active. This may not be acceptable to all users.

A.7.2 Pragma CONTROLLED

The pragma CONTROLLED restricts the performance of automatic storage reclamation for objects designated by values of an access type, such that it can only be performed upon leaving the body in which the access type was declared (reference LRM Appendix B).

This capability is useful whenever automatic storage reclamation is implemented, and should only apply within the scope of the relevant access type. (See Sections A.3.3.7 and A.5.4.)

A.7.3 Pragma INLINE

The pragma INLINE specifies that subprogram bodies should be expanded inline at each call (reference LRM Appendix B).

Use of pragma INLINE is intended to eliminate the processing speed overhead of a call/return mechanism for a procedure invocation. On the other hand, it will also increase memory utilization if invoked more than once for the same code. Accordingly, the system design engineer should consider the tradeoff between memory utilization and speed. In general, the pragma INLINE should be used.

A.7.4 Pragma INTERFACE

The pragma INTERFACE allows Ada language programs to include code that is written in other languages. It is necessary for the compiler to implement the INTERFACE pragma in order to support the inclusion of assembly language code.

A.7.5 Pragma OPTIMIZE

The Pragma OPTIMIZE allows optimisation of code based on memory or speed. (Reference LRM Appendix B).

A.7.6 Pragma PACK

The pragma PACK specifies to the compiler that storage minimisation, rather than access speed, should be the criterion when selecting the representation of a record or array type (reference LRM Appendix B).

COMMENTARY

Without this pragma, a large amount of memory may be wasted under certain conditions (e.g. the compiler default is word alignment for arrays and records).

The system designer should carefully evaluate the impact on access speed for any use of PACK.

A.7.7 Pragma PRIORITY

The pragma PRIORITY allows the programmer to specify the priority of the task(s) or the priority of the main program (reference LRM Appendix B).

The number of task priority levels necessary for embedded systems will vary from application to application, and even from one implementation of a particular application to another. In selecting the number of priority levels to implement, consideration must be given to the task scheduling approach. One should also consider the difference in priority scheduling of the various functions, and the possible performance penalty incurred through having an excess of priority levels.

In general, embedded systems should not require a large number of different priority levels. In order to promote portability, applications should use no more than fifteen priority levels. In the same spirit, Ada language compilers should support a minimum of fifteen priority levels. (See Section A.10.4.)

A.7.8 Pragma SUPPRESS

The pragma SUPPRESS provides for the elimination for certain checks normally performed by the Run-Time Environment (RTE) (reference LRM Appendix B).

In general, during development, checks should be enabled for embedded code, and handlers should be implemented for any exceptions which may be raised. However, since elimination of these checks does improve the processing speed of the embedded system, there may be a temptation to use SUPPRESS in the production code.

This should not be done, however, unless it can be demonstrated that an unacceptable runtime overhead results from specific checks, and that the specific error condition being suppressed can never arise.

If the system designer elects to use SUPPRESS, the software or system testing documentation should demonstrate that the omission of checks does not compromise reliability. In all events, an exception handler should be in place to handle the error, whether or not the pragma SUPPRESS is used.

> COMMENTARY
>
> The use of the SUPPRESS pragma should be approached with caution.
> The use of the pragma does not, of course, guarantee that the exception
> will not occur.

With appropriate precautions, the pragma SUPPRESS can be applied to the following checks:

```
ACCESS_CHECK
DISCRIMINANT_CHECK
INDEX_CHECK
LENGTH_CHECK
RANGE_CHECK
DIVISION_CHECK
OVERFLOW_CHECK
STORAGE_CHECK
ELABORATION_CHECK
```

This pragma, with each option listed above, should be supported by all compilers.

A.7.9 Pragmas SYSTEM_NAME, STORAGE_UNIT and MEMORY_SIZE

The LRM describes three pragmas related to package SYSTEM: (1) SYSTEM_NAME, (2) STORAGE_UNIT, and (3) MEMORY_SIZE. Each pragma can be included before the beginning of the first compilation unit in a program to explicitly redefine the corresponding constant.

According to the LRM, compilation of any of these pragmas causes an 'implicit recompilation' of the package SYSTEM. This means that any other unit in the program that names the SYSTEM package in a **with** clause becomes obsolete, and must subsequently be recompiled. In addition the LRM states that implementation-dependent considerations may create additional complications.

Package SYSTEM contains the constants SYSTEM_NAME, STORAGE_UNIT, and MEMORY_SIZE. If any of these constants are used, they should be accessed directly from package SYSTEM.

> COMMENTARY
>
> Some compiler vendors use these constants as a mechanism to select a target code system configuration. The system designer should determine if this is the case for a selected compiler.

A.7.10 Interrupt optimization pragmas

Some compilers support nonstandard pragmas such as FAST_INTERRUPT, FAST_INTERRUPT_ENTRY and INTERRUPT_HANDLER_TASK. These pragmas allow the programmer to specify restrictions that are observed by the accept bodies for interrupt entries.

They direct the compiler to generate code which minimises the hardware interrupt response time. The result is a considerable reduction in the time between the interrupt and the time of servicing the interrupt.

The pragma FAST_INTERRUPT may be used to specify that a particular task entry has only accept bodies that execute with the interrupts disabled, and that none of these accept bodies performs operations that may lead to task switches away from the accept body.

These pragmas, if supported, should be used whenever appropriate in avionics equipment.

> COMMENTARY
>
> The Ada Run-Time Environment Working Group (ARTEWG) is considering the adoption of these pragmas. However, the designated names for these pragmas may be different from those above.

A.8 Attributes

A.8.1 Introduction

An attribute denotes a basic operation of an entity given by a prefix (reference LRM 4.1.4). The following two attributes are considered to be extremely useful in embedded applications. The other Ada attributes are not addressed in this document.

A.8.2 Attribute P'ADDRESS

The attribute P'ADDRESS is a representation attribute which yields the first of the storage units allocated to the prefix P (reference LRM 13.7.2). This attribute is predefined in the package SYSTEM.

The ability to determine the address of the machine code associated with any program unit, label or entry should be supported by means of the address attribute. For an entry for which an address clause has been given, the value should refer to the corresponding hardware interrupt.

COMMENTARY

The address specified by the P'ADDRESS attribute is implementation defined (reference LRM 13.7). It may not be obvious whether this is consistently a virtual, logical, or absolute address, but the result of P'ADDRESS appears as an address in the virtual user's space. The linker/loader tools are responsible for translating this address specification into a physical address on the host and/or embedded system target.

A.8.3 Attribute P'COUNT

The attribute P'COUNT is a task entry attribute which yields the number of entry calls presently queued on the entry P (reference LRM 9.9).

If tasking is used it should be possible to determine the number of entry calls queued on an entry. This facility is provided by means of the COUNT attribute.

It is important to note that this attribute can be unreliable since the result of COUNT can fluctuate rapidly. As the number of entry calls can quickly change (e.g. due to timed entry calls) COUNT may not be a reliable means to determine an execution path.

A.9 Compile-time processing

A.9.1 Static expressions

Static expressions are defined to be certain expressions of a scalar type. Also, some discrete ranges can be static expressions (reference LRM 4.9). The value of real static expressions should be computed by the compiler with a precision at least as high as that of the most accurate predefined floating point type supported on the host. If the static expression is a universal expression, the evaluation should be exact.

A.9.2 Generics

There are two ways for a compiler to instantiate a generic unit (reference LRM
12.0), depending on the compilation strategy and the particular parameters:

1.   The instantiation is produced as an additional copy of all the object code (the
       'macro expansion' method).
2.   The instantiation is produced with only the required unique data objects or
       object code (the 'shared bodies' method).

The former method uses more memory than the latter, but the compilation
technique is simpler. The latter can be considered as an optimization for space,
although execution time may be increased. Compiler vendors should provide
information about the trade-offs underlying such optimisation, and allow programmers to select from these methods. Software designers should be aware of the
resource implications of generic instantiation in terms of memory and speed.

> COMMENTARY
>
> The use of generics does not eliminate the need to test every instantiation
> of the code. In other words, the testing of a single instantiation does not
> confirm the validity of all instantiations.

A.10 Tasks

A.10.1 Introduction

In the Ada language, tasking is the segregation of software into one or more separate
components which can be independently scheduled for execution (reference LRM
9.0). Some performance penalties can be expected due to the supporting Run-Time
System (RTS) overhead. The programmer determines the overhead associated with
a task rendezvous, entry queue maintenance and other similar features, and avoids
designs in which the overhead becomes unacceptable.

A.10.2 Ada language versus assembly for task management

Occasionally a system designer may consider the use of tasking to define a
foreground/background executive versus the use of assembly language to accomplish
the same results. For example, avionics software typically employs an executive to
manage execution-time resources between a primary (foreground) and secondary
(background) application. This situation can be effectively programmed in the Ada
language, and is both more maintainable and portable than traditional assembly
language implementations.

However, the inevitable overhead of tasking should be considered. If, for example a particular compiler implementation of tasking requires two milliseconds per context switch between foreground and background tasks, and if this switch must be made every 10 ms, 20 per cent of the system executive resources are consumed by task overhead.

In general, cyclic execution, written in the Ada language, should be used rather than the tasking model for implementing foreground/background processing.

A.10.3 Dynamic task allocation

The rules of task creation are similar to those for procedures and packages, i.e. they can be declared at any nesting level. Tasks are activated at the run-time elaboration of the declarative region containing them unless they are created dynamically by use of the access type allocator operator (i.e. use of a statement containing the qualification 'new'). In this case tasks are created and activated at execution of the statement which contains the allocation operator 'new'.

Consequently, the execution overhead incurred by task creation and the associated storage allocation can occur unpredictably during execution. Similarly, when the task terminates and control leaves the master unit, an indeterminate amount of time may be consumed by the associated storage reclamation. In general it is difficult to determine whether or not a given task actually gets created, and it is therefore difficult to make allowances for the time consumed.

Therefore, dynamic task allocation is generally considered inappropriate for real-time commercial avionics. Consequently, when tasking is used, all tasks should be declared at the highest lexical level or within a unit which is entered at system initialisation and is not exited during post-initialisation operation of the program. There should be no task creation or termination during any phase or normal operation where time or space constraints may be critical. In the same spirit, the use of **terminate** (reference LRM 9.7.1) alternatives on select statements, or use of the **abort** (reference LRM 9.10) statement is considered inappropriate.

A.10.4 Task scheduling and priorities

Although task scheduling and priorities are discussed briefly in the LRM (reference LRM 9.8), it does not explicitly define a mechanism for task scheduling. Regardless, commercial avionics software requires pre-emptive priority task scheduling. Accordingly, the Run-Time Environment (RTE) should implement this type of task scheduling. As a minimum, the RTE should check to determine if a context switch is needed at every synchronisation point, delay expiration, interrupt, and task queueing.

A.10.5 Delay statement

The **delay** statement specifies a minimum time delay before the execution of a task is permitted to resume (reference LRM 9.6).

The actual duration of the delay will depend on the activity of other tasks and the type of scheduling implemented. The delays experienced may differ from one execution to the next. This indeterminacy is largely dependent on the priority of the delayed task. Such a task operating at the highest priority will pre-empt other tasks to regain control when its delay has expired. It will be necessary for lower priority tasks to compete for the processor when it is ready, and the task may experience additional latency.

This effect should be considered when using the **delay** statement.

A.10.6 Select statement

The **select** statement is used to wait for and select from any of several accept alternatives (reference LRM A.9.7.1). A satisfactory implementation should ensure that any queue of tasks, which may be on each accept alternative, receives adequate service, and none are treated preferentially. A truly random choice is permissible, but a program relying for correct operation on a particular selection is unacceptable.

If the selective wait is used, it should be shown that only one accept alternative is available for the rendezvous. Criteria for proof of this (e.g. the use of guards) should be documented.

The use of **select** with other language features (delays, terminates, and guards) may degrade system performance significantly, and should be carefully evaluated to determine if the degradation if acceptable.

A.11 Exceptions and error handling

A.11.1 Use of exceptions and error handling

In general, exception handlers (reference LRM 11.4) should be used to handle unexpected conditions; that is, computational errors such as range error or numeric error, etc. It is considered poor programming practice to use exceptions to redirect program execution for expected conditions, i.e. unexpected data inputs such as those which are normally handled by **if** or **case** statements in embedded code.

For example, the exception usage in the cycle counter:

```
begin
    TOMORROW := DAY'succ(TODAY);
exception
    when CONSTRAINT_ERROR = >
        TOMORROW := DAY'first;
end;
```

is not appropriate and should be replaced with:

```
if TODAY = DAY'LAST THEN
    TOMORROW := DAY'first;
else
    TOMORROW := DAY'succ(TODAY);
end if;
```

Since only a few predefined exceptions are used to signal all error states produced by the underlying code, it may be impossible to confidently trace the exact cause of a fault. There may be many spots in a single line of code where the predefined exception CONSTRAINT_ERROR can be raised. Predefined exceptions, therefore, should not be relied upon to signal oriented faults, but rather, applications should explicitly check for their own faults.

Many run-time errors are detected without explicit detection code in the application. The strongly typed design of the Ada language (in particular, its ability to identify a range of values associated with a class of variables) allows the compiler to generate code that can check all scalar values on assignment for variable type conformity. To take full advantage of this feature, each program variable should be associated with only the range of values which it can logically assume. This is done by specifying a range or enumeration type in the variable declaration:

```
subtype DECIMAL_DIGIT is INTEGER range 0 .. 9;
DISPLAY_POSITION : DECIMAL_DIGIT;
```

DISPLAY_POSITION can be manipulated like an integer object, but can only take on values in the range 0 to 9. Consider the following:

```
DISPLAY_POSITION := DISPLAY_POSITION + 1;
```

The statement above would raise an exception if DISPLAY_POSITION = 9. This exception flags the problem and provides the program with an opportunity to recover.

Many other run-time inconsistencies are implicitly recognised by the Ada language. Such inconsistencies include faulty array subscripts, computational underflow and overflow, failure to return a functional value, and exhausted storage space. The recognition of these faults can be difficult if they are not recognised implicitly through predefined exceptions.

The operation of selected exceptions may be inhibited by the use of the SUPPRESS pragma. Although suppression of the predefined exceptions may yield a performance improvement, the practice is discouraged for two reasons. First, the predefined exceptions are usually enabled during software development and maintenance. To suppress these exceptions in the deliverable code, a program change may be required which could require regressive testing. Second, this facility provides the security and assurance that the software is reliable. See Section A.7.8 for information on preferred use of this pragma.

COMMENTARY

At the time of writing, the use of exceptions in deliverable embedded code is an open issue. One school of thought holds that, while exceptions and handlers are useful during the development and testing phases, they should be removed prior to final downloading. This, of course, requires extensive regression testing after the removal of the exceptions. It is also thought by this group that predefined exceptions, which indicate abnormal computing conditions, cannot be realistically handled within an embedded environment.

Another school of thought believes that exceptions should be used both in development and in the final product. This group considers exceptions to be fundamentally similar to normal (**if** statements) error detection methods. In this case, the RTS overhead resulting from exceptions would be acceptable.

Explicitly detected application faults can be handled either locally with conventional programming techniques, cr more globally by raising an exception. Program-defined exception handling is appropriate whenever:

1. The response to the condition must be handled non-locally.
2. Each instance of an exception is to be handled identically.
3. A predefined exception is to be propagated to an enclosing or parent block.
4. Exceptions can guard against inadvertent omissions.

To illustrate the use of exceptions, consider a package containing a subprogram to implement a pushdown stack in an array. Implicit underflow and overflow detection will occur when the array index exceeds the bounds of the array and the CONSTRAINT_ERROR exception is raised. Since CONSTRAINT_ERROR may be raised for other reasons in this routine, associating this exception with the overflow and underflow conditions is undesirable. Such detection should be implemented explicitly.

An unexpected error indication can be returned to the calling program by parameter or propagated exception. Exceptions are generally preferred.

The use of exceptions:

1. simplifies the calling sequence (no error indicating parameters are required);
2. is usable for blocks and functions (where no output parameters are allowed), as well as procedures;
3. enhances readability by separating error handling code from application code;
4. reduces the amount of check code required when many invocations are made of a routine, and guards against accidentally omitting the error parameter check.

Application defined exception names should be nouns that reflect the function performed by the enclosing entity. Exceptions raised by the previous stack example could be descriptively called 'STACK_ERROR' or 'STACK_OVERFLOW'.

Many aspects of predefined exceptions are implementation dependent. These exceptions should not be relied upon except where the user lacks access to information needed to perform those checks. Predefined exceptions should be handled within the region in which the identification of their cause can be determined. If propagation is required, an application oriented exception should be raised. For example:

```
     . . .
exception
    when NUMERIC_ERROR = >
        raise SINGULARITY;
end . . .;
```

A.12 Representations

A.12.1 Introduction

Several types of representation clauses should be supported for practical Ada language implementations.

Representation clauses specify how the types of the language are to be mapped onto the target machine (reference LRM 13.1). Representation clauses have various forms and are used to provide an Ada language compiler with specific, detailed information about how particular entities are to be represented. A representation clause can apply to a type, an object, or a subprogram. The use of representation clauses improves standardisation and portability by minimising the use of processor specific assembly code.

In general, the following recommendations apply to the use of representation clauses:

1. If representation clauses (or any other machine/implementation-dependent features) are anticipated, the implementation(s) to be used should be examined carefully before program design begins. Some very specialised features (e.g. storage boundary alignment for record representation clauses) may be rejected by a particular compiler if they cannot be handled in the proper manner. Also, they may be handled differently from one implementation to another. Other features may simply not be supported.

2. The Ada code containing representation clauses should be consolidated into packages according to function. This type of organisation is helpful for isolating implementation dependent clauses from other parts of the program.

COMMENTARY

Note that Ada compiler validation does not assure proper handling of representation specifications.

———

COMMENTARY

Note that the Ada language does not prescribe the bit numbering. Therefore, it is essential to check that the Ada compiler interprets bit numbers in record representation clauses in the same way as the computer manufacturer. Validation does not guarantee this.

A.13 Predefined units

A.13.1 The package SYSTEM

The package SYSTEM is a predefined library package which is highly implementation-dependent (reference LRM 13.7). Each Ada language implementation is required to include this package. This package contains certain target system-dependent values and declarations. It includes, for instance, the name of the system (represented as an enumeration constant), the number of bits a system storage unit requires, and the maximum number of storage units available for the configuration.

It is anticipated that the package SYSTEM will be useful in embedded systems, principally in the interest of code portability. The SYSTEM-dependent 'Named Numbers' will be needed to permit general purpose code to make allowance for variations between implementations, particularly in MIN_INT and MAX_INT.

A number of representation attributes may be needed. 'SIZE, 'STORAGE_SMALL, and 'SMALL are necessary because length clauses are needed. 'POSITION, 'FIRST_BIT, 'LAST_BIT for components of a record type are needed to allow manipulation of record types which do not need length clauses associated with them.

For increased clarity, qualified (dotted) notation should be used when referencing any entity from package SYSTEM. (Accordingly, a program unit should not contain a **use** clause for this package – see Section A.4.6.) In other words, the number of bits for a system storage unit should be represented with 'SYSTEM.STORAGE_UNIT'.

A.13.2 Procedure UNCHECKED_DEALLOCATION

UNCHECKED_DEALLOCATION is predefined generic library procedure (reference LRM 13.10.1). It is used to execute unchecked storage deallocation of an object designated by a value of an access type.

Some Ada language compilers may not implement automatic storage reclamation or garbage collection. The temptation may then exist where memory is limited to reclaim storage by means of this procedure. Unfortunately, in this type of deallocation, there is significant potential for deallocating objects referenced by more than one access object and leaving dangling references. (See Sections A.5.4 and A.6.3.)

Performing tests of this process are considered very difficult. Therefore UNCHECKED_DEALLOCATION should not be used.

A.13.3 Function UNCHECKED_CONVERSION

UNCHECKED_CONVERSION is a predefined generic library function (reference LRM 13.10.2). It is used to return the uninterpreted parameter value as a value of the target type. Essentially, it is a work-around for the strong typing of the Ada language.

Unchecked type conversions are extremely useful for data bus manipulation, I/O wraparound tests, CPU tests, device drivers, self-test and self-monitor type functions. It is strongly recommended that the compiler selected support this function.

A.14 Use of other languages

A.14.1 Introduction

In this document, foreign code is considered to be software which is not written in the Ada language. Since the Ada language checking mechanisms are not applicable to foreign code, some degree of consistency can be maintained by incorporating foreign code only as separate procedures and functions.

If used, other languages should be restricted to bodies, with Ada specifications defining how they will be seen by the rest of the program. This applies whether the other language is operative (such as Fortran, C, or assembler) or semantic (such as UDL or Z).

The potential problems associated with using foreign code in an Ada environment are significant. Unless it can be shown that there is a benefit to using foreign code, Ada code is recommended. The use of foreign code will generally result in higher life-cycle costs attributed to maintaining the compiler, documentation and expertise in the foreign code. Also, interface implementation, debugging, and code validation will contribute to higher costs. Therefore, the use of foreign code is not recommended.

For these reasons a cost–benefit analysis should be included in the consideration of foreign code use. However, and in general, the use of foreign code is not recommended.

A.14.2 Waivers

While definition of specific waiver criteria should be administered by individual companies, some general recommendations can be made. Since it is the intent to use the Ada language as the standard HOL, waivers should only be considered when:

1. It is not cost-effective to use Ada code.
2. The use of Ada code causes an unacceptable schedule impact.
3. The use of Ada code increases project risk.

Alternative languages should be limited to assembler and system implementation languages which do not require run-time support in excess of that required of the Ada language. Careful design and processor selection, coupled with the availability of production-quality compilers, should limit the need for waivers.

Individual airframe manufacturers and airlines should establish specific waiver criteria as early as possible in the design and proposal phases.

A.14.3 Use of assembly code

Where assembly code is used, it should be inserted in Ada programs by using the pragma INTERFACE or machine code insertion (i.e. code statements). The code statement is used in conjunction with the LRM optional package MACHINE_CODE (reference LRM 13.8). However, the structure and constraints enforced by the use of the Ada language can be destroyed by the use of assembly code. Therefore, the use of assembly code should be minimised.

A.14.4 Use of other high-order languages

The use of other High-Order Languages (HOLs) in the same application with Ada code may create difficulties in common exception handling, numeric representation, parameter passing, and data scoping. While such issues are not insurmountable, they levy a significant additional burden on the system designer, which should be weighed against the cost of converting these into Ada code. The use of other HOLs in common processors should be minimised. If other HOLs are used, the Ada package specifications should be written for the non-Ada bodies.

A.15 Compiler issues

A.15.1 Introduction

This section discusses compiler issues associated with the use of the Ada language.

A.15.2 Compilation order

An important distinction between the Ada separate compilation facility and that of most other languages is the concept of compilation order. In more traditional languages like Fortran, the modules that make up a program can be compiled in any order. (The order selected has no particular significant and will not affect overall construction of the program image). This is not the case in the Ada language, where definite rules apply (e.g. packages must be compiled before any subprograms that reference them).

The source code for an Ada program of moderate size may consist of a large number of compilation units and subunits. If a program is to be completely reconstructed from source code, a correct compilation order can be ascertained by examining the source code for each unit. However, there may be many possible correct orders, and determining one in this way could take a substantial amount of time and effort. In addition, a certain order might be preferred because of the particular implementation (e.g. the amount of time it takes to compile the entire program, or effect on configuration of the program library).

To reconstruct an Ada program from source code, supplementary information about compilation order should be maintained. This information should be consolidated in one place (e.g. a separate text file); and organised so that it clearly indicates a specific order in which the various units and subunits of the program should be compiled. The following items might be included:

1. Names of text files in which source code for compilation units and subunits are contained.
2. The names of package specifications, package bodies, subprograms, etc., contained in each of the files.
3. A description of the program library and status of its contents (which could be used to verify that the program has been reconstructed properly).
4. Some indication as to which procedure represents the main program, and the text file in which its source is located.
5. Various automatic tools should be available to support this process.

A.15.3 Compiler validation

The intent to avoid Ada language supersets and subsets is supported by the existence of a formal compiler validation test suite. Formal DoD validation of an Ada language compiler is the process of testing the compiler to ensure that it completely implements the LRM. This formal validation is performed by an Ada Validation Facility (AVF). All AVFs are under the control of the Ada Validation Office (AVO) which in turn reports to the director of the Ada Joint Program Office (AJPO), US Department of Defense.

The Ada Compilation Validation Capability (ACVC) is the set of programs (the test suite) that tests the compiler for validity. Validation is performed for the base configuration, that is, the host machine, host operating system, target architecture and target operating system (if any).

Upon successful completion of the ACVC, the compiler vendor is awarded a Certificate of Conformity, a document that specifies that the given compiler, in the base configuration, is in conformity with the official Ada language standard. At the time of this writing it is DoD policy to require revalidation of Ada language compilers (used on DoD projects) every twelve months. It is possible that this revalidation period will be extended in the future.

Of course, the DoD has no authority over the development of commercial avionics software. Nonetheless, it is recommended that only validated Ada language compilers be used.

—

A.15.4 Quality and performance

Compiler performance is determined by the speed, memory size, compactness and efficiency of the target code. Compilers can vary in ways which may impact their performance in a specific production environment. Speed of compilation, error recovery, quality of error messages, amount of code optimisation performed, size of runtime support required, and the method of implementation of various language features all contribute to the overall quality of a compiler.

The ACVC tests for completeness and correctness of the compiler. It does not test for any performance characteristics of the compiler (i.e. speed, memory utilisation, efficiency, etc.). Note that successful validation of a particular compiler does not guarantee that compiler's suitability for any specific purposes.

The proposed Ada Compiler Evaluation Capability (ACEC), is a collection of tests in the public domain which performs some performance checks. However, at the time of this writing, these tests are quite limited. Both the ACVC and ACEC test suites are available for compiler evaluation.

It is recommended that any compiler selected for an avionics application be thoroughly evaluated prior to project development.

A.16 Run-time issues

In order to reduce memory utilisation, a Run-Time System (RTS) should be selectively loadable, i.e. with the capability to load only those RTS features which are actually used. In this way, it is anticipated that for non-tasking applications, a support system of approximately the size employed for current languages (e.g. Pascal, Jovial) can be achieved.

In selecting a run-time system, it is essential that all relevant aspects be considered by the system designer. Table A.1 lists several issues which may be useful for evaluating run-time systems.

Table A.1 Run-time system evaluation topics

1.	Availability of source code
1.1	Ownership
1.2	Implementation
1.2.1	Ada language
1.2.2	Other high-order language
1.2.3	Assembly
1.3	Tracing and documentation
2	Maintainability
2.1	Modifiability
2.2	Modularity
2.3	Readability
3	System clock
3.1	Resolution
3.2	Tick size or period
3.3	Delay duration resolution
3.4	Clock maintenance
4	System size
4.1	Delineation based on function
4.2	Dynamic memory requirements
4.3	Loading restrictions
4.4	Application code size
5	Speed
5.1	System throughput (e.g. how many tasks can be handled simultaneously)
5.2	Interrupt response time
5.3	Execution time
5.4	Exception propagation overhead
5.5	Task creation/destruction overhead
6	Floating point implementation
6.1	Precision
6.2	Representation
6.3	Arithmetic implementations
7	Generic expansion implementation

A.17 Recommended Ada features for avionics

Appendix D of ARINC Report 613

This appendix discusses Ada features which should be supported by all compilers, and features whose efficient implementation is considered essential.

A.17.1 Optional features that should be supported

The following Ada language features are important to avionics software development, and should be supported by all compilers:

A   Pragmas

1.   CONTROLLED
2.   INLINE
3.   INTERFACE
4.   OPTIMIZE
5.   PACK
6.   PRIORITY
7.   SUPPRESS

B.   Predefined units

1.   Package SYSTEM
2.   Package MACHINE_CODE
3.   Function UNCHECKED_CONVERSION

C.   Attributes

1.   P'ADDRESS
2.   A'COUNT

D.   Pre-emptive priority task switching.

E.   Some mechanism (as part of the linker or as a pragma) to allocate memory space for specific tasks.

F.   Some mechanism (as part of the linker or as a pragma) to allocate a task to a particular processor in a multiprocessor environment.

A.17.2 Features that should be supported efficiently

Immediate efficient implementation is needed for the following Ada language features:

A.   Declaration of and reference to and assignment to scalar entities.
B.   Declaration of and reference to and assignment to composite entities.
C.   Subprogram invocation including parameter linkages.
D.   Exception handlers
1.   The presence of an exception handler should not increase the execution time of the containing block, subprogram, or package item when the exception is not raised.
2.   Exception propagation should take no longer than twice the time required to return and process an error flag parameter of a subprogram or block.

E.   Short circuit control forms.

F.   Expression forms which have equivalents in Pascal should execute with corresponding efficiency.

G.   All statements (except **goto**) which have equivalents in Pascal should execute with corresponding efficiency. Execution of block statements should incur little, if any, overhead.

H.   Interface to assembly language code. Assembly code routines should only be allowed to access global (main program) objects as passed parameters. Note that this approach would supersede the rules of scope for assembly language routines only.

I.   Task switching overhead should be minimised. If tasking is not used, no overhead should be incurred.

J.   Generics should be implemented using both shared bodies and macro expansions.

K.   A selectively loadable Run-Time Environment such that only the routines which are actually used are included.

L.   Task elaboration and destruction mechanisms should exist so that static tasks can be defined and used.

M.   Elaboration of data should occur at either compile time or link time, when possible.

N.   Optimisation such that only those subprogram units which are accessed by the application code are included in the executable image.

O.   Slices.

P.   Default procedure parameters.

Q.   User subprogram overloading.

R.   User operator overloading.

(ARINC 613 contains several other appendices, which are not reproduced here, including a glossary, sample data-type declarations, stylistic recommendations, and the use of the Ada programming language in flight simulators.)

Appendix B
Health and Safety Executive guidance
for programmable electronic systems

THE HEALTH AND SAFETY EXECUTIVE (HSE) has published guidance for the design of safety-related systems involving computers, which are generically described as 'Programmable Electronic Systems' (PESs). The following summarises the HSE guidelines, and shows the relevance of the design and checking techniques we have described.

The HSE makes a deliberate separation between the control of a safety-related system and a safety protection system, according to the following definitions:

> A *Safety related system* is a system upon which the safety integrity of the plant is to be assured. For the purposes of the guidelines, the SRS is presumed to include programmable electronics, either alone or in some combination with non-programmable constituents.

> A *Protection system* is a system designed to respond to conditions in the plant (which may be hazardous in themselves or could eventually give rise to a hazard if no action were taken) and to generate outputs that will prevent the hazard or mitigate the hazardous consequences.

The HSE Guide analyses the sources of failure in these systems, and strategies that should be used against them. Three basic sources of failure are identified, which are:

(a) errors or omissions in the safety requirements specification;
(b) random hardware failures;
(c) systematic failures (including software).

The resistance strategies against them also fall into three categories: configuration, hardware reliability and overall quality. The influence of Ada on a safety system is through the last of these. The HSE strategies are summarised in the sections below.

B.1 Configuration

The HSE rules for a safe configuration are as follows:

(a) There must be sufficient safety-related systems to be capable, independently, of maintaining the plant in a safe state or of bringing the plant to a safe state when required.

(b)   No single failure of hardware in any of the PE components should cause a dangerous mode of failure of the total configuration. (Systematic hardware failures may affect all identical designs of PE components.)

Hence, in addition to a programmable element in an SRS, there should be at least one additional means of ensuring safety, which may be non-programmable, a well-established similar programmed design, or a diverse programmed design.

(c)   No single failure of software in any of the PEs should cause a dangerous mode of failure of the total configuration. (A software fault will affect all identical software.)

Hence safety should not depend on a single design of software: there should always be at least one additional means of ensuring safety in the event of a failure arising because of software.

(For example, there might be physical constraints to ensure safety of a moving part, or containment for dangerous fluids.)

B.2 Hardware reliability

Bearing in mind that random hardware failures may result in a dangerous mode of failure, the rule is that the overall failure rate in a dangerous mode of failure of the whole SRS in combination must be below an adequate figure; in other words, the probability that the SRS fails to operate on demand must be adequate for the safety of the system. This overall failure rate is to be determined by:

(a)   Qualitative appraisal of the SRS, including appropriate aspects of PES, using engineering judgement.
(b)   Quantified assessment of the reliability of the SRS. (The PE may be shown not to dominate the overall reliability.)
(c)   Overall quantified safety assessment of the plant, to ensure that the overall plant reliability is adequate.

B.3 Overall integrity and quality

This heading covers qualitative, non-quantifiable aspects of safety integrity. These are the quality of the procedures used in manufacture (specification and design), implementation and operation, including precautions taken against errors or omissions in the specification of the safety system(s) and systematic failures from all causes including software. This is the aspect of safety to which Ada is relevant, and underlies the discussion of quality levels in Section 4.3.

(a)   Quality of manufacture: to an established quality assurance system, such as
      BS5750. (Note that while such standards give assurance that an espoused
      quality system is actually being used, they do not determine what quality of
      product is intended or achieved.)

(b)   Quality of implementation: engineered by competent and experienced persons
      having an understanding of PES safety engineering principles.

(c)   For a higher degree of reliability, each procedural and engineering aspect of
      the PES should be carefully and systematically examined to ensure that the
      level of quality is appropriate. This corresponds to the categoristation of Ada
      packages (Section 8.3) and the checking described in Part III.

Appendix C

DO-178A guidance

THE RADIO TECHNICAL CORPORATION OF AMERICA's document DO-178A (which has been endorsed by the European Organisation for Civil Aviation Electronics) gives guidance and recommendations concerning software in airborne systems and equipment certification. The major recommendation is for all the information needed to support regulatory approval (concerning software) to be written in fourteen documents with defined contents. Some of these must be made available to the regulatory agency as the applicant's records, and various others (depending on the risk factor of the software concerned) must also be available to support the particular certification plan (See Section C.3). The details are given below.

C.1 Defined documents

The documents defined in DO-178A are the Certification Plan and others determined by the risk factor, as follows:

1. Configuration index (always required); see Section C.4.
2. Software requirements (must be available for Risk Factor 1).
3. Design description (must be available for Risk Factors 1 and 2).
4. Programmer's manual (not needed for certification approval).
5. Software Configuration Management and Quality Assurance Plans (always required, and must be available in case of re-certification after any modification); see Section C.5.
6. Source listing (must be available for Risk Factor 1).
7. Source code (not needed for certification approval).
8. Executable object code (not needed for certification approval).
9. Support/Development system configuration (must be available for Risk Factor 1).
10. Accomplishment Summary (always required); see Section C.2.
11. Software Test Plan, Procedures and Results (required for Risk Factors 1 and 2); see Section C.7.
12. Software design standards (must be available for Risk Factor 1).
13. System requirements (required for Risk Factors 1 and 2, and must be available for Risk Factor 3); see Section C.6.

14.   Plan for software aspects of certification (always required); see Section C.3.

The last of these (document 14), may be included in the overall Certification Plan or may be provided as a distinct document. The following sections explain the major documents.

C.2 Accomplishment Summary (document 10)

This is considered to be the primary document for certification, identifying and summarising all other documents concerned. A preliminary issue of the Accomplishment Summary may satisfy the requirement for document 14. The full document contains the following information:

(a)   Description of equipment or system, including organisation of software (summarising document 3).
(b)   Criticality categories and software risk factors.
(c)   Design disciplines (summarising document 12).
(d)   Development phases.
(e)   Software verification plans and results (summarising document 11).
(f)   Configuration management (summarising document 5A).
(g)   Quality assurance (summarising document 5B).
(h)   Certification plan (possibly expanded in document 14).
(i)   Organisation and identification of documents (summarising document 1).

Depending on the risk factor, the Accomplishment Summary may be accompanied by other documents. In the case of Risk Factor 2, a summary description of each verification process and a Statement of Compliance is required.

C.3 Certification Plan (document 14)

Each certification process is conducted in accordance with a plan, which is normally prepared by the applicant and approved by the regulatory authority. When software is involved, the software aspects of the certification process must be covered by this document or a preliminary issue of the Accomplishment Summary, Section (h). When the equipment or system to be certified performs an essential or critical function, the Certification Plan should cover:

(a)   the criticality categories for each item to be certified, and the associated software risk factors;
(b)   the nature of the certification sought (i.e. Initial Type, Supplemental Type, Equipment Approval);
(c)   the software development, test, configuration management and quality assurance programmes to be conducted;
(d)   the specific sections of certification regulations to be applied;

(e) any special conditions to be levied by the regulatory authorities;
(f) the documentation needed to support certification, including software docu-
     mentation.

Particularly when software of Risk Factor 1 or 2 is involved, the software aspects
must be treated explicitly in document 14, including

- brief description of equipment or system;
- criticality categories and software risk factors;
- activities to be carried out in support of certification;
- documentation plan;
- schedule;
- definition of organisations involved with their distinct responsibilities.

This document complements the general Certification Plan.

C.4 Configuration index (document 1)

This is the major control document for documents and software, providing a
historical reference for all items under configuration control, indicating the current
status of each.

The documents concerned include subsidiary configuration index documents
(CIDs), particularly the System CID as the root of a tree of Unit CIDs. The system
is expected to consist of a set of Line Replaceable Units (LRUs), some of which
employ software; each of these would have its own Unit CID that identifies the LRU
hardware, the software it contains, and all documents for the LRU that are currently
applicable.

C.5 Software control plans (document 5)

Software Configuration Management and Quality Assurance Plans are required as
document 5 or separately as documents 5A and 5B. These provide asssurance that
the end products will function as specified. The main contents are defined in DO-
178A, but further guidance is available in IEEE Standards 828-1983 (Software
Configuration Management Plans) and 730-1984 (Software Quality Assurance
Plans).

If, as recommended in this book, the software is written in Ada, a number of
important points can be made in these documents concerning the features of Ada
that support configuration management and assure quality: the recompilation rules,
governed by context clauses, and the strong type checking for consistency between
provision and use of facilities (achieved by having explicit specifications). An Ada
compiler and supporting tools check comprehensively, giving a much stronger
assurance of quality than the sample checking that is the best achievable by
conventional testing.

C.6 System requirements (document 13)

The description of the overall system to be certified must be submitted as evidence for certification when the software concerned has Risk Factor 1 or 2. The description must be available, but need not be submitted as evidence, if all the software has Risk Factor 3. The document should contain:

(a)   System description, identifying hardware Line Replaceable Units (LRUs) and functional components, with a description of each component to be certified.

(b)   Certification requirements, according to the regulations concerned (as in the Certification Plan, Section (d)). If the system being certified is part of a larger system, then the requirements and criticality of that larger, enclosing system should be summarised or referenced.

(c)   Proposals and actual achievements for system development, validation, testing, design error detection and correction, and documentation.

(d)   Proposed and actual design techniques, such as monitoring, redundancy or functional partitioning.

Note that, although the document is called 'System Requirements', it is really a description rather than a statement of required characteristics, which emphasises constituents of the system rather than the effects or behaviour to be achieved by cooperation among these constituents. Each Line Replaceable Unit is a constituent which would be distinctly tested, and replaced *en bloc* if found faulty.

C.7 Software verification (document 11)

The test plans, procedures and results of software verification are required in this document for software which has Risk Factors 1 and 2. Verification (in DO-178A) comprises analytical and test activities, which are discussed in Part III of this book. Thus document 11 (for a specific project) contains the plan for applying the principles explained in Part III, the particular verification procedures to be used, and the results of applying them to the software concerned.

Appendix D
Procurement of safety-critical systems containing software

THE MINISTRY OF DEFENCE draft Interim Standard 00–55 'For the procurement of safety critical systems containing software' lays down the respective responsibilities of the MoD Project Manager and the Design Authority for such a system. The document defines the information that must be passed between them at the start and completion of the project, and the ways in which such a project must be carried out, emphasising that the practices and procedures used must be over and above those of conventional software engineering.

The MoD Project Manager must be involved from the concept stage, before any software development contract is let. Any likelihood of safety-critical Software must be identified, and the Project Requirement Specification written in plain text. The MoD Project Manager will be the MoD Software Safety Authority: this responsibility cannot be delegated or assigned to the Design Authority. If it has been established that software is likely to be critical to safety, the broad goals are to treat the software safety risk in the context of the system safety risk, so that it is **identified** and **minimised**, to such an extent that it is **acceptable**.

The Design Authority must appoint an independent Software Safety Assessor, who will monitor all relevant activities during the software development. On completion, the Design Authority must certify that the prescribed safety assurance activities have been carried out satisfactorily, and the independent Software Safety Assessor must confirm this by countersigning the certificate.

The Safety Certificate, with the Safety Plan and Safety Records for the project (explained below) is the evidence on which the MoD Project Manager will decide whether to accept the developed software.

The Design Authority has the responsibility for ensuring that the personnel involved are suitably qualified and properly trained in the techniques. Similarly, the Design Authority has the responsibility for ensuring that the software tools used are properly validated and evaluated. The independent Software Safety Assessor must have full access to the software, and must receive the reports of design reviews at each stage of development.

This combination of prescribed techniques, responsibilities for management and assessment, with documentary evidence, gives the Safety Assurance required by the Ministry of Defence (Procurement Executive). The status of the document, as a draft interim standard, indicates the Ministry's current approach to software development in safety-related systems, but its implementation is uncertain because of the need for trained staff (in the Procurement Executive as well as in the industrial suppliers) and suitable software tools.

D.1 Safety assurance

The Design Authority has the responsibility for Software Safety Management, which means using the techniques appropriate for the system. The techniques selected must be recorded in the Safety Plan, with the associated activities and milestones. As they are carried out, an Audit Trail of the work must be recorded in the Safety Records as documentary evidence for certification.

A number of techniques have been identified for use in high integrity computing systems, with various degrees of fault-sensitivity, according to the criticality of the system. An early draft of the standard (but not the published version) listed a number of techniques which were classified as mandatory, default, application-dependent or not necessary, depending on whether the system is 'Safety critical',

Table D.1 Criticality-dependent analyses (from a STARTS working paper)

	Safe Cat 1	High Cat 2	Norm Cat 3	Ada	Section number	
Dynamic Analysis	★	/	/	A	14	
Hazard Analysis	★	/	?			
Independent V & V	★	/	?			
Static Analysis	★	/	?	A	12.3	12.4
Approved Tools	★	/	?			
Automated Config. Control	★	/	?	A	7.3	
Safe Subsets	★	/	–	A	8.3	12.3
Formal Review (animation)	★	?	?			
Defensive Programming	★	?	?	A	9.3	
Fail Safe Operation	★	?	?	A	5.3	10.8
Formal Specification	★	?	–	A	7.6	8.4
Formal Proof	★	?	–	A	11.5	13.3
Independent Assessment	★	?	–			
Certification	★	?	–			
Safety Certification	★	–	–			
Safety Integrity Analysis	★	–	–	A	11.3	12.3
Safety Plan	★	–	–			
Safety Records Log	★	–	–			

Key: ★ Mandatory
  / Default: to be used unless contractor justifies non-use
  ? Application-dependent
  – Not applicable or not necessary
  A Ada-specific interpretation in listed section(s) of this book

'High integrity' or 'Normal'. Where the techniques have any special characteristics related to Ada we have discussed them in the main text, summarised in the references below. The techniques without the annotation are equally relevant to software, whether in Ada or not. The categorisation does not occur in the present interim standard, so the following notes are given for guidance rather than definitively (Table D.1).

Appendix E
EWICS TC7 guidelines for
industrial computer systems

THE GENERAL PRINCIPLES for the design of safety related software are given by TC7 in terms of human understanding. The basic rule is:

> The program structure should be easy to understand, both in its overall design as well as in its details. The program should be readable from start to end.

Only if this rule is followed can we expect to be able to detect possible faults or dangers. From this rule a number of derived recommendations can be formulated, which closely match the concepts and practices of Ada:

(a) The program should be divided into modules: in Ada these are packages.

(b) Good documentation must be provided: in Ada much of the information is automatically checked for consistency. We explain where additional information is needed.

(c) Retrospective attempts to optimise memory space or execution time should be avoided: Ada allows an overall programming style to be chosen that localises such decisions, with disciplined evolution for improvement of performance characteristics when found necessary.

(d) The program should be written in such a way to allow easy testing: Ada package bodies have this property.

(e) Programming tricks should be avoided: programmers resort to these when they cannot express their design in the language used. Ada provides facilities to render this unnecessary, but checks are still necessary.

(f) A central idea of system structure should be adopted: again, Ada packages, with their context clauses and subunits, provide precisely this. Ada establishes a uniform approach to the kinds of program unit and data types used. It also provides for clear identification of the parts of programs in which different tasks or processes can compete for resources, and where they refer to the potentially dangerous devices.

The architecture of a program in Ada is discussed in Chapter 8, including the way of handling system-wide (or global) data in a widely accessible data-base. The packages that encapsulate the data make it available to any other package by the use of the context clause, which imposes disciplined use through the access facilities provided in the package. This principle of encapsulation is exactly what is needed for safety and security.

E.1 Development style

All software qualities, not only safety, are affected by the approach used in its development. The STARTS Guide explains steps to be taken at each stage in the software life-cycle for real-time systems, but with no specific attention to safety. The TC7 Guide presents two apparently conflicting recommendations for the design of safety related software systems:

- a top-down or mixed approach is preferred to a bottom-up one;
- they should incorporate verified and previously used components.

The second is a bottom-up approach which appears to contradict the first. (The TC7 Guide says 'as far as it is consistent with the first' which is in effect no guidance!) These can be resolved in Ada by distinguishing package specifications from package bodies. The first recommendation refers to package specifications used in the system architecture; the second to their bodies.

E.2 Appropriate programming language

Although the TC7 Guide does not recommend a specific programming language, the basic rules it gives all point to Ada, with a properly validated compiler and a supporting environment:

(a) Only languages with a thoroughly tested translator should be used. (Not that any vendor would admit to a product not being thoroughly tested; the validation process for Ada is much stronger than this.)
(b) Problem-oriented languages are strongly preferred.
(c) The language should be completely and unambiguously defined.
(d) A programming language and its translator should preferably provide
  - error limiting constructions (subtypes in Ada);
  - compile time type checking (types in Ada)
  - run-time checking of parameters, type matching and array bounds (all in Ada).
(e) Automated testing aids should be available.

Bibliography

ACARD (1986) *Software: A key to UK competitiveness*. ISBN 0 11 630829 X, HMSO.

Anderson, T. (ed.) (1985) *Software – Requirements, Specification and Testing*. ISBN 0–632–01309–5, Blackwell.

Anderson, T. (ed.) (1985) *Resilient Computing Systems*. ISBN 0–00–383039–X, Collins.

Anderson, T. (1987) 'Design fault tolerance in practical systems'. In *Software Reliability – Achievement and Assessment*, B. Littlewood (ed.), ISBN 0–632–01573–X; Blackwell Scientific Publications.

Anderson, T. (ed.) (1989) *Dependability of Resilient Computers*. ISBN 0–632–02054–7, Blackwell Scientific Publications.

Bache, R. and Tinker, R. (1988) 'A rigorous approach to metrication – a field trial using Kindra'. In *Proceedings of Software Engineering 88*, Conference Publication Number 290, pp. 28–31. ISBN 0 85296365 0, Institution of Electrical Engineers.

Baudoin, L. (1986) In *Supplement to Safety of Computer Control Systems 1986 (Safecomp '86)*, W.J. Quirk (ed.). ISBN 0–08–034801–7, Pergamon Press, Oxford.

Bishop, P.G., Esp, D.G., Barnes, M., Humphreys, P., Dahll, G. and Lahti, J. (1986) 'PODS – an experiment in software reliability'. *IEEE Transactions on Software Engineering*, vol. SE-12, nr 9 (Sept).

Bishop, P.G., Esp, D.G., Pullen, F.D., Barnes, M., Humphreys, P., Dahll, G., Bjarland, B., Lahti, J. and Valsuo, H. (1987) 'STEM – a project on software test and evaluation methods'. In *Achieving Safety and Reliability with Computer Systems*, B.K. Daniels (ed.), pp. 100–15. ISBN 1–85166–167–0, Elsevier Applied Science.

Bishop, P. (ed.) (1989) *Dependability of Critical Computer Systems – Techniques Directory*. Elsevier Applied Science.

Björner, D. and Jones, C.B. (1980) *Formal Specification and Software Development*. Englewood Cliffs, Prentice Hall.

Booch, G. (1983) *Software Engineering with Ada*. Benjamin Cummings.

Bougé, L (1982) Modélisation de la notion de test des programmes – Application à la production de jeux de tests; Thèse de 3eme cycle, Université de Paris 6, Paris, France (October).

Bougé, L. (1983) *A Proposition for a Theory of Testing – An Abstract Approach to the Testing Process*, DAIMI PB–160. Computer Science Department, Aarhus University, Denmark (May).

Carré, B.A. and Jennings, T.J. (1988) *SPARK – The SPADE Ada Kernel*. Department of Electronics and Computer Science, University of Southampton.

Cullyer, W.J. and Goodenough, S.J. (1987) *The Choice of Computer Languages for Use in Safety-critical Systems*. Royal Signals and Radar Establishment, Memorandum Nr. 3946 (October).

Cullyer, W.J. and Kershaw, J. (1984) 'Viper, a new microprocessor for safety-critical applications', *Proceedings of Colloquium on Design and Advanced Concepts of Avionics/ Weapons Systems Integration*. Royal Aeronautical Society, London.

Daniels, B.K. (1987) *Achieving Safety and Reliability with Computer Systems*. ISBN 0 85166 167 0, Elsevier Applied Science, London.

Dobson, J.E. and Martin, M.J. (1986) 'Modelling the real issues in dependable communications systems'. In *Safety of Computer Control Systems 1986 (Safecomp '86)* W.J. Quirk (ed.). ISBN 0–08–034801–7, Pergamon Press, Oxford.

EWICS (1985) *Safety Related Computers – Software Development and System Documentation*. European Workshop on Industrial Computer Systems, TC7: Systems Reliability, Safety and Security. ISBN 3–88585–204–7; Verlag TUV Rheinland.

Fussel, J. (1976) 'Fault tree analysis – concepts and techniques'. In *General Techniques in Reliability Assessment*, E. Henley & E. Lynn (ed.). Noordhoff Publishing Co., Leyden, Holland.

Goldsack, S. (ed.) (1985) *Ada for Specification and Design – Possibilities and Limitations*. Cambridge University Press, Ada Companion Series.

Gordon, A.M. (1988) 'Introducing Ada at GEC Sensors Ltd.' *Ada User*, **9** (3), 127–8, Ada UK.

Gordon, A. (1990) Software Reliability; 2nd European Conference on Quality Assurance, Oslo, May/June.

Halstead, M.H. (1977) *Elements of Software Science*. Elsevier, North-Holland.

Hamer, P.G. and Frewin, G.D. (1982) 'M.H. Halstead's software science – a critical examination'. *Proceedings of 6th International Conference on Software Engineering*, Tokyo, Japan.

HAZOP (1987) *A Guide to Hazard and Operability Studies*; Chemical Industry Safety and Health Council of the Chemical Industries Association; Alembic House, 93 Albert Embankment, London SE1 7TU.

Helps, K.A. (1986) 'Some verification tools and methods for airborne safety-critical software'. *Software Engineering Journal*, **1** (6), 248–53.

Hill, A. (1984) 'Asphodel, an Ada compatible specification and design language'. *Proceedings of the 3rd Joint Ada Europe AdaTEC Conference*. Cambridge University Press, Ada Companion Series.

Hill. A. (1988) 'The formal specification and verification of reusable software components using Ada and Asphodel'. *Ada User*, **9** (3), 113–23.

Hoare, C.A.R. (1981) 'The Emperor's old clothes – The 1980 ACM Turing Award Lecture'. *Communications of the ACM*, **24** (2), 75–83.

Holzapfel, R. and Winterstein, G. (1988) 'Ada in safety critical applications'. In *The Use of Ada in High Integrity Systems*, Cranfield Information Technology Institute, and in *Ada in Industry* S. Heilbrunner (ed.). Cambridge University Press.

HSE (1987) *Programmable Electronic Systems in Safety Related Applications* (2 volumes) Health and Safety Executive. Volume 1: *An Introductory Guide*, ISBN 0 11 883913 6, HMSO. Volume 2: *General Technical Guidelines*, ISBN 0 11 883906 3, HMSO.

Humphreys, P. (1987) 'Diversity by design – reliability aspects of systems with embedded software'. In *Software reliability – Achievement and Assessment*, B. Littlewood (ed.). ISBN 0–632–01573–X, Blackwell Scientific Publications.

IEE (1985) *Guidelines for the Documentation of Software in Industrial Computer Systems*. ISBN 0 86 341046 4, Institution of Electrical Engineers, Savoy Place, London.

IEE (1989) *Joint IEE/BCS Study*: Report on Safety Critical Systems Employing Software,

DTI reference IT/24/27/39. Institution of Electrical Engineers, London.

Jennings, T.J. and Carré, B.A. (1988) 'A subset of Ada for formal verification (SPARK)'. *Ada User*, **9**, Supplement, 121–6, Ada UK.

Jones, C.B. (1980) *Software Development – A Rigorous Approach*. Englewood Cliffs, Prentice-Hall, London.

Jones, C.B. (1986) *Systematic Software Development Using VDM*. Prentice-Hall International, London.

Kelly, J.P.J., Avizienis, A., Ulery, B.T., Swain, B.J., Lyu, R-T, Tai, A. and Tso K-S (1986) 'Multi-version software development'. In *Safety of Computer Control Systems 1986 (Safecomp '86)*, W.J. Quirk (ed.). ISBN 0–08–034801–7, Pergamon Press.

Lamport, L. (1980) 'The "Hoare Logic" of concurrent programs'. *Acta Informatica*, **14**, 21–37.

Lehmann, M.M. (1988) Software's time-bombs, reported by T. Durham, *The Guardian*, Thursday 23 June 1988.

Leveson, N.G. (1986) An outline of a program to enhance software safety. In *Safety of Computer Control Systems 1986 (Safecomp '86)*, W.J. Quirk (ed.), pp. 129–36. ISBN 0–08–034801–7, Pergamon Press.

Leveson, N.G. (1987) 'Building safe software'. In *Software Reliability – Achievement and Assessment*, B. Littlewood (ed.), ISBN 0–632–01573–X, Blackwell Scientific Publications.

Leveson, N.G. and Stolzy, J.L. (1984) 'Software fault tree analysis applied to Ada'. In *8th International Computer Software and Applications Conference – COMPSAC 84*. IEEE Computer Society Press, USA.

Littlewood, B. (ed) (1987) *Software Reliability – Achievement and Assessment*. ISBN 0–632–01573–X, Blackwell Scientific Publications.

Luckham, D.C, von Henke, F.W., Krieg-Brueckner, B. and Owe, O. (1984) *ANNA, A Language for Annotating Ada Programs (Preliminary Reference Manual)* Technical Report Nr 84–248, Stanford University Computer Systems Laboratory (June).

Manuel, G. (1990) 'Untouched by human hands'. In *The Engineer*, 19/26 April, p. 19.

Maxion, R.A. (1986) 'Towards fault-tolerant user interfaces'. In *Safety of Computer Control Systems 1986 (Safecomp '86)*. W.J. Quirk (ed.). ISBN 0–08–034801–7, Pergamon Press, Oxford.

McCabe, T.J. (1976) 'A complexity measure'. IEEE *Transactions on Software Engineering*, **SE-2** (4), 308–20.

McCabe, T.J. (1982) 'Structured testing – a software testing methodology using the cyclomatic complexity metric'. *NBS Special Publication 500–99*, December.

McCormick, F. (1988) *Ada Scheduling in Integrated Civil Avionics*; position paper for the Second International Workshop on Real-Time Ada Issues. Moretonhampstead, Devon, England.

McGettrick, A. (1982) *Program Verification Using Ada*. ISBN 0 521 24215 0, Cambridge University Press.

MoD (1987) The development of safety-critical software for airborne systems. *Interim Defence Standard 00–31/1* (August).

NCC (1987) *The STARTS Guide – A Guide to Methods and Software Tools for the Construction of Large Real-time Systems*; 2nd edn (2 vols). ISBN 0 85012 619 3, NCC Publications (September).

NCC (1989) *The STARTS Purchasers' Handbook – Procuring Software-based Systems*; 2nd edn. ISBN 0 85012 799 8, NCC Publications.

O'Neill, G and Wichmann, B.A. (1988) *A Contribution to the Debate on Safety-critical*

Software. National Physical Laboratory, Report DITC 126/88 (September).

Oxford (1986) *Dictionary of Computing*. ISBN 0–19–853913–4, Oxford University Press.

Pickard, L. (1987) 'Analysis of software metrics', *CSR 87 Conference proceedings*; Centre for Software Reliability.

Pierce, R.H. and Webb, J. (1989), 'Analysing Ada programs with MALPAS'. In *Proceedings of the 7th Ada UK Conference, York*; *Ada User*, **10** Supplement, Ada UK.

Pierce, R.H. and Wichmann, B.A. (1989), 'Analysis techniques for Ada programs'. *Ada User*, **10** Supplement, Ada UK.

Pyle, I.C. (1984) 'Limits on the use of Ada for specifications', pp. 251–260. In *Proceedings of the 3rd Ada Europe Conference, Brussels* J. Teller (ed.). ISBN 0 521 30102 5, Cambridge University Press, Ada Companion Series.

Pyle, I.C. (1987) 'Designing for safety using Ada packages'. In *Achieving Safety and Reliability with Computer Systems*, B.K. Daniels (ed.), pp. 29–35. ISBN 1–85166–167–0, Elsevier Applied Science.

Pyle, I.C. (1987) 'Designing for safety using Ada', pp. 56–64. In *Software Quality Assurance, Reliability and Testing*; C. Summers (ed.). Unicom Seminars, ISBN 0–291–39732–8, Gower Technical Press.

Pyle, I.C. (1989) 'Safety implications of integrated avionics systems'. In *Military Avionics Architectures for Today and Tomorrow*. ERA Report 88–0437; ISBN 0 7008 0386 6; ERA Technology Ltd., Leatherhead, Surrey, England.

Randell, B. (1975) 'System structure for software fault tolerance'. *IEEE Transactions on Software Engineering*, **SE-1** (2), 220–32,

Redmill, F.J. (ed.) (1988, 1989) *Dependability of Critical Computer Systems – vols. 1 and 2*. ISBN 1–85166–203–0, Elsevier Applied Science.

Rex, Thompson and Partners Ltd. (1987) *The Capabilities of MALPAS – a Software Verification and Validation Tool*, report RTP/4002 (April).

RTCA (1985) *Software Considerations in Airborne Systems and Equipment Certification*. Document Nr RTCA/DO-178A, Prepared by SC-152, Radio Technical Commission for Aeronautics (March).

Shepperd, M. (1988) 'A critique of cyclomatic complexity as a software metric'. *Software Engineering Journal*, **3** (2), 30–36.

Somerville, I. and Morrison, R. (1987) *Software Development with Ada*. ISBN 0–201–14227–9, Addison Wesley.

Theuretzbacher, N. (1986) 'Using AI methods to improve software safety'. In *Safety of Computer Control Systems 1986 (Safecomp '86)*, W.J. Quirk (ed.). ISBN 0–08–034801–7, Pergamon Press, Oxford.

Tooby, B. (1986) 'Opinion – the word "Coding" considered harmful'; *Ada User*, **7** (3).

Walsh T.J. (1979) 'A software reliability study using a complexity measure', [USA] *National Computer Conference*, IEEE.

Watt, D.A., Wichmann, B.A. and Findlay, W. (1987) *Ada Language and Methodology*. ISBN 0–13–004078–9, Prentice-Hall International.

Wichmann B.A. (1988) 'Notes on the security of programming languages'. In *10th Advances in Reliability Technology Symposium*, G.P. Libberton (ed.). Elsevier.

Wichmann, B.A. (1989) *Insecurities in the Ada Programming Language*. National Physical Laboratory, Report DITC 144/89.

Wichman, B.A. (1990) private communication.

Wirth, N. (1977) 'Towards a discipline of real-time programming. In Commun. ACM (US) **20**, nr. 8, pp. 577–83 (August).

Index